Development Challenges Confronting Pakistan

Development Challenges Confronting Pakistan

Edited by

ANITA M. WEISS AND SABA GUL KHATTAK

AMERICAN INSTITUTE OF PAKISTAN STUDIES

Kumarian Press

An Imprint of Stylus Publishing
Sterling, VA

Published by Stylus Publishing, LLC
22883 Quicksilver Drive
Sterling, Virginia 20166–2102

Bulk Purchases
Quantity discounts are available
for use in workshops and for staff
development.
Call 1–800–232–0223

Library of Congress Cataloging-in-Publication Data

Development challenges confronting Pakistan / edited by Anita M. Weiss and Saba Gul Khattak. — First edition.
   pages ; cm
  Includes bibliographical references and index.
  ISBN 978-1-56549-552-4 (cloth : alkaline paper) — ISBN 978-1-56549-553-1 (paperback : alkaline paper) — ISBN (invalid) 978-1-56549-554-8 (library networkable e-edition) — ISBN (invalid) 978-1-56549-555-5 (consumer e-edition) 1. Economic development—Pakistan. 2. Human security—Pakistan. 3. Pakistan—Politics and government. I. Weiss, Anita M., editor of compilation. II. Khattak, Saba Gul, editor of compilation.
  DS389.D48 2012
  38.95491—dc23

2012022876

Printed in the United States of America

∞All first editions printed on acid free paper that meets the American National Standards Institute Z39-48 Standard.

First Edition, 2013

1 0   9   8   7   6   5   4   3   2   1

Contents

Part Three
Challenges of Human Security

Part Four
Ongoing Challenges of Militancy, Insecurity, and Political Paths

Acknowledgments

This volume is the culmination of intellectual discussions and heated debates among a wide spectrum of scholars of Pakistan that have gone on for many years. These debates led us to organize a conference, Development Challenges Confronting Pakistan, in May 2011 with the purpose of articulating the distinct circumstances and identify the unique blend of factors prevailing in Pakistan at this time that affect its development prospects. The conference organizing committee consisted of Anita M. Weiss, Saba Gul Khattak, S. Rifaat Hussain, and S. Akbar Zaidi. We want to thank the conference steering committee for its excellent recommendations and selection of conference participants who represented a wide spectrum of scholarly and practical expertise in various arenas of development concerns.

This volume would not have been possible without the many dimensions of support provided by the American Institute of Pakistan Studies (AIPS), a member of the Council of American Overseas Research Centers (CAORC) that supports research on issues relevant to Pakistan. Then AIPS president, J. Mark Kenoyer, was consistently supportive and helped obtain a grant for AIPS, "Reviving American Scholarship in Pakistan," to cover conference and publication expenses. We appreciate the invaluable support provided by AIPS staff Nadeem Akbar and Ghulam Rasool, who paid close attention to all logistical details, and Laura J. Hammond and Salima Currimbhoy, who helped manage the conference and publication accounts.

University of Oregon International Studies graduate student Patrick Jones was indefatigable in his efforts to assist with organizational details and format all the chapters to Kumarian Press specifications. We appreciate the extra effort Patrick went to, especially in trying to format the various charts and figures for this volume.

Anita Weiss, a longstanding supporter of Kumarian Press and member of the Kumarian Press Advisory Committee, is delighted finally to have the opportunity to work with Jim Lance on the publication of a book with Kumarian Press.

Working together, Anita Weiss and Saba Gul Khattak came to experience the trials, tribulations, and periodic sense of accomplishment of working with colleagues in putting together this volume. Finally, we want to acknowledge the extra efforts of all volume contributors, not just for the chapters you see in front of you, but for everything they do on a daily basis to work for a better future for Pakistan as both scholars and practitioners. It is to that envisioned future we dedicate this volume.

ANITA M. WEISS AND SABA GUL KHATTAK
ISLAMABAD, FEBRUARY 2012

1

Introduction

ANITA M. WEISS

The global scholarly community concerned with development and social transformation has identified explicit "structural impediments" that constrain countries' efforts to alleviate poverty and promote sustainable social development. The United Nations Development Programme (UNDP), in launching its Millennium Development Goals, contends that there are "practical, proven solutions" to breaking out of the poverty traps that entangle poor countries. Today, donors everywhere talk about linking states' efforts to promote good governance, human rights, and civil society, and to combat violence against women to the giving of aid. However, delving into practical experiences worldwide shows that the myriad of these "solutions" interact with local culture, prevailing political realities, a state's relationship and interactions with the global political economy, and various other factors in critical ways to affect a state's development prospects enormously. Nowhere is this truer than in the case of Pakistan.

There has been limited substantive research conducted about Pakistan to identify the unique blend of structural impediments to development that prevail in the country at this time. However, just glancing at the country today we can see that Pakistan's prospects to promote viable, sustainable social development appear bleaker than even a decade ago. This volume seeks to rectify this void in research by bringing together scholars and practitioners in order to develop a substantive understanding of the structural impediments, or barriers, that are having a negative impact on Pakistan's ability to eliminate poverty, promote social justice, and implement policies to promote equity. It also seeks to promote an understanding of the synergy among local institutions, development, and social transformation. We recognize that many more issues need to be included in our discussion, such as the ongoing energy shortage, agricultural transformation, and how corruption and impunity threaten to compromise all accomplishments. While acknowledging that far more issues need addressing, we seek to begin a dialogue with this volume and hope the work presented here will be constructively built upon by others.

When we think of the goals of development, we are reminded of how Gunnar Myrdal had extended the definition of "development" that had been used by modernization theorists in the 1950s and 1960s, one that focused solely on closing the gap between the rich and poor in underdeveloped economies to something more comprehensive. Myrdal, in his 1968 seminal work *Asian Drama*, argued that development is more than increasing economic growth and a material betterment of the human condition. It must also imply a deepening of the human potential, increasing access to many goods and services, and bringing about higher literacy rates, better health-care systems, and freedom from poverty, famine, and social injustice.[1] How has this played out in Pakistan?

Many factors contribute to affecting how people think about national identity, the role of the state, and an envisioned ideal society in Pakistan. For example, consider the country's size: Pakistan is the sixth most populous country in the world—soon to become the fifth most populous—with a 2010 population estimated at 177 million.[2] Its population is not evenly distributed throughout the country, but ranges dramatically from sparsely populated Balochistan to some of the highest densities in the world in parts of Karachi and the Walled City of Lahore. High population growth rates, even in urban areas, will result in the country's population nearly doubling by 2050 as Pakistan becomes the world's fourth most populous country, with 335 million persons.

While there are many formidable structural problems confronting Pakistan, such as its burgeoning population growth, it is the challenge of living in the shadow of the nearly daily bomb blasts and suicide attacks—which affect all realms of life and have become a norm of social life today—that poses the greatest challenge to Pakistan's development prospects. Pakistan at this time is in crisis, not only beset by infrastructural problems (lack of electricity, clean water, waste disposal, and aging buildings) and limited employment and economic growth options, but especially by the violence that is ripping the nation apart. These bode poorly for the country. Violence, while exacerbated by infrastructural problems and limited jobs, emerges mostly from identity politics and promotes further tension and contestation among ethnic, social, religious, and economic communities. Indeed, the unrelenting violence in Pakistan often emerges from narrow views of community, a divisive cleavage that ostensibly pits the poor, the disempowered, those who cannot afford a government education and who know that receiving one won't alleviate their poverty and disenfranchisement, with one another. These are the people who identify with their groups wholly, whether due to tribal identity, sectarian identity, kinship, locale, or other ascribed factors.

Given the above, how can we think about Pakistan's development prospects and identify possible solutions to the challenges it faces? This volume is not meant to offer prescriptive solutions—do this and that will successfully occur—but rather seeks to frame Pakistan's development challenges in light of specific arenas concerning the economy, politics, and society. While identity politics seems to be a major driver affecting outcomes of various initiatives, this is interwoven with the myriad economic and political difficulties that Pakistan is facing and that, combined, create very real obstacles to Pakistan's social development efforts.

Historical Backdrop

Pakistan was definitively an agricultural space at the time of independence in 1947, home to only one of British India's port cities (Karachi) and a few other urban areas, mostly in Punjab. An overwhelming majority of factories and other kinds of industries were in areas of British India that went to the new country of India at partition. There was little political unanimity at that time either, as debates and divisiveness over a shared vision arose at the outset among Pakistan's leaders. Mohammed Ali Jinnah—a British-trained lawyer who rose to be the founding father of the country, the Quaid-e-Azam (Father of the Country)—and other Western-oriented professionals envisioned a multiethnic, pluralistic, democratic state free from the hegemony of any one sectarian group. The hope for this is evident in Jinnah's inaugural presidential address to the Constituent Assembly of Pakistan three days prior to Independence when he declared, "If we want to make this great State of Pakistan happy and prosperous we should wholly and solely concentrate on the well-being of the people, and especially of the masses and the poor."[3] Jinnah encouraged the rise of a vigorous civil society, one in which ethnic and religious divides would be set aside so as to promote the overall well-being of the new country.[4] Jinnah regarded Pakistan as the culmination of what had finally become a mass-based grassroots movement, extending out to consist of partisans from a range of ethnic, class, regional, and religious backgrounds, a profusion of groups working together for the overall well-being of the state regardless of these divisions. Differences were to be resolved within a constitutional context, as Jinnah and other leaders of the new state shared the conviction that a popular consensus existed on its necessity, viability, and structure. Most citizens of the new state, whether from areas deemed in the 1947 partition to become part of Pakistan or the huge numbers of migrants (*muhajirs*), some twelve million, who left everything behind in those areas ceded to India as they boarded trains for Pakistan, shared a conviction that they had achieved something pivotal for the Muslims of South Asia.

The havoc and chaos that ensued after partition in 1947 kindled a unifying spirit among much of the public of the new state. Pakistan's future held great promise for many, according to the mainstream, populist narrative. While substantive political and economic challenges confronted the new state, most shared the conviction that these would be surmounted over time.

Even then, at the outset, alternative viewpoints also existed. There were some factions that initially wanted no part of Pakistan, but for different reasons. Supporters of the Punjab Unionist Party placed their loyalties with the British; many of their successors still identify with global culture as they educate their children in British-style schools, speak English among themselves, and value indigenous aesthetics only as quaint historic relics. Many Pakhtuns, from the outset, refused to accept the international boundary between Pakistan and Afghanistan as the Durand Line dividing them had been determined by the British; most Balochis weren't sure what the new country held for them. Distinct *madrasas*,[5] particularly those run by the Deobandis,[6] initially opposed the demand for Pakistan on the grounds that Islam could not be confined within the borders of a nation state as a Muslim's identity is first and foremost with the religion. After the 1947 partition, however, many adherents of this view migrated to the new country from India. Once arriving there, many then began to conceptualize the possibilities of creating a *dar-ul-Islam* in which Islamic laws and values would be predominant. Not all members of this group, however, shared a common vision either.

Indeed, despite the assumptions of the Two Nations theory,[7] Pakistan's formidable Muslim population came from diverse practices and heritages. These ranged among the majority Sunnis from the austere Deoband school, the Sufi-oriented Berelvi[8] school, the orthodox Ahle Hadith, to the modernist Aligarh school, and among Shi'as from the followers of the Twelve Imams, the disciples of the Aga Khan, to members of the Dawoodi Bohra and Memon communities. Notwithstanding these formal divisions, Sufi teachers who had spread Islam throughout the subcontinent still had their followers, and most Bengali Muslims, accustomed to a more syncretic Islamic tradition, found little in common with the rest.

Jinnah died of cancer a year after the new country was born, and his successor, Liaqat Ali Khan, was assassinated three years later. The ensuing political instability combined with the social cleavages noted earlier, the absence of a charismatic civilian leader with strong national standing, and the military threat from India, created an opening for military rule to be widely condoned, at least for a while.

Landed, wealthy families that embraced innovation and educated their children became successful; those who did not, along with the vast majority of the country that started out poor, have seen their options diminish over the years. The Harvard Advisory Group came to Pakistan in 1959 and essentially retained a presence in Karachi until 1963, arguing that Pakistan's economy could take off if given large injections of capital, either in the form of joint ventures or loans. Many in the U.S. development community considered Pakistan their great experiment, and its economic success would prove the assumptions of Simon Kuznets and modernization theory: that income differentiation was greater in poorer countries than in the richer ones, and that large injections of capital into an economy would enable this gap to be closed, thus prompting substantive economic development. However, when this failed to occur—and Pakistan became a poster child for this failure in the early 1960s—U.S. policymakers, in recognizing that capital was not sufficient to promote a country's economic development, argued that institutions had to exist so as to make a compatible environment for the Western form of industrialization. These new structures could range from forms of political legitimacy to the reorganization of the family from the basic unit of production to the basic unit of consumption. In Pakistan, the United States urged President Ayub Khan to implement political reforms that resulted in the Basic Democracies introduced in the 1962 Constitution. The idea was that previously disenfranchised groups would be empowered to become involved in the political process and have their voices heard. However, while the goals were certainly laudable, the implemented reality fell far short. Industrialists emerged as a key class in this era and were able to contest the political might of the feudal groups given the unprecedented expansion of their economic clout along with their newfound alliances with the military.

The industrial elite, those who benefited from this aid, regards the 1958–68 era as the "Golden Age" of Pakistan's development. But ethnic and class divisions became so exaggerated in this era due to such uneven growth—the rich getting much richer and the lot of the poor either hardly changing or getting worse—that one of the end results was the dismemberment of the country in 1971 (due to the unrelenting poverty and alienation experienced by East Pakistanis) and the coming to power of Zulfiqar Ali Bhutto's Pakistan Peoples Party (PPP) on a platform of Islamic Socialism.

Jinnah's pluralistic view of Pakistani society was shaken somewhat in the mid-1960s and 1970s as divisions and distinctions among different ethnic and class groupings became more conspicuous. Animosity grew between *muhajirs* and Punjabis, the two most powerful economic-ethnic groups in the country. The end result of that era was the dismemberment of the country in 1971, separatist movements in Balochistan and the Northwest Frontier Province (NWFP)[9] in the ensuing decade, and sectarian feuds overflowing into the national arena that remain potent concerns.

Zia's Islamization program, introduced in 1979, further alienated many Pakistani communities from one another as it legislated a more orthodox interpretation of Islam than that which had been adhered to in the area traditionally. The escalation of *dawah*[10] teachings throughout the country resulted in contestations between different groups positing that one was more or less "Muslim" than the other. After the Soviet invasion of Afghanistan in December 1979 and the ensuing proxy war between the United States and the USSR over Afghanistan, Pakistan witnessed a virtual invasion of over three million refugees from Afghanistan. Mostly Pakhtuns, these refugees officially were to remain in the border areas of NWFP and Balochistan, where they had an immediate impact on local economies, politics, and development processes in both provinces. Many eventually migrated throughout Pakistan, plying trucks and working on construction sites that brought them to Pakistan's biggest cities. Karachi, in becoming the most popular destination point, now became home to two large immigrant communities: *muhajirs* (originating in 1947) and their descendants, and Pakhtuns.

By the time the USSR invaded Afghanistan in December 1979, Pakistan had become of limited interest to the United States. With the invasion, its importance was suddenly rejuvenated and it quickly became a Frontline State in the U.S. proxy war with the USSR over Afghanistan. The U.S. government quickly put together a nonmilitary aid package to Pakistan for US$3.2 billion dollars for 1982–87; this was followed with an allocation of US$4.1 billion for 1988–93. Full details on the total amount of military support given to Pakistan remain unclear, but it was far greater than the nonmilitary support.

Was this the period when Pakistan's development focus became truly distracted? The United States overwhelmed Pakistan's economy with politically driven development assistance, while Zia instituted policies and laws that affected local culture at its very core, transforming state and society in unprecedented and wholly unpredictable ways. Throughout the 1980s, Pakistan's political and economic fortunes were affected more by geopolitical pressures from outside than from within; its domestic politics did not function independently. However, this is not to say that they were manipulated by only one force; instead, a combination of geopolitical, economic, and even cultural pressures resulted in limiting how the state would address its development imperatives and options.

The ensuing decade, a period between 1988 and 1999 that can be termed a democratic interregnum, saw Benazir Bhutto, leader of the Pakistan Peoples Party, jockeying for power with Nawaz Sharif, scion of an industrial family who had revived the Pakistan Muslim League and created his own faction, the PML(N). Despite each government declaring its commitment to improving the lives of Pakistan's poor and moving Pakistan's economy forward, each regime seemed more intent with staying in power than with taking chances to enact substantive change. There were no major political transformations, alliance-building efforts, or even major catastrophes during this period, other than Pakistan's nuclear-weapons test in May 1998 and the Kargil incident with India in the summer of 1999. Nawaz Sharif, a protégé of Zia ul-Haq, brought Pakistan into a decidedly more conservative, Middle East–focused orbit during his two periods in power. He continued the process begun under Zia in the 1970s and 1980s to move Pakistan symbolically closer to the Middle East—not by prioritizing *sharia*, but rather by prioritizing practices that had not actually been a part of Muslim traditions in this area as well as empowering Islamist political forces. Unlike Zia, Nawaz and his party, the PML(N), had been democratically elected. During Benazir Bhutto's two tenures, while not proceeding further with this agenda, neither did the PPP even attempt to undo any of the draconian edicts passed during the Zia regime. Social conditions continued to deteriorate, while each government was dismissed twice on charges of corruption, and it soon became evident that the military was fed up with the democratic experiment.

In October 1999, democratic processes were once again repudiated as Pakistan witnessed yet another coup d'etat. This time, a relatively modernist-oriented general, Pervez Musharraf, proclaimed this was going to be a different kind of military government than that of Zia ul-Haq. Referring to himself as the chief executive instead of chief martial law administrator, his rhetoric initially appeared similar to Ayub Khan's efforts to modernize Pakistan in the 1960s, especially in promoting economic development and the writ of the state. However, it is important to remember that Musharraf operated in a very different global context: the Soviet Union had been repelled from Afghanistan, leaving the United States as the world's sole super power; both India and China were emerging as global economic powers; and the pervasive globalization of the world's economy limits the influence a given country, like Pakistan, can have in asserting itself in external economic negotiations. Pakistan's economic prospects with regard to the global economy had never before been as weak.

The events of September 11, 2001, further reinforced the global community's influence in Pakistan, forcing the country, its leadership, and its people to reconsider its place in the world. Musharraf quickly supported

U.S. efforts to overthrow the Taliban government in Afghanistan and banned some of the most extreme Islamist groups in January 2002, although most Pakistanis had far more mixed reactions. The myriad implications of Pakistan's new geostrategic situation has had profound consequences on its development prospects in the past decade, which is the focus of the chapters in this volume.

Situating Development Today in Pakistan

Pakistan's four major provinces were initially created to reflect how language is divided in the country: Balochistan, NWFP, the Punjab, and Sindh. In early 2010, the Northern Areas became a fifth province, Gilgit-Baltistan; in March 2010, NWFP was officially renamed Khyber Pakhtunkhwa. Provincial residence no longer denotes either ethnicity or language, particularly as Punjabis and Pakhtuns have settled outside of the respective provinces associated with their language. For example, nearly half of all Pakistanis (48 percent) speak the provincial language Punjabi, while over two-thirds identify as being ethnically Punjabi. Therefore, a sizable number of ethnic Punjabis do not speak the Punjabi language. We must presume that, in this case, many who identify as being ethnically Punjabi but who don't speak the Punjabi language may be speakers of Saraiki (a dialect of Punjabi), who comprise 10 percent of the population. In response to the creation of Gilgit-Baltistan there have been demands not only for renaming other provinces—resulting in NWFP being renamed Khyber-Pakhtunkhwa—but also for carving out new ones. The Punjabi language distribution is important here. The population of the province of Punjab (84.8 million) would make it the fifteenth largest country in the world if it were a separate national entity.[11] A political movement in southern Punjab to separate that area from Punjab as a Saraiki-speaking province is gaining strength. Riots have also broken out in Abbottabad and other non-Pakhtun Hindko-speaking areas of Khyber-Pakhtunkhwa as Hindko speakers feel divested of their provincial citizenship under the new name and are agitating to carve out a separate province of their own.

We can see how politics, ethnicity, and development priorities are uniquely intertwined in Pakistan from such demands. The family as a primary social concern in Pakistan extends out to ethnic identity, and ethnicity is a key influence in political attitudes. Ethnic identity is the primary foundation of provincial divisions in Pakistan, albeit residence in a province is by no means an exclusive domain of only one distinct ethnic group. Indeed, some of the greatest initial political divisiveness occurred over the question of which province distinct districts should join. For example, many Balochis had championed having Dera Ghazi Khan be a part of Balochistan, although it ended up being in Punjab. Numerous Pakhtuns live in villages abutting GT (Grand Trunk) Road between Rawalpindi and Attock, but one does not enter Khyber-Pakhtunkhwa until the Attock Bridge is crossed. One of the key reasons for the delay in enumerating the 1991 census (it was finally held in 1998, seven years late) is that popular knowledge held that the influx of millions of Afghan Pakhtun refugees into Balochistan had caused the majority ethnic group in the province to change; stating definitively that Baluchis no longer composed the majority ethnic group in Balochistan would provide further fuel for open provocation among groups in the province. In addition, clearly articulating that the city of Karachi had indeed experienced a very high growth rate would have brought demands for commensurate representation in the national parliament and higher quotas for government jobs, university admissions,and other benefits, further aggravating hostility between the political party of most *muhajirs*, the Muttahida Qaumi Movement (MQM), and other groups. Punjab, the most populous province, would have seen its share of federal jobs and funding affected— whether its count was too high *or* too low—further antagonizing groups in other provinces and fueling anti-Punjabi sentiment (either from others, or from Punjabis who thought they were deliberately undercounted by anti-Punjabi entities). An associated outcome would be that rural landholding elites would lose seats in the National Assembly if the census proved that there had been significant population growth in urban areas. Furthermore, it was feared that sectarian disputes between Sunni and Shia groups would escalate further (they did, regardless) as each group would certainly decry the over counting of the other, thereby fueling the ravaging, widespread, and random acts of terrorism that these disputes have wrought. Finally, showing population growth rates hovering at about 3 percent would have undermined economic growth in the country and serve to underscore the state's failure to raise the status of women. This, in turn, would have further antagonized the brewing "culture war" between Western-oriented groups demanding that the state actively pursue the empowerment of women versus Islamist groups demanding that the state suppress those forces which seek to exploit women and lead them away from their prescribed roles as commonly perceived within the tradition.[12] Not surprisingly, when the delayed census was finally taken, the ethnic distribution officially recorded was remarkably similar to that recorded in the previous census, despite the very real social transformations that had occurred.

These are not symbolically imagined communities either. Ethnic orientations toward social hierarchies, toward the state, even toward Islam differ markedly among groups. Being cognizant of the most salient ways that ethnicity influences political and economic stances enables us to gain a fuller view of how the different segments that make up Pakistan interact. There are also significant cultural differences among major ethnic groups in Pakistan that contribute to interprovincial misunderstandings and very real tensions.

Separatist movements and ethnic crises have plagued Pakistan since its inception, though the nature and composition of such conflict has changed over time. At Independence, there was a definable fear that Pakistan might cease to exist; East Pakistan's secession in 1971 further aggravated that anxiety. More recently, separatist movements in what was then NWFP (now Khyber Pakhtunkhwa), Balochistan, and Sindh have given way to demands for greater power and autonomy.

Political dissent and control is a key factor in demands for restructuring FATA, the Federally Administered Tribal Areas. This legacy of British colonialism, traced to the Frontier Crimes Regulation Act of 1901, comprises seven tribal agencies and six frontier regions. While administered directly by the federal government, it enjoys a great deal of local autonomy. Here, tribal leaders' power holds sway over their members' lives to a considerable extent, and federal institutions and constitutional laws are essentially irrelevant. Political agents, representatives of the federal government, rarely wield even limited influence; they are essentially couriers. A common sentiment in FATA is the disdain with which most residents regard the federal government; this has grown exponentially in the past decade as residents see themselves as physical targets of drone attacks in the U.S.–Pakistan anti-terrorism alliance. Development projects that have sought to build modern roads, schools, and new kinds of economic enterprises are often viewed locally as insidious efforts to dominate the tribal areas. It is erroneous to assume that the federal government of Pakistan maintains effective power and influence in FATA.

The growing "nuclearization" of the family in Pakistan is substantively affecting the country's social character as well, as values today are increasingly imparted in schools, through the media, and on the streets. The old urban *havelis* have given way to self-contained flats, and it is now common not to know one's neighbors. As high population growth rates and rampant urbanization provide greater challenges than opportunities, younger generations of Pakistanis are now questioning the priorities of their elders in wholly unprecedented ways. Yet the failure of government schools to provide viable education is further eroding a sense of national community. Education in the colonial era had been geared to staffing the civil service and producing an educated elite sharing the values of and loyal to the British colonizers. It was unabashedly elitist and divisive. Contemporary education—reforms and commissions on reforms notwithstanding—usually shares the same bias.

Until the late 1970s, an excessive amount of educational spending went to the middle and upper levels. The elitist nature of education was evident in the glaring gap between the country's public and private schools, which were nationalized in the late 1970s in a leveling effort to increase access. While access to students from poorer class backgrounds has increased in the nationalized schools over the past twenty years, teachers and school principals alike bemoan the decline in quality education that has concomitantly occurred.

The resultant curriculum is often heavily biased. This bias stems not only from the political philosophy of the current regime in power, but also from past ones, as revising curriculum tends to be a lower priority for democratic administrations. A study conducted by the Sustainable Development Policy Institute (SDPI) in Islamabad found that especially during the Zia ul-Haq regime (1977–88), political bias had an untoward influence on what was taught in schools:

> In the educational sphere, this amounted to a distorted narration of history, factual inaccuracies, inclusion of hate material, a disproportionate inclusion of Islamic studies in other disciplines, glorification of war and the military, gender bias, etc. Subsequent governments either failed to check these harmful deviations, or willingly perpetuated them.[13]

Curricula and textbooks are largely insensitive to the religious diversity of Pakistani society. The entire curriculum is "heavily laden with religious teachings, reflecting a very narrow view held by a minority among Muslims that all the education should be essentially that of Islamiat." In both curriculum documents and textbooks, "Pakistani nationalism is repeatedly defined in a manner that excludes non-Muslim Pakistanis from either being Pakistani nationals or from even being good human beings. Much of this material runs counter to any efforts at national integration." Even the constitution of Pakistan "is cited but misrepresented."[14]

Furthermore, despite Pakistan having one of the lowest female literacy rates in the world, there has never been a systematic, nationally coordinated effort to improve female primary education in the country. Overall adult literacy rates are nearly 60 percent, although female literacy rates hover at 32 percent.[15] The scenario today, however, is changing remarkably. UNICEF reports an overall youth literacy rate (ages 15–24) at 80 percent; the female youth literacy rate is 60 percent.[16] One cannot decry cultural reasons for the low adult female literacy rates, as the South Asian regional norm is over two-thirds.[17] Research conducted by the former Ministry for Women's Development[18] and a range of international donor agencies has revealed that *access* is the most crucial concern that parents have about educating their daughters. Indeed, reluctance turned to enthusiasm when parents in rural Punjab and rural Balochistan could be guaranteed their daughters' safety and, hence, their honor. In research I have conducted in a wide variety of areas in Pakistan—from the Walled City of Lahore, to metropolitan Islamabad and Peshawar, to small towns in Swat—I have found educated women being the vanguard of change in Pakistan and the most secure about their future. Over twenty years ago in the Walled City of Lahore, an impoverished widow who saved every rupee she earned from sewing *panchas* (hems) at the bottom of *shalwars* (loose-fitting pants) so she could educate her daughters told me, "Land and gold can always be taken away, but no one can steal a good education."[19] Despite enormous strides made in access for urban females nationwide and rural girls in Punjab to get that desired education, few effective programs have been put in place to enhance female literacy levels elsewhere in the country.

Pakistan lags behind countries with comparable per capita income in most social indicators. The lifestyle of the educated and relatively well-off urban population is similar to counterparts in other countries of similar income range. However, the poor and rural inhabitants have been left with limited resources, clamoring for jobs and decent schools for their many children, plagued by inflation, and living—quite literally—in the dark. Poverty remains a serious concern in Pakistan. Even more threatening to social stability, however, is that differences in income per capita across regions have persisted or widened.[20] Over one-third of children under age five are inappropriately underweight, a telling statistic of the failure of development efforts to promote equity in development and opportunity. Over two-thirds of Pakistan's population currently live on less than US$2 a day; over one-third live below the national poverty line. Its ranking in the UNDP's Human Development Index has slipped from 120 in 1991, to 138 in 2002, and to 141 in 2009, worse than the Congo (136) and Myanmar (138), and only just above Swaziland (142) and Angola (143), all countries with far weaker economies.

How to enable all members of the society to contribute openly to the country's future and to reap the benefits of development equitably is by far Pakistan's greatest challenge. People need to be able to access the state on their own merits, not solely through the systems of power and patronage in place today, which results in the view that corruption is rampant in Pakistan—it *is*, because this is the only way to get things done. The Government of Pakistan's draft National Population Policy recognizes that a huge societal shift is now under way:

Societal changes such as rapid urbanization, increased female achievements in education and employment market, related expansion of opportunities for women, proliferation of information through electronic and other media, and improvements in economic situation have set in a process of changes in social values.[21]

With greater numbers of people demanding goods and services in the country, and a growing majority of them living in densely populated cities difficult to navigate (physically as well as politically), the Government of Pakistan seems to be struggling with identifying how to create new kinds of economic and political space. Between growing numbers of literates in the country, growing numbers of economic migrants working throughout the world, and the expansion in media and social networking, nearly all Pakistanis today are aware of what transpires elsewhere, and they are expecting—and will ultimately demand—more options for engagement. We have already seen the violence that emerges from narrow views of community; unless the Government of Pakistan initiates more dialogue and more options, such violence is likely to escalate, and the hope for creating greater social cohesiveness resulting in positive social development in Pakistan will further diminish.

The phenomenon of development assistance has grown to enormous proportions in the world today, and its priorities are undergoing a great deal of transformation. In Pakistan, at the Official Development Assistance (ODA) Donors' Conference for earthquake relief in Islamabad in November 2005, shortly after the devastating earthquake had hit the country, while *more* aid was pledged than was asked for (US\$5.8 billion/US\$5.3 billion), nearly every donor raised the issues of transparency and accountability about how the funds would be dispersed. This issue is ongoing as Pakistan still seeks to recover from that catastrophe, though donors are reluctant to commit aid that might find its way into the coffers of extremist groups in the country (the Tehrik-e-Taliban Pakistan and the Haqqani network, among others). At the November 2010 ODA Donors' Conference organized to address relief from the mega-flood that had hit parts of Pakistan on July 29, 2010, while the need for donor support was as great (if not greater) as after the earthquake, the situation and donor response were profoundly different. While development assistance to Pakistan was now exponentially greater than five years earlier, little could be said about its effectiveness. The entire two-day conference was replete with Pakistani government officials trying to reassure the global donor community about the growing strength of its economy, how development assistance can help it, and efforts being made to ensure accountability—but the last fell short in being convincing.

This occurred with the backdrop of the United States' commitment of $2.376 billion in total aid to Pakistan for 2010–11, to go through both the government and nongovernmental organizations; it includes $700 million in the spring supplemental budget for Pakistan's Counterinsurgency Capability Fund (PCCF). Former U.S. ambassador Anne Patterson (who stepped down in October 2010) said that some of the anticipated nonmilitary aid would be "directly transferred to the government" and the remainder sent through government institutions and nongovernmental organizations. "Using a deliberate qualifying process, we will stream more funding through national, provincial, and local institutions, and build their capacity to work with us in the future ."[22] The United States tripled its development assistance budget to Pakistan—to a proposed $1.5 billion over the next year as per the Enhanced Partnership with Pakistan Act 2009— and this prompted debate on how much of the assistance should go directly to a government that had been often accused of corruption.[23] Transparency International, which has long reported that Pakistan is one of the most corrupt countries in the world, has questioned the utility of providing assistance to Pakistan: "How can one expect from any donor to come forward to assist Pakistan from its current financial crisis, when there exists no law against corruption."[24] Susan Epstein and Alan Kronstadt, writing for the Congressional Research Service in July 2011, argued that Pakistan, the second-ranking U.S. aid recipient and important to U.S. national security interests, would see its funding reduced given its lack of accountability and that

> corruption is endemic to South Asia and to Pakistan in particular. It presents a persistent and serious problem for the national economy, harming both domestic and foreign investment rates, as well as creating skeptical international aid donors.[25]

Indeed, this came true when U.S. assistance was reduced for fiscal 2012 as the U.S. Congress made both economic and security assistance conditional on Pakistan's cooperation in fighting militants and, presumably, accountability in its aid expenditures.[26]

Organization of the Volume

This volume brings together scholars and practitioners from a wide range of backgrounds to identify explicit "structural impediments" that constrain Pakistan's efforts to alleviate poverty and promote sustainable social development as well as to offer suggestions for "practical solutions" to move forward to do so. The volume is organized in four sections: "Economic Challenges," "Challenges of Infrastructural Transformation," "Challenges of Human Security," and "Ongoing Challenges of Militancy, Insecurity, and Political Paths." The focus of the various chapters is on the past decade as well as on recommendations for the future, something deemed imperative for Pakistan's long-term survival and sustainability.

The first section, "Economic Challenges," brings together three political economists, Shahrukh Rafi Khan, Aasim Sajjad Akhtar, and Abid Qaiyum Suleri. Shahrukh Rafi Khan, a former executive director of the SDPI in Islamabad, argues that while advocates of growth diagnostics have shown it to be a preferable alternative to other methods of formulating growth strategies, it also suffers from problems and demands a high level of economic sophistication from its practitioners. He instead proposes using a "weakness diagnostics" paradigm as a much broader, simpler, and forward-looking alternative. In applying this method to address the puzzle of Pakistan's lagging per capita gross domestic product (GDP) relative to India's, he argues that the lack of technological upgrading and economic diversification in Pakistan may partly explain this puzzle. Aasim Sajjad Akhtar traces how Pakistan's polity and economy have been militarized and made dependent by a politics of aid that has evolved through successive eras starting in the early 1950s. He argues that the political economy of aid has become even more stifling in recent years, and total external debt will reach US$74 billion by 2013–14. This escalation of aid effectively has consolidated Pakistan's political and economic dependence on Western governments and international financial institutions while also bolstering the state security apparatus within the polity. Abid Suleri, current executive director of SDPI, analyzes how food insecurity has been a cause of unrest, conflict, and political instability, while political instability, conflict, and social unrest have in turn caused food insecurity, poverty, and marginalization. He argues that both food insecurity and conflict erode people's resilience to any external or internal change, and vice versa. He explores the relationship among these challenges in Pakistan's context, arguing that insecurity breeds insecurity and that unless individual security is given precedence over national, regional, and global securities, it will be difficult to break the vicious cycle of insecurities facing the people of Pakistan.

The second section, "Challenges of Infrastructural Transformation," looks at various institutions in Pakistan—law, politics, and the bureaucracy—with an eye toward understanding how they can—and must—be transformed to contribute constructively to Pakistan's future. Aitzaz Ahsan, former head of the Supreme Court Bar Association and leader of the Lawyer's Movement in Pakistan, focuses on salient aspects of Pakistan's legal system that must be changed to facilitate positive development in the country. He argues that identification, however, is but a first step; the even greater challenges are to conceive of what would work better and develop a strategy to incorporate these changes into Pakistan's legal structure. Hasan Askari Rizvi analyzes what he sees as an increasingly dysfunctional political system that threatens Pakistan's long-term viability as a coherent and stable political entity. He argues that the dilemma is not the state's failure to identify solutions but rather to create a consensus on them, their priorities, and how to implement them. After reviewing major political obstacles to development as well as reviewing party dynamics in the country, he addresses constitutional discontinuities, the political threat of religious extremism and militancy, and other political challenges affecting Pakistan's development prospects. He concludes that the compelling reason behind how politics affects development is based on how political leaders and parties manage their affairs, as their priorities are dominated by narrow partisan interests and power politics. Saeed Shafqat follows on this political thread as he addresses the issue of the workability of Pakistan's bureaucracy and questions the impact the recently enacted Eighteenth Amendment, which devolved many responsibilities from the federal level to the provinces, may have on the effective running of the bureaucracy in the future. Following an overview of the civil service in Pakistan, he reviews the reports of four commissions tasked between 1972 and 2009 with reforming Pakistan's bureaucracy. He evaluates each report in the context of the prevailing sociopolitical environment, the regime type (democratic or military) that initiated it, and the state's imperative, arguing that both democratic and military rulers' reform efforts have been driven by considerations of subordinating the bureaucracy rather than changing its behavior, improving service delivery and citizen welfare, and enhancing professional skills, managerial capacity, and public accountability. He also explores why reform efforts have been only on the higher bureaucracy and not the provincial governments. Finally, he assesses how the recently enacted Eighteenth Amendment is reshaping the federation, especially by offering provincial governments an opportunity to revamp the capacity of their bureaucracies and improve governance.

This is followed by "Challenges of Human Security," which includes various scholars' and practitioners' interpretations of the human security threats that Pakistan lives under on a daily basis. They conceptualize how best to protect the poor, develop tourism both to bring in foreign exchange as well as to promote a sense of cultural heritage, move forward with a population policy that can effectively lessen the country's high population growth rates (which threaten to compromise all other successes), and promote women's rights. Saba Gul Khattak, another former executive director of SDPI and currently a member of the Pakistan Planning Commission (and co-editor of this volume) addresses the concept and contested meanings of social protection with regard to social safety nets. She traces various policy measures instituted by the Government of Pakistan to mitigate people's vulnerabilities. Given the intensified challenges from increased population, poverty, under- and unemployment, and insecurity, she delves into questions about the usefulness of targeting social protection and subsidies along with the associated tools of poverty, head-count ratios, and caloric intake. In highlighting Pakistan's allocations for social-sector social protection programs, she compares these with allocations for the "hard" sectors including infrastructure and security and argues for increasing investment in the social sector rather than building on welfarist band-aid approaches. John Mock, in his provocatively titled chapter, "No American, No Gun, No BS": Tourism, Terrorism, and the Eighteenth Amendment," is echoing a statement he has frequently heard in Pakistan regarding tourists. In his discussion of the state of tourism and tourism trends in Pakistan, he identifies potential strategies for mitigating impacts and conflict, and how best to foster tourism to play a salient role in contributing to Pakistan's future as it has done in many other areas of the world. Zeba Sathar and Peter C. Miller note that despite Pakistan having been one of the earliest countries to have a clearly articulated population policy, it is one of the last countries in Asia to experience the onset of a fertility decline. This has been compounded by the stalling use of contraception, leading to a recent deceleration in the rate of fertility decline. Sathar and Miller examine various explanations for this decline, including macroeconomic conditions—particularly per capita income and poverty—and human development factors, particularly educational enrollment, literacy, the status of women (particularly employment), and the provision or lack thereof of family-planning services. They argue that Pakistan's decision-makers never considered population policies seriously and that this neglect, further affected by the devolution of population planning responsibilities to the provinces, has now thrown the country's demographic destiny into further peril. Muhammad Khalid Masud, eminent historian and former chairperson of Pakistan's Council of Islamic Ideology, explores the historical relationship between the Ulema in Pakistan and development initiatives. He argues that the Ulema have an entirely different perspective on development from the mainstream population and analyzes the causes behind the Ulema's reluctance to support and become engaged with development projects. He identifies types of projects that the Ulema have and have not supported, and argues that "attempts to enlist the Ulema's cooperation have strengthened their authority at the cost of development targets." The section concludes with a chapter by Afiya Shehrbano Zia, who argues that while the initial framework for women's rights in Pakistan was loosely based on a universal human rights model, increasing Islamization of state and society have challenged practically all basic liberties, freedoms, and security for women. At the same time, the "theocratization" of development has seeped into the rationale of several post-9/11 donor-funded projects, in effect replacing universal minimal human rights with abstract conceptions of Islamic nationalism and culture. Zia argues that such recourse is not just defeatist and counterintuitive to the historical direction of women's rights in Pakistan, but that it also reinforces patriarchal traditions within Pakistan's gendered discourse. In addressing these new challenges to women's rights and development in Pakistan, she also focuses on the broader implications for feminism in the country.

The final section, "Ongoing Challenges of Militancy, Insecurity, and Political Paths," captures the various dimensions of the challenges Pakistan must address in the face of daily political turmoil, militarism, and extremism. Nazish Brohi's starting point is that the investiture of power at the center, among other acts, has been a consistent grievance of the provinces. She suggests that "these centrifugal and centripetal forces do not exist as binaries" and that impunity toward violence against women has created nationwide narratives of national honor and autonomy that have promoted "a masculinist solidarity across sub-nationalist cleavages." Women on the peripheries have responded by sometimes attempting to break through boundaries of the private sphere by locating themselves in the public realm and claiming state protection or, more commonly, by circumventing the state altogether. Brohi suggests that in the current debate in Pakistan over devolution, cast in the center-periphery paradigm, the tectonic plates of the country's power structures are shifting and may offer new possibilities to address violence against women. The next chapter in this section, by Ashley J. Tellis, explores various factors that have impeded the development of democratic institutions in Pakistan and examines what might be done to strengthen the prospects of success, internally and externally, in the future. Finally, Moeed Yusuf's chapter examines the intersection of development, politics, and security in Pakistan, taking "the anomalous civil-military relations" as his starting premise. He briefly traces the roots of this anomaly before analyzing its impact on development outcomes. He argues that the impact of the civil-military disconnect goes far beyond the failure to consolidate democracy; it is responsible for having created a security-centered narrative that has never allowed Pakistani leaders to approach development holistically, thereby skewing the very priorities of the state, which are further reinforced by weaknesses on both the military and civilian sides.

In the end, our goal has been to initiate a discourse. We recognize that much more could have been included herein, but the imperative to move forward and begin taking up these issues precluded adding even more chapters. Even within each chapter, there was much more that could have been explored, but then this volume would have become untenable. In the end, it is with good heart that we move forward with this undertaking, with sincere hopes that somehow these various chapters will get people thinking about Pakistan's development prospects and how we can reconceptualize issues, dilemmas, and prospects to help build a better future for all Pakistanis.

Notes

1. Gunnar Myrdal, *Asian Drama: An Inquiry into the Poverty of Nations* (New York: Twentieth Century Fund, 1968).

2. UNDP *Human Development Report* data are available on the hdrstats.undp.org website. The UN Population Division estimated Pakistan's population at 180.8 million, while the World Bank estimated it at 173.6 million. However, figures in the Ministry of Population Welfare's "Draft National Population Policy 2010" estimated Pakistan's population at the same time as 171 million.

3. Reprinted in C. M. Naim, ed., *Iqbal, Jinnah, and Pakistan: The Vision and the Reality*, South Asian series no. 5 (Syracuse, NY: Syracuse University Maxwell School of Citizenship and Public Affairs, 1979), 212.

4. Ibid., 212–13.

5. Islamic religious schools, centered around the teachings of a distinct school of thought within Islam.

6. This sect emerged when Sunni Muslims, opposed to British rule in South Asia, established a religious school, the Dar-Ul-Ulom, in 1867 in the northern Indian city of Deoband. Deobandi teachings espouse a very literal interpretation of Islam.

7. Allama Iqbal, in the early twentieth century, reasoned that two distinct nations—now manifest as Hindus and Muslims—have existed simultaneously in South Asia, with different historical backgrounds, traditions, cultures, and social orders. The Two Nations theory was one of the foundations of the demand for Pakistan at independence.

8. Barelvi Sunnis make up about half of Pakistan's population; their greatest concentration is in the Punjab. Founded in the early nineteenth century, Barelvi teachings espouse a *pir*-centered, populist understanding of Islam, prioritizing communal practices over texts.

9. In 2010, the Northwest Frontier Province was renamed Khyber Pakhtunkhwa.

10. While the global *dawah* movement has the goal to teach Muslims worldwide how to adhere to a more authentic Islam, in practice it is spreading Wah'habi interpretations more commonlhy found in Saudi Arabia. Funding for *dawah* missions is popularly perceived to originate in Saudi Arabia as well.

11. CIA *World Factbook*. This would place Punjab between number 14–ranked Ethiopia (85.2 million) and number 15–ranked Germany (82.3 million).

12. For further discussion of the various factors that constrained the Pakistan government from holding a census, refer to Anita M. Weiss, "Much Ado about Counting: The Conflict over Holding a Census in Pakistan," *Asian Survey* 39/4 (1999): 679–93.

13. "The Relationship between Education and Religious Discrimination in Pakistan: Analysis of Curriculum and Pedagogy in Pakistani Schools." Information on this SDPI report is available on the sdpi.org website.

14. Ibid.

15. Statistics Division, Population Census Organization, *1998 Census: Demographic Indicators* (Islamabad: Government of Pakistan).

16. UNICEF, "Basic Indicators: Pakistan," available on the unicef.org website.

17. UNDP, "Country Brief, South Asia Region, Pakistan," 2003, compares Pakistan's female literacy rate with that of other countries in the region with similar per capita income levels.

18. The responsibilities of the Ministry of Women's Development devolved to the provinces in 2010 with the implementation of the Eighteenth Amendment.

19. This was conveyed to me when I was conducting research for *Walls within Walls: Life Histories of Working Women in the Old City of Lahore* (Boulder, CO: Westview Press, 1992).

20. The World Bank first expressed this as a concern in its "Pakistan Country Update" in 2004.

21. Ministry of Population Welfare, *Draft National Population Policy 2010* (Islamabad: Government of Pakistan, 2010), 7. However, with the implementation of the Eighteenth Amendment and the devolution of population matters to the provinces, this draft policy was not implemented.

22. BBC News, "US Gives $3bn in Aid to Pakistan," September 17, 2009, available on the news.bbc.co.uk website.

23. For more details on the Enhanced Partnership with Pakistan Act, refer to USAID's website, at usaid.gov.

24. Transparency International–Pakistan, transparency.org.pk website (September 2009).

25. Susan B. Epstein and K. Alan Kronstadt, *Pakistan: U.S. Foreign Assistance*, Congressional Research Service (Washington DC: 2011): 32.

26. Susan Cornwell, "U.S. Foreign Aid Escapes Slashing Cuts in Fiscal 2012," *Reuters*, December 19, 2011.

Part One

ECONOMIC CHALLENGES

2

Explaining the Puzzle of Pakistan's Lagging Economic Growth

Shahrukh Rafi Khan

Pakistan in its short history has suffered from political upheavals, wars, natural disasters, and terrorism, and so it has had to fight the odds. Despite this, its per capita GDP was higher than India's until 2006. The puzzle this chapter addresses is why a crossover occurred, and "weakness diagnostics" is introduced as a simple tool to address this puzzle.

India is used by most Pakistanis and their government to track their own progress even though India of late has viewed itself in another league and looks to China for comparison. Notwithstanding India's aspirations, Pakistan's comparison to India makes sense because at least the initial economic conditions were similar though they were slanted in favor of India based on asset and resource distribution at the time of independence in 1947.[1] Size and political developments, notably a maturing democracy in India and military interventions in Pakistan, distinguish the two countries. Also notably different due to military interventions is the state of higher education, with India's benefiting from a relatively free democratic system and Pakistan's suffering from military-led bureaucratization and repression. These differences may be much more telling in the next sixty odd years than they have been to date, because comparisons in the early twenty-first century show relative parity in many respects, as will be demonstrated.

The next section of this chapter presents weakness diagnostics as a prelude to fuller growth diagnostics. The following section presents and discusses

---

This chapter draws from "Growth Diagnostics: The Puzzle of Pakistan's Lagging Economic Growth," *Global Economy Journal* 11, no. 4 (December 2011): 1–17.

the associated empirics, and the last section makes suggestions as to what might be done and how.

Weakness Diagnostics

Growth diagnostics (GD) is getting the attention of macro-development economists to address puzzles such as what constrains catch-up growth in a particular country.[2] This line of inquiry was initiated in various articles, including Hausmann and Rodrik 2005, Hausmann, Rodrik, and Velasco 2008, and Hausmann, Klinger, and Wagner 2008. There are three components of this approach, as summarized in Dani Rodrik's *One Economics, Many Recipes* (2009): use diagnostics to identify the most binding constraint(s); design policy to address the constraint(s); and institutionalize the process so that as the growth process begins other constraints that become the most binding can be addressed.

Growth diagnostics has many strengths, including providing a place to start the analysis, being country specific, using economic intuition and all available evidence, and emphasizing pragmatic policy prescriptions. Since only a few prescriptions are suggested for the identified constraint, administrative ability is not overburdened. The decision tree posited draws on a whole spectrum of approaches, both orthodox and heterodox. However, it also has a number of weaknesses, such as being very demanding in the level of analytical skill required of practitioners (Khan 2011). We therefore propose weakness diagnostics as a prelude to narrow down the options for rigorous evaluation using growth diagnostics. This tool is forward looking in exploring whether growth can be sustained even if it is robust and what might be some of the key roadblocks looking ahead.

The data search is driven by the particularities of the country in question and can be broad, covering all relevant evidence and approaches, informal and formal. Those with a finger on the economic pulse of a country can explore the data to see if what are identified as the major economic constraints by businesses are indeed so in a comparative context. The data can provide heuristic diagnostics of major weaknesses and also identify the intensity of the problems. For example, in Pakistan's case, judging from business complaints in the media, the key constraints might be the shortage of credit and poor infrastructure. Other constraints are evident just from living in the country. For example, experiencing blackouts and brownouts would suggest looking at the data to identify the intensity of the energy constraint. Anyone who has worked in the science and technology or higher-education sectors in a low- or middle-income country knows about the acute shortage of talented people with doctorates and how local talent is poached by international organizations like the World Bank and the UNDP.

Alternatively, one could use theory to identify the extent of or the lack of development. Those defining development as access to entitlements and building capacities would look at social indicators to identify key weaknesses (Sen 2000). Macro-stabilization is viewed as a precondition for attaining a higher sustainable growth path by orthodox economists, and this could be explored (World Bank 2005).

One view of the development process suggests that healthy social indicators can be an input, but they are much more likely to be a complement and an outcome rather than fundamental process of development. In this view the development process is about attaining an indigenous and endogenous technological capacity for diversifying the economy, which will concomitantly lead to both higher human development and macroeconomic stability.[3] To start with, the empirics could simply be creatively processing raw data into comparative tables. However, more sophisticated empirical methods can subsequently be used to pursue leads with the caveats suggested above.

To sum up, weakness diagnostics is broad based and forward looking. While in growth diagnostics, recent economic history is tracked to identify binding constraints, weakness diagnostics uses the most recent data available to scan for hints of what the main problems might be. The approach is much more humble and promises much less certainty. Since it is much less demanding of analytical skills from practitioners than growth diagnostics, it can serve as a useful prelude.

Weakness diagnostics entails the following five-step process: (1) as with GD, start the process with a research question or puzzle; (2) select a good set of comparators to construct tables; (3) use anecdotal evidence, observation, the media, theory, or broad conceptual frameworks for data gathering; (4) identify the glaring weaknesses revealed by scanning the tables; (5) if needed, do in-depth follow-up analysis of key weaknesses.

Weakness Diagnostics: The Case of Pakistan

The puzzle we address using weakness diagnostics is illustrated in Figure 2–1.[4]

As the trend lines of per capita GDP for India and Pakistan show, both countries started with virtually identical per capita GDPs in 1960, but Pakistan quickly took the lead and moved on to a higher per capita GDP trajectory and maintained this lead until 2006.[5] However, India shifted to higher per capita GDP trajectory in the late 1970s and again, after the turn of the century.[6] Figure 2–1 suggests a structural break in the per capita GDP

Figure 2–1. Real Per Capita GDPs for India and Pakistan (Constant 2000 US$s)

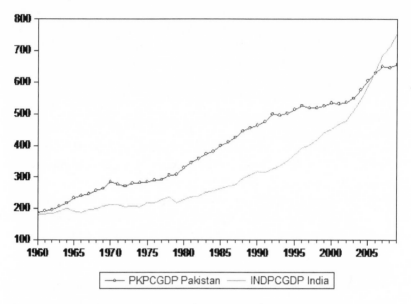

Source: Online World Development Indicators

series around 1979 and again in 2002. Rodrik and Subramanian present formal evidence to argue that the structural break occurred in 1979, and we replicated this result via two of the methods proposed (2004). Following a test proposed in the article "Growth Accelerations," we found that the year 2002 represents a break year following which India experienced growth acceleration (Hausmann, Pritchett, and Rodrick 2005).

By comparison, the trend line for Pakistan shows three stagnations in the periods from 1970 to 1977, 1992 to 2002, and 2007 to the present. While the first stagnation corresponds with Prime Minister Zulfiqar Ali Bhutto's administration, viewed as a period of great economic disruption induced by nationalizations,[7] there is no neat fit with a regime for the second lost decade. Economic historians could engage in period analysis to try to understand trajectory shifts; however, our goal in this chapter is more limited.

Pakistan's per capita GDP in 2008 was US$980 compared with US$1,070 for India. As earlier indicated, the two countries had similar initial conditions in 1960, and both economies still appear to be structurally similar, as indicated by the percentage distribution of agriculture, industry, and services shown in the Appendix, Table A-1. However, these broad aggregates mask important variations, and this is one of the key issues we emphasize in this chapter.

China is clearly in a different league on all counts other than governance, particularly in voice and accountability, as indicated in the Appendix, Table A–4. However, because it has been the most dynamic emerging economy for the last three decades, its comparative achievements are instructive. The average of the low-middle-income countries (LMICs) is also used for comparison. Since Pakistan has just barely graduated into LMIC ($976–$3,855) status, comparing its numbers with the averages of other LMICs is a reach. However, the comparison does indicate what Pakistan needs to strive for to secure its position in the LMIC category and move on to upper-middle-income status.

Following from country particularities and frameworks identified above, the Appendix, Tables A–2 through A–5 presents the associated comparative statistics. Table A–1 provides country background data to set the stage for the comparisons to follow in the remaining tables: Table A–2 explores the stories that emerge from anecdotes or observations; Table A–3 pursues the human development story; Table A–4 details the structural problems and reforms story; and Table A–5, the technology and economic diversification story.

The numbers in Table A–1 reveal some surprises. For example, Pakistan has much higher labor productivity in agriculture ($696) compared to India ($392) and even China ($407), though it is way below the average of LMICs ($2,721). Table A–1 also demonstrates that much more is made of India's recent strength and Pakistan's recent weakness than is suggested by numbers. For example, India's annual average growth rate since the turn of the century is 7.9 percent, which is below the LMIC average of 8.3 percent average and 2.5 percent below China's rate, which is 10.4 percent. However, it is a whole two percentage points higher than Pakistan's rate.

Positives for Pakistan are an open unemployment rate of 5.5 percent, which is about half that of India's. It has the least inequality of the comparators in that the share of the poorest quintile in national consumption is the highest and it has the lowest Gini coefficient, 31, compared with 37 for India and 42 for China during 2005. Again, poverty is about half that of India's. However, unless Pakistan addresses its weaknesses it is likely to fall further and further behind in its ability to provide a decent standard of living to its more rapidly growing population (2.3 percent compared with 1.4 percent for India).

The numbers in Table A–2 show that the commonly heard complaints by businesses concerning credit and power have substance. Domestic credit provided by the banking sector as a percentage of GDP in 2008 was 40 percent, which was about half that of India and about one-third that of China. The cost of capital inferred from the interest rate on a ten-year government bond was 11.22 percent, which was almost one-fourth greater than India and about three-fifths greater than China. Similarly, there is substance to the complaints about power shortages. The value lost due to electric outages as a percentage of total sales for Pakistan in 2007 was about 10 percent, double the losses in 2002. Although at 6.6 percent India also had high losses, this percentage still marked a reduction of losses from 2002's 8.1 percent. Using quality of ports and percentage of total roads paved as proxies for infrastructure, there seems less reason for businesses in Pakistan to complain on this score, at least in a comparative context.

The numbers in Table A–3 explore the human development story, and Pakistan shows some surprising strengths in a comparative perspective. It matches India on life expectancy, has more than twice the level of improved sanitation, and shows better maternal mortality statistics. However, the Achilles' heel remains low adult literacy rates (about half the population). Since two-fifths of those attending primary school do not complete, compared to only 14 percent for India, matters do not look as though they are going to improve any time soon.

The numbers in Table A–4 explore the structural problems and reform stories. Pakistan demonstrates serious structural flaws, including a high trade and fiscal deficit and also a high level of external indebtedness. However, these are also problems that India faces. Also, along with India, Pakistan faced double-digit inflation, 13.7 percent, in 2010. The tax effort in both countries and also in China—and in fact the average of other LMICs—is between 9 and 12 percent, which is very low by high-income country standards.[8]

Other structural problems and their symptoms (trade and fiscal deficits and inflation) that induce the International Monetary Fund (IMF) to impose structural adjustment reforms are similar to those that India faces, and so this is not the place to find what differentiates the two countries. In any case, scholars such as Chang have convincingly demonstrated that emerging economies such as Korea faced similar structural problems in the initial phase of their economic take-off and that the improvement on these indicators is endogenous to the economic take-off rather than a precondition (2006).

The cost of business and good governance are viewed as the second generation of structural reforms, and Pakistan outranks India and is, in fact, closer to China with regard to ease of doing business. As a percentage of profit, its tax rate is 31.6, which is about half that of India or China. Thus, relative to India, it is much more business friendly. However, on governance, India outranks Pakistan on all measures, including government effectiveness, regulatory quality, rule of law, and voice and accountability.

An important part of the structural reform story is that ease of doing business, and good governance will promote foreign direct investment (FDI).

Again, whether or not FDI helps the economy is not straightfo[rward] and Grabel 2004, 138–48). However, in any case, the differe[nce] India and Pakistan is one percentage point despite Pakistan's a[b]centile ranking on political stability and the absence of terrorism. Pakistan's percentile rank on this indicator dropped from 15.87 in 0.47 in 2009, about as low as it can go.

So far, we have demonstrated that Pakistan reveals some surp[rising] strengths relative to its comparators in labor productivity in agriculture in the human condition of its population (unemployment, poverty, inequality), though its low per capita GDP trajectory may make improvi[ng] the human condition or social indicators difficult. The main weakness i[n] human development is in basic education; this is one problem that Pakistan has had to contend with for a long time and the numbers show that this weakness is likely to persist. We also found that there is strong support for business complaints about the shortage of credit and power, though Pakistan is much more business friendly than India. It suffers from much weaker governance and political instability. Once again, improvements here are likely to be endogenous to a take-off and a virtuous cycle beginning such that success breeds success.

The question then is, other than education, where should Pakistan focus to reverse its lagging per capita GDP relative to India? Due to our adoption of indigenous technological capacity and economic diversification as the definition of the development process, the variables associated with this process are of interest, and it is here that Pakistan shows the greatest weakness, as the numbers in Table A–5 demonstrate. Gross capital formation, an essential complement to technological development and economic diversification, was 18 percent of GDP in Pakistan in 2008, which was approximately half that of India's 35 percent. Another complement to technological development is Internet access and use. While Pakistan has higher overall Internet access (11.1 per 100 people) relative to India's surprisingly low 4.5, it has almost five time less fixed broadband Internet service per 100 people and three times less secure Internet servers per million people than India.

More important for technological development and economic diversification is evidence of effective research and development (R&D). The issue is not inputs but outcomes, since the data show Pakistan was spending about the same amount as a percentage of GDP (0.67) on R&D as India (0.80). Pakistan has more researchers per million (152) than India (137), though many times less than the average for LMIC (479) and even more for China (1,071). However, it is the outcomes that are sizably lower. Patent activity provides an indication of the prevailing scientific and innovative buzz.

Domestic applications for patents by residents in 2006 in China were 122,318 compared with 5,314 in India and only 91 in Pakistan.

Technological development enables a country to diversify. Most nations start with the textiles and clothing industry and then move up the technology ladder. Thus, by 2003, this industry only accounted for 2 percent of the total manufacturing value added in China and 9 percent for India. By comparison, in the period from July 2009 to April 2010, 53 percent of total exports in Pakistan were textiles, making them the largest export by percentage (Government of Pakistan 2010, 89). Another indicator of economic diversification is high-technology exports as a percentage of the total. For China and India these are 29 percent and 6 percent, respectively, compared to 2 percent for Pakistan. Thus, Pakistan is seriously lagging scientifically and technologically and has a much less diversified economy compared to India, and this may partly account for its lagging per capita GDP.

We now explore technological sophistication in more detail, given its importance. Table 2–1 presents the weights used by the respective statistics bureaus of India and Pakistan in computing large-scale manufacturing sector indices.

While the industry groups are not identical, it is quite clear from this data that India has a much more technologically sophisticated economy.[9] Pakistan's largest group is textiles and apparel, more than one-quarter of manufacturing and double India's percentage. Its other big group is food, beverage, and tobacco, and that also is low on the technology ladder. Engineering goods represent less than one-half of 1 percent of total manufacturing weight (0.45). By contrast, about half of India's economy is now basic chemicals and products, including pharmaceuticals, basic metals, and machinery and equipment.

Another technological insight can be gleaned from exploring patenting activity of domestic residents in more detail. The *World Development Indicators* reports the absolute amounts of applications. We standardized these for population and computed average ratios for patent applications in India relative to Pakistan for the periods for which data were available. Between 1964 and 1969, the ratio was 1.4; between 1971 and 1980, it rose to 3.9; and between 1990 and 2006, it rose to 7.1. This series shows a steady rise for India and a steady decline for Pakistan.[10]

What Needs to Be Done?

Economic history suggests that the development process is about moving up the technology ladder and diversifying the economy (Chang 2002; Reinert 2007). In Pakistan's case this also means addressing the acute shortage of

Table 2–1: Large-Scale Manufacturing Sector Weights in India and Pakistan

Group Pakistan	Pakistan	India	Groups India
Textile and apparel	26.41	13.79	
Food, beverage, tobacco, and related products	14.35	14.45	
Petroleum	5.23	7.22	Rubber, plastic, petroleum and coal products
Pharmaceuticals	5.03		
Chemicals	2.88	17.64	Basic chemical and chemical products
Nonmetallic mineral products	4.19	5.54	
Automobile	3.95		
Fertilizers	3.38		
Electronic	2.49		
Leather products	2.27	1.44	
		3.40	Wood and wood products, furniture and fixtures
Paper and paper board	0.60	3.34	
Engineering products	0.45		
Tires and tubes	0.30		
		9.39	Basic metals and alloy industries
		3.55	Metal products and parts
		12.05	Machinery and equipment
		5.02	Transport equipment and parts
Other	28.55	3.22	

Notes: The large-scale manufacturing groups are not identical for the two countries and rather than force items into groups, they are separately reported when they do not match. For Pakistan, these group weights have been used to compute changes in production by groups between 2008–9 and 2009–10. For India, they have been used to compute index numbers of industrial production from 2004–5 until 2007–8. Totals are slightly greater than 100 due to rounding.

Source: Government of Pakistan (2010, p. 42), and India, Ministry of Statistics and Programme Implementation, available online.

highly educated personnel in the science and technology sectors. Resources are an issue, but simply throwing resources at the problem, as was done by the well-meaning minister of science and technology during General Musharraf's administration, created perverse incentives. An important lesson of the East Asian development experience is that incentives must be tempered by performance criteria to attain goals (Wade 2004). To avoid the "bean counting" that resulted from incentives in Pakistan (more publications, more local PhDs), the incentives need to be conditioned by the quality of the research, publications, and patents.

Again, diversifying the economy needs entrepreneurship that is nurtured in an environment of incentives and fierce competition. We start with the presumption that in most low-income countries entrepreneurship is distributed as in any other population, though opportunities to realize potential varies by country income level.[11] The state needs to discover what is working despite its lack of support or where it needs to step aside.[12] A possible tool for identifying "successes" could be the scrutiny of foreign-trade statistics or disaggregated manufacturing-sector data. Activities identified as successful could be urged up the technology ladder by relaxing credit, information, or infrastructural constraints based on performance criteria such as meeting export targets. Thus, an important component of industrial policy could be nurturing successes by understanding and relaxing constraints. Here, open channels of communication between the public and private sectors are highly relevant.[13]

Peter Evans suggests the possibility of using "pockets of efficiency" in the bureaucracy as a mechanism of support (1995, 61). An alternative is to restructure the Planning Commission into a Bureau of Economic Activity with a one-point mandate of nurturing promising activities. This task entails supportive interministerial roles to ensure upstream and downstream activities are in place.[14]

While one might anticipate the most dynamic efficiencies to be in the manufacturing sector, as the name Bureau of Economic Activity suggests, there may be promising nonindustrial activities like information technology that qualify for conditional support. Much of the bureau's work would be interfacing with other agencies and ministries to ensure that support systems are in place. It bears repeating that all advocates of industrial policy acknowledge the importance of the ability of such an agency to set and monitor performance criteria such as exports and employment growth and to have the political strength to sanction or withdraw support if need be.[15]

A fair question would be how one could rely on economic bureaucrats to execute incentives efficiently. First, there are many competent and efficient officers willing to work in the national interest even if they are themselves subject to poor incentives. Second, open competition for incentives and transparency with open access to information to the media and civil society could limit rent-seeking.

Planning commissions used to have prestige and draw the best and brightest, but over time, particularly with the sway of neo-liberalism, they have lost their sheen. A revamped and relevant bureau could change that.[16] As Chang points out, such a bureau needs to have power over other related ministries, be immune from the funding veto of the finance ministry, and be answerable directly to the chief executive but with a cabinet-level check on economic practice (2006, 98).

Conclusion

Pakistan and India had virtually identical per capita GDPs in 1960, the first year for which we have data, but there was a quick divergence after which Pakistan gained and maintained a lead until 2006. India's trend line initially shows a slow and steady increase, much like the proverbial turtle to Pakistan's hare, but it subsequently experienced an upward trajectory shift in per capita GDP around 1979 and again in 2002. The puzzle we address in this chapter, by using "weakness diagnostics" as a prelude to more rigorous investigation, is why Pakistan was unable to maintain its lead.

In Pakistan's case, future growth is likely to be hindered by many noneconomic composite variables. In addition, political administrations have to deal with a complex interplay of ethnic, sectarian, regional, and class tensions. All of these have consequences for external and internal investment. Finally, they have to contend with a military that has assumed most of the state's power and that can dictate budget and off-budget allocations. Getting beyond these obstacles, economic growth is likely to be determined by intangibles, such as the motivation for collective action, premised on inclusion and social justice. Thus, it seems that diagnostics may be of limited assistance; perhaps good luck is what really counts (Dixit 2007, 149).

However, our presumption is that even limited and predatory democracies seek survival or reelection by trying to deliver something to the public, particularly knowing that the military is not shy when it comes to assuming state power directly and that rioting or popular uprisings are possible. If national cohesion and a reasonably responsible leadership set the stage for sustained growth for a historically created geographic entity, it is worth pointing out what glaring weaknesses we should pay attention to.

Based on our historically informed definition of the development process, our weakness diagnostics suggests that the most glaring shortcomings relative to India as our main comparator are in education and the low levels of technological upgrading and industrial diversification. Both factors may be viewed as endogenous based on some process, but that could be argued to be the case for all variables. The issue here is finding where to initiate a virtuous cycle.

So many have harped for so long on the need for quality education in Pakistan at all levels, starting with Mohammed Ali Jinnah as Pakistan's first governor general, that it is difficult to add much to that. However, until elites see education as an investment in people to build and draw on the potential of the whole nation rather than as a threat to their class interests, particularly in agriculture, little will change. An inverse association between landed power and rural education has been established in the literature. More broadly, quality education may be perceived as enhancing competition, already fierce, for access to opportunities and positions for the children of elites.[17]

Technological development is embodied in broader economic and social development, but progress is always jagged and uneven, and movement with the right social incentives might be possible. Our prescription based on weakness diagnostics is for a fuller exploration of technology policy as a key determinant of growth. If our hunch proves right by more rigorous evaluation, a range of associated policies would follow.

Since technology policies need to be embedded in associated supportive industrial policies, such as those for infrastructure, training, institutions, trade, technology, finance, and fiscal incentives, it is easy to lose focus very quickly. Hence, our recommendation is a partnership with businesses such that with open channels of communications and rudimentary data analysis the government can discover what is working well under difficult circumstances and facilitate those activities. Further, this process would need to be institutionalized so that there is conditional support for continued movement up the technology ladder with the associated diversification of the economy.

The presumption behind the use of weakness diagnostics to address the puzzle of India moving to a per capita GDP trajectory in the late 1970s and the turn of the century is that India clearly did something right that Pakistan did not.[18] Further, enough time has elapsed so that some of the differentiating steps should show up in the current comparative data using the alternative approaches identified above for data collection. We recognize that many of the reasons that probably account for India's higher per capita GDP trajectory are historic and intangible, and they are therefore unlikely to show up in the data; hence, any conclusions reached are suggestive. Our choice of variables is primarily driven by policy. Others may be motivated to generate alternative comparative tables using alternative frameworks for data collection, and in this regard we view the method and the case study to have value.

Notes

1. Refer to Oldenburg (2010).

2. Two articles in the December 2010 issue of the *Journal of Economic Literature* 48/4 suggest a broader acceptance and use of such diagnostics.

3. Unfortunately, production systems are often environmentally dirty without policy nudging, even if there are win-win possibilities; this important issue has been extensively addressed in the literature and additional important work is under way (Zarsky 2010).

4. While this puzzle had already motivated this chapter, the issue was brought into sharper focus by the comparative per capita GDP figure for Bangladesh, India, and Pakistan reported as Figure 11 in Hausmann, Klinger, and Wagner (2008).

5. We deliberately use per capita GDP in constant dollars rather than the purchasing power parity (PPP, constant 2005 international dollars). Apart from methodological problems in constructing PPP estimates (Reddy 2009), it is actual and not PPP$ that are used by LICs (low-income countries) and LMICs to purchase capital equipment, raw materials, and technology on international markets to enhance their economic growth. Also, PPP estimates only extend back to 1980. Using these PPP estimates also shows a sharp trajectory shift for Indian per capita GDP for 2002, though the crossover year is 2003 rather than 2006.

6. The 1991 market-oriented structural reforms are often cited as the cause of the Indian take-off, and the evidence reported here would suggest about a decade for these and subsequent reforms to take effect fully. While that is plausible, these reforms could not explain the trajectory shift in 1979. Rodrik and Subramanian challenge the reform story (2004).

7. Other causes for the low economic growth could include an oil shock and a subsequent global economic slowdown as well as nature (floods and droughts).

8. Again, Pakistan should take little comfort from performing at the level of its peers in this regard, even if statements by the IMF, which enforced structural adjustment of the economy between 2008 and 2011 (see imf.org website) do not indicate cognizance of this parity.

9. Almost one-third of Pakistan's total weight (28.6 percent), compared with only 3.2 percent for India, fits into the "other" category. It is therefore difficult to say anything definitive about economic diversification, but judging from the listed product groups, India has a much more diversified economy.

10. With some data massaging, it would be possible to construct a series from 1964 to 2006 and use this and other proxies such as manufacturing exports as a percentage of GDP to examine more rigorously the impact of technology on economic growth using time series analysis. I leave this exercise to others. For an analysis of the state of technology in Pakistan's large-scale manufacturing industries and its impact on productivity growth, refer to Mahmood and Siddiqui 2000. Using data from 1973 to 1997, they attribute slow productivity growth to an ailing science-and-technology apparatus. For a review of the state of technology in India, refer to Dutz 2007.

11. Sociologists have rightly argued that the incidence of entrepreneurship may be higher as a self-defense mechanism among some minority communities like the Parsis in the Indian subcontinent (Kilby 1971).

12. Most LICs are likely to focus initially on imported technologies, adaptation, and imitation.

13. This issue has been elaborated on in detail by Evans (1995) in terms of the concept of embedded autonomy. Johnson (1982, 267), in exploring various forms of "deliberation councils" used in Japanese industrial policy, describes the Industrial Structure Council of 1964, which included the economic bureaucracy, business, and finance to keep open channels of communication among stakeholders. Shapiro expresses reservations with this "top down" policy (2010).

14. This would include coordination for social and environmental investments and safeguards.

15. Refer to the concise summary by Chang and Grabel (2004, 77–80). Chang points to the importance of retaining flexibility regarding targets to address contingencies while resisting undue lobbying for advantage, a universal trait of businesses (2009, 26).

16. Refer to Singh for a new agenda for the Indian Planning Commission (2009).

17. Refer to Hossain and Kabeer 2004 for the role of governing elites in being instrumental in boosting basic education way beyond Pakistan's achievements starting from a similar base in 1970. Bangladeshi elites identify with the rural masses from where many of them came and see an investment in basic education as foundational for nation-building and for poverty alleviation. This political commitment is backed by appropriate resource allocations.

18. At the time of writing (summer 2012), India's growth rate has slowed down relative to its earlier blistering pace. However, it is still higher than Pakistan's by a wider margin and enviable even for most middle income countries. In this regard, a long view needs to be taken, and I stand by the assertion in this chapter that India's economic diversification and technological development are part of what is needed for a solid economic growth foundation.

Reference List

Chang, H-J. *Kicking Away the Ladder: Development Strategy in Historical Perspective.* London: Anthem Press, 2002.

———. *The East Asian Development Experience: The Miracle, the Crisis, and the Future.* London: Zed Books; Penang: Third World Network, 2006.

———. "Industrial Policy: Can We Go beyond an Unproductive Confrontation?" Plenary Paper for the Annual World Bank Conference on Development Economic. Seoul, South Korea. 2009.

Chang, H-J., and I. Grabel. *Reclaiming Development: An Alternative Economic Policy Manual* London: Zed Books, 2004.

Dixit, A. "Evaluating Recipes for Development Success." *The World Bank Research Observer* 22/2 (2007): 131–57.

Dutz, M. A., ed. *Unleashing India's Innovation: Towards Sustainable and Inclusive Growth.* Washington DC: World Bank, 2007.

Evans, P. *Embedded Autonomy: States and Industrial Transformation.* Princeton, NJ: Princeton University Press, 1995.

Government of Pakistan, Economic Advisor's Wing, Finance Division. *Pakistan Economic Survey 2009–2010.* Islamabad, 2010.

Hausmann, R., B. Klinger, and R. Wagner. "Doing Growth Diagnostics in Practice: A 'Mindbook.'" Center for International Development Working Paper no. 177 (2008).

Hausmann, R., and D. Rodrik. "Self-Discovery in a Development Strategy in El Salvador." *Journal of Latin America and Caribbean Economic Association* 6/1 (2005): 43–101.

Hausmann, R., D. Rodrik, and A. Velasco. "Growth Diagnostics." In *The Washington Consensus Reconsidered: Towards a New Global Governance*, edited by N. Serra and J. E. Stiglitz. New York: Oxford University Press, 2008.

Hausmann, R., L. Pritchett, and D. Rodrik. "Growth Accelerations." *Journal of Economic Growth* 10/4 (2005): 303–29.

Hossain, N., and N. Kabeer. "Achieving Universal Primary Education and Eliminating Gender Disparity." *Economic and Political Weekly* 39/36 (2004): 4093–4100.

Johnson, C. *MITI and the Japanese Miracle*. Stanford, CA: Stanford University Press, 1982.

Khan, S. R. "Growth Diagnostics: The Puzzle of Pakistan's Lagging Economic Growth." *Global Economy Journal* 11/4 (December 2011): 1–17.

Kilby, P., ed. *Entrepreneurship and Economic Development*. New York: Macmillan, 1971.

Mahmood, Z., and R. Siddiqui. "State of Technology and Productivity in Pakistan's Manufacturing Industries: Some Strategic Directions to Build Technological Competence." *The Pakistan Development Review* 39/1 (2000).

Oldenburg, P. *India, Pakistan and Democracy: Solving the Puzzle of Divergent Paths*. New York: Routledge, 2010.

Reddy, S. G. "The Emperor's New Suit: Global Poverty Estimates Reappraised." UN-DESA Working Paper no. 79 (2009). Available on the UN website.

Reinert, E. *How the Rich Countries Got Rich and Why Poor Countries Stay Poor*. New York: Carroll and Graf, 2007.

Rodrik, D. *One Economics Many Recipes: Globalization, Institutions and Economic Growth*. Princeton, NJ: Princeton University Press, 2009.

Rodrik, D., and A. Subramanian. "From 'Hindu Growth' to Productivity Surge: The Mystery of the Indian Growth Transition." National Bureau Working Paper Series no. 10376 (2004). Available on the ksghome.harvard.edu website.

Sen, A. K. "What Is Development About?" In *Frontiers of Development Economics: The Future in Perspective*, edited by G. M. Meier and J. E. Stiglitz, 506–13. New York: Oxford University Press, 2000.

Shapiro, H. "The Pernicious Legacy of the Rent-Seeking Paradigm." In *Towards New Developmentalism: Market as Means Rather than Master,* edited by S. R. Khan and J. Christiansen, 89–99. New York: Routledge, 2010.

Singh, A. "The Past, Present, and Future of Industrial Policy in India: Adapting to the Changing Domestic and International Environment." In *Industrial Policy and Development: The Political Economy of Capabilities Accumulation*, edited by M. Cimoli, G. Dosi, and J. E. Stiglitz, 277–302. Oxford: Oxford University Press, 2009.

Wade, R. H. *Governing the Market: Economic Theory and the Role of Government in East Asian Industrialization*. Princeton, NJ: Princeton University Press, 2004.

World Bank. *Economic Growth in the 1990s: Learning from a Decade of Reform*. Washington DC: World Bank, 2005.

———. *World Development Report 2010*. Washington DC: World Bank, 2010.

Zarsky, L. "Climate Resilient Industrial Development Paths: Design Principles and Alternative Models." In *Towards New Developmentalism: Market as Means Rather than Master,* edited by S. R. Khan and J. Christiansen, 227–51. New York: Routledge, 2010.

Appendix

Table A–1. General comparative overview

Indicator	Pakistan	India	China	Average LMIC
Per capita GDP $ (2008)	980	1,070	2,940	2,078
Average annual growth, %, 2000–2008	5.8	7.9	10.4	8.3
Agricultural value added per worker, 2003–5, (2000$s)	696	392	407	2,721
Agricultural value added as a % of GDP, 2008	20	18	11	14
Industrial value added as a % of GDP, 2008	27	29	49	41
Service sector value added as a % of GDP, 2008	53	53	40	45
Unemployment rate, 2011	5.5 (July 2010)	10.8 (2010)	9.6 (2009)	na
Population below international poverty line ($1,25 per day) %[a]	22.6 (2004–5)	41.6 (2004–5)	15.9 (2005)	na
Share of poorest quintile in national consumption, %, 1990–2007[b]	9.1	8.1	5.7	na
Gini coefficient (2005)	31	37	42	na
< 5 malnutrition (2000–2007)	31.3	43.5	6.8	na
Annual average population growth rate, 2000–2008	2.3	1.4	0.6	1.2

Source: World Bank (2010, 380–87) and online World Development Indicators, available on the databank.worldbank.org website. Data on unemployment taken from the economic and financial indicators of The Economist (March 12–18, 2011).

Notes: a. The validity of the World Bank's international poverty lines is disputed. Refer to Reddy 2009. b. Comparator year may not be the same. na = not available.

Table A–2. Following the anecdotes

Indicator	Pakistan	India	China	Ave. LMIC
Value lost due to electric outages, % of sales, 2002	4.93	8.14	1.13	na
Value lost due to electric outages, % of sales	9.92 (2007)	6.62 (2006)	na	na
Domestic credit provided by the banking sector, % of GDP, 2008	40	70	126	98
Interest rate, %, (10 year government bonds), 2011	11.22	8.25	4.02	na
Quality of port infrastructure, (1–7, 7= well developed)	3.96	3.47	4.27	3.71
Roads paved as % of total	65.36 (2006)	47.40 (2002)	na	36.30 (2001)

Source: Online World Development Indicators, available on the worldbank.org website. Data on unemployment taken from the economic and financial indicators of The Economist *(March 12–18, 2011).*

Table A–3. The human development story

Indicator	Pakistan	India	China	Average LMIC
Life expectancy at birth (females), 2007	66	66	75	66
Life expectancy at birth (males), 2007	65	63	71	70
Adult literacy, 15 and older, 2007	54	66	93	81
Primary completion rate, 2007	63	86	101	90
Ratio of girls to boys in primary and secondary school, %, 2007	80	91	100	94
< 5 mortality rate, per 1000, 2007	90	72	22	65
Maternal mortality rate, per 100,000, 2007	320	450	45	370
Improved sanitation, % population, 2006	58	28	65	82

Source: World Bank (2010, 380–87) and online World Development Indicators, available on the databank.worldbank.org website.

Table A–4. Structural problems, reforms, and associated stories

Indicator	Pakistan	India	China	Average LMIC
Trade deficit, % of GDP, 2008	−10	−6	7	1
Present value of external debt, % of GNI	25	20	0	na
Consumer price inflation (2010)	13.7	16.1	5.7	na
Fiscal deficit, % of GDP, 2010	−6.7	−5.0	−1.7	na
Tax revenue as a % of GDP, 2007	9.83	11.83	9.92	11.39
Ease of doing business index, 1–183 (most difficult), 2010	83	134	79	na
Total tax rate, % of profit, 2010	31.6	63.3	63.5	na
Government effectiveness, percentile rank, 2009	19.04	54.28	58.09	na
Regulatory quality, percentile	33.33	44.28	46.19	na
Rule of law, percentile rank, 2009	19.34	55.66	45.28	na
Voice and accountability, percentile rank, 2009	20.85	60.18	5.21	na
Political stability and the absence of violence/terrorism, percentile rank, 2009	0.47	13.21	29.72	na
FDI, net inflows as % of GDP, 2009	1.47	2.64	1.57	0.80

Source: Online World Development Indicators, available on the databank. worldbank.org website. Data on unemployment taken from the economic and financial indicators of The Economist (March 12–18, 2011).

Table A–5. The Technology and Economic Diversification Story

Indicator	Pakistan	India	China	Average LMIC
Gross capital formation, % of GDP, 2008	18.96	35.05	47.66	36.72
R&D, % of GDP, 2007	0.67	0.80	1.49	1.24
Internet access, per 100 people, 2008	11.14	4.54	22.5	13.67
Fixed broad-band Internet subscribers, per 100 people, 2008	0.10	0.46	6.29	2.59
Secure Internet servers, per one million people, 2009	0.62	1.55	1.18	1.81
Patent applications, local residents, 2006	91	5,314	122,318	na
High-technology exports as % of total, 2007	1.88	5.69	28.66	22.13
Textile and clothing as % of value added, 2003	na	8.68	2.21	na

Source: Online World Development Indicators, available on the databank. worldbank.org website.

3

Dependency Is Dead:
Long Live Dependency

Very soon after the end of the Cold War an apparent "consensus" was forged in mainstream academic and political circles with regard to the eminent desirability and durability of the "free market" and "liberal democracy" (Amin 2000). However, even before the end of the 1990s, this "consensus" was subject to a prominent legitimacy crisis within the Western countries themselves, let alone the rest of the world.[1] In the subsequent decade or so the crisis of what is widely known as neo-liberalism has deepened, even while the political and intellectual alternatives required to challenge it have remained conspicuous by their absence.[2]

Since 2001, Pakistan has served as one of the major laboratories for neo-liberal economics. For most of this time, an unelected military ruler remained in power—the third such extended spell in the country's sixty-three years of existence—with a weak elected government restored only in 2008. As such, then, Pakistani-style neo-liberalism has not, at least until 2008, even required "liberal democracy" to coexist alongside the "free market." Just how long the current experiment with (procedural) democratic rule will last—and, for that matter, whether or not a long-term process of genuine democratization of state and society is really under way—is beyond the scope of the present contribution. What I wish to show in this chapter is that, the return of some semblance of democracy notwithstanding, Pakistan's recent political and economic tribulations are but the latest phase of a much more drawn-out story of geopolitics, militarization, and social upheaval.

Until 2007 or so—around the time that the anti-dictatorship movement against General Musharraf's regime found its feet—Pakistan, particularly its economy, was enjoying the good graces of Western governments and multilateral institutions alike. A team of economic managers led by Prime Minister Shaukat Aziz had pried open the Pakistani economy for foreign capital, reduced the state's control over economic decision making, and opened up avenues for a burgeoning and ruthless urban middle class to partake in the benefits afforded by the twenty-first-century information economy. In short, the structural adjustment agenda, championed since 1988 by the international financial institutions (IFIs), appeared to be reaching its logical and triumphant conclusion. Growth rates were robust, foreign reserves were at an all-time high, and large amounts of liquid cash were in circulation, free from the constraints of government regulation. It scarcely seemed to matter that rural landlessness, urban squalor, and social conflict of various kinds were all increasing. The Citibanker-turned-prime minister announced in 2006 that the country had forever broken the begging bowl and was well on its way to self-sufficiency.

However, the neo-liberal bubble burst spectacularly. In February 2008, following almost a year of uninterrupted street protests, Musharraf, Aziz, and their political clients were routed in general elections in the face of rampant food inflation, soaring unemployment, and acute shortages of electricity, gas, and sugar. By the time the coalition led by the Pakistan Peoples Party (PPP) took power after the general election, all macroeconomic indicators had reached rock bottom and the government was virtually insolvent. Unsurprisingly, the International Monetary Fund (IMF) came to the rescue, offering a US$11.3 billion loan over thirty-four months replete with what was by now a well-known set of conditionalities.[3]

If multilateral donors have been major players in Pakistan's political economy in recent times, bilateral donors, and the United States in particular, have been even more so. Since 9/11 the United States has disbursed a total of US$19 billion to Pakistan, which constitutes approximately half of all aid in the corresponding period. Only after George W. Bush's departure from the White House, however, has any meaningful debate taken place within the United States about the merits of this aid. That 75 percent of total American aid (until at least 2008) has gone straight into the hands of Pakistan's powerful military has been a subject of concern for many Pakistanis for much of the past decade, long before serious questions about the consequences of this aid started to be asked within the United States itself.[4]

Indeed, I will demonstrate that, long before the onset of neo-liberalism, aid and aid givers have been playing a crucial role in shaping the polity. To be more precise, the political economy of aid has evolved over the past six decades to facilitate the gradual militarization of the state and concomitantly encourage dependence on external handouts to subsidize a non-productive and inefficient security apparatus.

The framework that I employ to demonstrate this historical trend is that proffered by David Harvey, which emphasizes two competing logics of power in the operation of modern-day imperialism, or as he calls it, "imperialism of the capitalist sort" (2003). On the one hand, there is a "territorial logic" of power that is expanded by taking control of territories and the resources within them. On the other hand, there is the "capitalistic logic" of power that is expanded as control over economic capital increases. These two forms of power cannot simply be equated, although they are often closely related.

It is my argument that aid given to Pakistan by Western governments and the IFIs has been motivated *not* by the potentialities for capitalist development within the Pakistani social formation, but by the territorial imperative of increasing the influence of Western powers in the region.[5] While the engagement of donors with Pakistan has been somewhat erratic, the net effect of both bilateral and multilateral donors' strategically motivated exchanges with the Pakistani state has been to reinforce a narrow ruling clique in which the military stands out as arbiter.

Competing Logics Inherited From Colonialism

In describing the unique history of British colonialism in India while situating it within the context of a burgeoning international capitalist system, Harvey argues that there was a dialectical contradiction between logics insofar as the raison d'être of the Raj was *not*, in fact, to encourage the unfettered proliferation of the capitalistic logic in India, but rather the inherently political objective of establishing and maintaining a territorial empire that spanned the globe (139–40). India occupied a position of great significance in this grand design because it possessed valuable human and material resources while also being strategically located such that control over India greatly enhanced the British capacity to conquer swathes of territory across the vast Asian landmass. Insofar as there was potential for capitalism to develop organically within India, the British were keen to suppress this impulse in favor of the territorial logic of imperialist power.[6]

This was reflected in the role that the British Indian army played in conquering and then protecting British colonial possessions across the world. The notorious Great Game pitched British interests in Central and West Asia primarily against Russian influence from the North, and it was thus that the northwest frontier region of British India came to acquire crucial significance for the larger imperial project. Given the new geopolitical stakes that emerged after the end of British rule, many British colonial officers argued for the continuing use of Pakistan as a potentially powerful buffer state that could represent the interests of Western capitalism or at least stem the spread of the new threat from the north, Bolshevism (cf. Caroe 1951).[7] Excepting the ambiguous—some would even call it non-aligned—foreign policy of the Pakistani state in the first five years after Independence, Pakistan indubitably played the role of "client garrison state" to the United States and its Western allies in the struggle against communism (Alavi 1991).[8]

LaPorte breaks into three separate components the operation of U.S. power in Pakistan in the first two decades after the state's inception: (1) U.S. government operations (the activities of U.S. state department officials, USAID economic and technical advisers, U.S. military advisers and supply officers, and other U.S. officials); (2) private foundation operations (economic and technical advisers provided by such organizations as the Ford Foundation); and (3) U.S. business and private-sector operations (U.S. businesses with direct investment in banking, industrial, insurance, and other operations). He shows that private-sector operations are the least significant in terms of investment by American firms, and if anything, the influence of private American capital was limited to the parroting of the American firms by their Pakistani counterparts (143–47). White confirms this analysis in his exhaustive analysis of companies listed on the Karachi Stock Exchange by showing that foreign firms control only 9.2 percent of total assets in the Pakistani economy (153–58).[9]

Thus, aside from the existing stock of British capital that remained in Pakistan after the departure of the British themselves, the evidence suggests that there was little substantive activity on the part of metropolitan capital in the first few decades after formal independence.[10] This was not surprising given the greater attraction of India—both politically and economically—and the fact that at the time of partition, industry in Pakistan was conspicuous by its absence. However, politically motivated aid was much easier to come by. Following the signing of the first mutual defense agreement between the United States and Pakistan in 1954, aid started flowing freely into Pakistan, primarily to modernize the Pakistani military as a fighting force and to provide it with new hardware supplies in accordance with the American conviction that Pakistan needed to be stable and secure as one of the key members of its anti-communist network of states in the region. "During the period 1954 to 1965, the United States provided military grants assistance valued at $650 million, defense and support assistance valued at $619 million, and cash or commercial-based purchases of $55 million" (Lohalekar 1991, 47). This was a substantial sum and can be compared with military assistance given to other countries in the region such as India; 77.8 percent of all U.S. military aid to Pakistan, India, Saudi Arabia, and Nepal between

1947 and 1962 was allocated to Saudi Arabia and Pakistan. Between 1950 and 1960, 90 percent of aid to the Near East and South Asia went to Iran, Turkey, Greece, and Pakistan (Hashmi 1983, 106–7).[11]

Pakistan received economic aid as well, which was, and continues to be, a major pillar of the economy; total foreign aid received by 1968 was US$4.7 billion, which constituted 5.8 percent of the GDP.[12] The significance of aid is reflected in the fact that it was equivalent to 50 percent of total imports and 34 percent of total development expenditure. However, the importance of this aid must be put into context. Of the figure US$4.7 billion quoted above, only US$1.3 billion was in the form of grants, while the rest was offered as loans (Brecher and Abbas 1972, 24). In historical terms, the majority of the grants were offered in the 1950–55 period, whereas loans started to constitute a bigger share of total aid between 1955 and 1960. By 1960–65, "large loans with high interest rates and increasingly harsh conditions completely mortgaged the country" (Rashid 1983, 126). A British economist made the salient observation that the nature of lending by Western countries to Pakistan evolved coevally with the perceived geopolitical requirements of Western governments. This pattern manifested first in the shift from grants to loans, and then culminated in the termination of U.S. and other bilateral and multilateral aid entirely following the start of the 1965 war (Griffin 1965).

To be sure, a distinct pattern prevails throughout the history of the evolving relationship between Pakistan and its Western allies, namely, that military *and* economic aid levels are clearly contingent on the geopolitical considerations of the Western powers (Akhtar 2006). In other words, aid has been substantial when Pakistan has been deemed a Frontline State, and it has been considerably reduced at other times. For my purposes, a related point upon which considerable stress needs to be laid is that, inasmuch as aid—whether military or economic—has been used as a tool to achieve the clearly delineated political objectives of the aid giver, it matters little what form the aid takes. In other words, in line with the theoretical framework outlined above, economic—as much as military—aid to Pakistan has reflected imperialism's territorial logic of power. The direct result of this has been the consolidation of oligarchic domination within Pakistan. This territorial logic has prevailed regardless of the impact it may have had on the capitalistic logic of power.[13]

This situation is borne out in practice by considering the impact of this aid on the polity. It is important to bear in mind that beyond the technological gains from U.S. military aid, the large amounts of economic aid that were doled out to the state by the United States and other Western allies had other crucial effects. The military grew in confidence vis-à-vis political forces, while at a more general level it developed a commitment to modernizing the polity while according to itself the role of spearheading this process of modernization.[14] As an internal Department of Defense document published in 1967 testified: "From a political viewpoint, U.S. military aid has strengthened Pakistan's armed services, the greatest stabilizing force in the country" (Alavi 1991). Thus, there was a close link between the pretensions of the military to take direct control of government and the material and moral encouragement provided in this regard by the United States. Indeed, U.S. Ambassador James Langley was one of the few individuals both inside and outside of Pakistan who seemed to have advance notice of the October 1958 coup (Rizvi 2000, 83).

By the time of the 1965 war, when aid was suspended to Pakistan, the military had already established itself as the dominant force within the country and acquired the expertise and wherewithal to remain powerful despite the deterioration in bilateral ties with the United States. However, there was another important lesson to be learned from the breakdown in the U.S.-Pakistan relationship. By the mid-1960s, Pakistan's economy had become reliant on aid. This situation was underlined by the fact that foreign sources accounted for 3.24 percent of total capital receipts in 1955–60 and 52.57 percent by 1966–67 (Waseem 1994, 197). Aid had much to do with the impressive macroeconomic performance through most of Ayub Khan's tenure, but the fact that aid would subsequently dry up also illustrated the dangers of aid-dependence. By the mid-1960s, Pakistan was perceived as a model of third-world development only to suffer a dramatic collapse shortly thereafter due to serious internal contradictions and the fallouts of regional geopolitics.

The Emerging Politics of Jihad

The contradictions of the Ayub regime's modernization policies coupled with the trauma of the 1971 dismemberment of the country explain the rise of Bhutto's populism. In spite of the generally held perception that this was a period in which the relations between the metropole and Pakistan were at an all-time low, there was negligible conflict between the Bhutto regime and the Western capitalist countries. Bhutto's anti-imperialist tirades tended to be for domestic consumption. However, in practice, his government's relations with the United States and its allies were quite cordial. In particular, Bhutto's government was the major go-between for the Americans and the Chinese, and he took pride in the fact that it was under his leadership that the arms embargo imposed by Washington since 1965 was lifted (Shafqat 1997, 184).

Regardless of whether or not the United States was perturbed about the Fabian socialism being introduced into Pakistan by Bhutto,[15] there was little censure of the regime, except in the aftermath of Bhutto's announcement of Pakistan's nuclear program. But again this was a reflection of the "territorial logic of power" insofar as a nuclear Pakistan was a geostrategic liability for the Western world. On the other hand, Western governments at large seemed to be far less concerned with the nature of the internal convulsions that were perpetrated by the Bhutto regime, although this could be because it was clear, particularly toward the end of the PPP's time in power, that the regime had not made a rupture with national and international economic and political structures.[16]

In the aftermath of the coming to power of Zia ul Haq and the start of the Afghan War, Pakistan was once again raised to the status of Frontline State, and the military was once again elevated to a position of primacy in the geopolitical calculus of the metropole. The Afghan War hence constituted a fortuitous development for the military regime insofar as the latter was insulated from external pressures to revert to even a nominal democratic process and, indeed, provided a pretext for the brutalization of Pakistani society.[17] Secretary of State Alexander Haig apparently reassured Zia's Vice Chief of Army Staff K. M. Arif: "General, your internal situation is your problem" (Kux 2001, 257).

Between the fiscal years 1977–78 and 1981–82, the Pakistani defense budget increased from Rs. 155 crore to Rs. 429 crore, whereas between 1984 and 1989 Pakistan was allocated a large number of defense grants as well as loans specifically for arms sales to the tune of US$1500 million (Lohalekar 1991, 65–76). All told, American aid during the Zia tenure totaled US$4.2 billion.[18] Needless to say, this aid tremendously augmented the ability of the Zia regime to overcome its lack of popular legitimacy, and it offset the potential instability that would have arisen from economic woes. Importantly, net aid flows decreased because of the increasing debt repayment burden, which again indicates the cumulative effect of an aid-dependent economy (Noman 1988, 164). The inherent weakness of the economy was exposed following the drying up of aid in the period following the signing of the Geneva Accords, and it was the various governments in the 1990s that had to contend with another thaw in the relations between Pakistan and the Western countries.

The coming to power of the Zia regime also coincided with the neo-liberal reaction in the Western world, spearheaded by Ronald Reagan and Margaret Thatcher. This effectively signaled a shift in the basis of the global capitalist economy from production to finance as well as an attendant "disciplining" of post-colonial states that suffered from serious indebtedness by either metropolitan states and/or international financial institutions. Under the guise of what Harvey calls "accumulation by dispossession," a new wave of metropolitan capital has invaded the post-colonial world in an attempt to offset a serious crisis of over-accumulation of capital within the metropole itself (Harvey 2003).

Intriguingly, Zaidi insists that when compared with other third-world states, Pakistan's economic position did not mandate the rigorous fiscal stabilization, liberalization, and privatization measures that were pushed hard by the IFIs—thus the decision to continually adopt neo-liberal policies has been a political one rather than an economic one (2005, 348). Moreover, all but one of the various agreements signed with the IFIs since the first one in 1988 have been concluded by unelected governments, thereby suggesting that the IFIs and by extension Western governments—regardless of their continued resort to the rhetoric of "good governance"—have been directly complicit in the subversion of democratic norms within Pakistan (Gadi, Hussain, and Akhtar 2001). Meanwhile, the capitalistic logic of power within Pakistan remained relatively weak throughout the 1980s and 1990s as reflected in low investment rates. Growth rates in total investments actually plummeted to as low as -3.6 percent in 1998–99, while investment as a percentage of GDP steadily declined through the 1990s and was at 13 percent by the turn of the century (Zaidi 2005).

Frontline State Yet Again

Pakistan once again emerged as a Frontline State in the aftermath of the 9/11 attacks. This followed on the heels of a decade in which Pakistan not only fell out of favor with the United States and its Western allies, but at one time was even categorized as a rogue state.[19] Aid levels fell precipitously through the 1990s, at least partially because of the collapse of the Soviet Union in 1991, which reduced Pakistan's importance to the Western world as the hitherto omnipresent threat of communism had disappeared. Debt grew to alarming proportions, confirming that the structural reforms undertaken under the rubric of adjustment had neither done away with what the IFIs termed "distortions in the economy" nor reduced aid-dependence.[20] Once again a military ruler was in power who was initially unpopular with the Western countries; however, overnight his regime transformed into the most precious ally of the "free world."

And yet again, the most obvious indicator of this remarkable turnaround in Pakistan's fortunes was the aid that was pumped into the economy. Between 2002 and 2010, annual aid inflows from the United States alone averaged US$2 billion. As I stated at the outset, approximately 75 percent of this aid has been in the form of military assistance (Zaidi 2011).[21] This is a startling amount of aid, and the willingness of the United States to provide assistance induced the IFIs also to support Pakistan. The IMF, for example, provided thirty-seven countries with loans under the Poverty Reduction and Growth Facility (PRGF) between 1999 and 2004, with a total disbursement of US$6.88 billion. Pakistan received by far the biggest loan from this program, receiving more than 22 percent of this amount (Zaidi 2005, 318). Aid from both the World Bank and the Asian Development Bank exceeded US$8 billion in the same period.[22]

The aid provided came with the now standard set of prescriptions, with which the Musharraf government was generally willing to comply. Indeed, in comparison with the governments of the 1990s, the military regime was far less concerned with the negative fallouts of the neo-liberal policy framework it adopted; the only meaningful difference between the military and preceding governments was the intensity with which virtually the same policies were implemented.

The dichotomy between the territorial logic and the capitalistic logic is clear even in the post-9/11 period, despite the fact that the metropolitan capital has clearly increased its presence within the Pakistani social formation, primarily in high-return sectors such as telecommunications and oil and gas. The privatization of state-owned enterprises—which Harvey considers to be the most significant mechanism through which accumulation by dispossession is enforced—has entailed the growing presence of metropolitan capital. The total share of foreign capital in privatized companies between 1990 and 2000 was a miniscule 2.5 percent. Since 2000, foreign capital's share in privatized companies has increased markedly, to 51.2 percent, totaling Rs. 234.6 billion or approximately 3 percent of the GDP (Kizilbash 2007). Meanwhile, foreign direct investment increased by 238.7 percent from 2005–6 to 2006–7, totaling 2.7 percent of the GDP.

These figures do suggest a non-negligible increase in the capitalistic logic of power, and as the mobility of capital increases, the capitalistic logic may be expected to intensify further. However, it has become clear in the period following the end of Musharraf's regime that geopolitical whims continue to play a defining role in shaping not only the polity, but also the economy. According to the Government of Pakistan, total investment as a percentage of GDP decreased markedly from a high point of 22.5 percent in 2006–7 to 13.4 percent in 2010–11. It is all too easy to chalk this up, as most analysts tend to do, to the worsening security situation in the country and other objective economic shocks in the years in question. In fact, a deeper explanation for this economic downturn must be seen in the context of the dialectic of territorial and capitalistic logics of power.

To be sure, the post-Musharraf government has not made a fundamental departure from the neo-liberal policy framework that had, until 2006, produced results that were lauded by the IFIs and Western governments alike. Neither is it necessarily true that the law-and-order situation worsened within the country all that dramatically during the 2007–10 period. What has changed, however, is the tone and tenor of Western government rhetoric—and particularly the Obama administration—regarding Pakistan. The United States and other allies have been scathing in their criticism of the Pakistani military's apparent unwillingness to sever completely its ties with certain militant groups. This has precipitated a downturn in economic fortunes that cannot be attributed only to the objective economic and political conditions. In short, the territorial logic is once again dominating the capitalistic logic, as it has done throughout Pakistan's history.

Importantly, regardless of the pressure being exerted by Washington on the Pakistani military, there is no sign that American patronage of the Pakistani military will cease. Much has been made about the 2009 Kerry-Lugar civilian-aid package—US$7.5 billion to be disbursed over five years—that purportedly marks a departure from the historical trend. I have already demonstrated that nonmilitary aid given to Pakistan in the past has not necessarily made any dent in the power of the military. In any case, disbursements as part of the Kerry-Lugar package have been slow, and there is the additional "odd[ity] . . . that a civilian aid package has numerous military conditions, and given the Pakistani government's weak control over and fear of the military, one is not sure how these conditions will be enforced" (Zaidi 2011, 109). Indeed, if the U.S. Congress were to withhold aid to Pakistan under the pretext that the two militaries do not share strategic objectives, civilian aid would be just as likely to be cut as military aid.[23]

More generally, there is no obvious indicator that the overall policy calculus of Western governments and the IFIs has been changed fundamentally in the post-Musharraf period. Indeed, one cannot help but note just how much more pressure the PPP-led government is facing on economic and other fronts than the Musharraf military regime did. The lip service that the donor community—both bilateral and multilateral—continues to pay to "democracy" and "good governance" betrays the reality of the political economy of aid.

Conclusion: Dependency Is Dead?

Until the 1980s, there was a measure of consensus across the Western academy that post-colonial states such as Pakistan continued to suffer the long-term consequences of European colonial rule and forced subsumption into the capitalist world system. The so-called dependency school was a major intellectual pillar of the various attempts made by post-colonial states to reconstitute the international political and economic order, starting with the Bandung Conference in 1955 and culminating in the formation of the so-called Group of 77 (G-77) countries in the United Nations in the mid-1970s.

The emergence of neo-liberal politics and economics was accompanied, of course, by a relegation of neo-Marxist intellectual discourses to the dustbin of history. While the dependency school did suffer from its fair share of historical and logical inconsistencies, it is clear that many of its most obvious insights remain extremely pertinent. Yet post–Cold War orthodoxy has mandated that dependency be declared dead. The Pakistani case illustrates that dependency in fact lives on.

Nayak writing in the 1990s could just as well be writing in the second decade of the twenty-first century:

> These military alliances with the imperialist bloc have meant grave disasters to Pakistan. They have not only helped in building a political nexus between the state civil personnel and those in the military wing (over the years, the former yielding place to the latter) but what is worse, it tended to dictate terms of building and alignment of upper strata of the propertied classes in Pakistan. (1992, 27)

Notes

1. The first obvious manifestation of this crisis was the mass protest at the World Trade Organization (WTO) summit in Seattle in 1999.

2. The notable exception is in Latin America, where a host of left-of-center governments have been voted to power since the late 1990s. The most prominent and far-reaching alternative to neo-liberalism has been fashioned by President Hugo Chávez in Venezuela under the guise of a "socialism for the twenty-first century."

3. This agreement has been extended on at least two occasions due to Pakistan's inability to meet stringent reporting requirements.

4. See Zaidi (2011).

5. Until 1991 the major competitor to the Western world was communism. Pakistan was one of a number of countries in the region that were perceived as constituting a major anti-communist alliance in west Asia and that signed the so-called Baghdad Pact (CENTO). Other members included Turkey, Iran, and Iraq. After the end of the Cold War, the imperative of "fighting terror" has provided a mandate for support to Pakistan's security apparatus.

6. Harvey (2003) proves this assertion by noting that the actual amount of capital invested in India by the British was miniscule in comparison to what was invested in other regions, including the United States and other capitalist contenders.

7. For the American perspective on the "new great game," see Kux (2001, 62). See also Jalal (1990) for an exhaustive discussion of the negotiations and intrigue that characterized the new state's relationship with both the British and the Americans.

8. It is another matter that the Pakistani state oligarchy cultivated this perception even though its primary foreign policy concern was India, and it viewed its ability to achieve a limited form of parity with India as being contingent on the material impetus provided by the American alliance.

9. The analysis is based on numerous statistical estimates, and the figure of 9.2 percent is, according to White, probably an overestimation

10. Alavi (1983) points out that metropolitan capital did penetrate the Pakistani economy by way of tied credits through public financial institutions such as Pakistan Industrial Credit and Investment Corporation (PICIC) and Industrial Development Bank of Pakistan (IDBP) and also through investment in state-led development projects. However, there is no suggestion that the magnitude of this penetration is substantive, at least in comparison to the interventions of metropolitan states, particularly the United States.

11. Hashmi (1983) makes the important point that these are only officially quoted figures, whereas actual disbursements are most likely far in excess of the official disbursements.

12. This figure was as high as 7.5 percent in 1964.

13. In any case, aid given to Pakistan in the initial years after formal independence was subject to a startling dynamic which meant that Pakistan was actually paying for the military "aid" it received; this was at least partially because the United States insisted on differentiating Mutual Assistance Program (MAP) forces, or in other words those forces supplied by the United States, and non-MAP forces, which Pakistan funded itself (Alavi 1991).

14. As Cohen (1998) has noted, the generation of military officers that was exposed to American ideas and training in the 1950s and 1960s ensured that the secular—and elitist—traditions of the military inherited from the British remained intact. Importantly, they also imbibed the bias within parts of American foreign policy establishment that the military was potentially the preeminent political force in third-world countries.

15. IFIs and the World Bank, in particular, were far from satisfied with the PPP government's adopted policy framework. While aid did not dry up as a result, lending terms became much harsher (Noman 1988, 90–93).

16. Jalal (1994) points out that the astoundingly well-funded Pakistan National Alliance (PNA) movement was widely reputed to have received at least some support from the United States, and that this might be considered the Americans' method of punishment for Bhutto's insistence on carrying on with the nuclear program. The popular perception that the Americans directly supported the July 1977 coup was based in part on Bhutto's own claims to this effect during the two years between the coup and his hanging. Even if the United States did have a part in the ousting of Bhutto, the fact that the Zia regime was not censured for continuing the nuclear program—ostensibly because of the changed geopolitical needs of the United States in the region after the start of the Afghan War—indicates the clearly functional nature of the American policy toward Pakistan.

17. Rather perversely, "Zia's admirers proudly presented his formulation of Afghan policy as the most significant contribution of his era" (Shafqat 1997, 206).

18. The breakdown was US$2.5 billion in economic and US$1.7 billion in military aid. The initial aid package agreed upon totaled US$3.2 billion and lasted from 1979 till 1986, whereas a five-year aid package from 1986 to 1991 worth US$4.02 billion was incomplete when the military regime gave way to the PPP government (Haqqani 2005, 152).

19. Toward the end of the 1990s, the Clinton administration started using this term extensively to describe states that had connections with international terrorist networks.

20. Outstanding debt as a percentage of GDP reached 51.7 percent in 1998–99 (Zaidi 2005, 364).

21. Nearly 60 percent of total military aid has been disbursed as part of the Coalition Support Fund (CSF), which covers logistical costs incurred by the Pakistani military in its support of the American war effort in Afghanistan.

22. See www.worldbank.org/pakistan and www.adb.org/prm.

23. This is not to suggest that civilian aid has necessarily in the past, or will in the future, contribute greatly to the welfare of Pakistan's people.

Reference List

Akhtar, Aasim Sajjad. "Le Pakistan, Etat de la ligne de front." In *Atlas Alternatif.* Paris: Le Temps des Cerises, 2006.

Alavi, Hamza. "Class and State in Pakistan." In *Pakistan: The Unstable State*, edited by Hasan Gardezi and Jamil Rashid. Lahore: Vanguard Books, 1983.

———. "The Origin and Significance of the Pak-U.S. Military Alliance." In *Indian Foreign Policy*, edited by Satish Kumar. New Delhi: Manohar, 1991.

Amin, Samir. "Economic Globalism and Political Universalism: Conflicting Issues?" *Journal of World Systems Research* 6/3 (2000): 582–622.

Brecher, Irving, and S. A. Abbas. *Foreign Aid and Industrial Development in Pakistan.* London: Cambridge University Press, 1972.

Caroe, Olaf. *Wells of Power: The Oil Fields of Southwestern Asia.* Westport, CT: Greenwood Press, 1951.

Cohen, Stephen P. *The Pakistan Army.* Karachi: Oxford University Press, 1998.

Gadi, Mushtaq, Khadim Hussain, and Aasim Sajjad Akhtar. *Taking the Poor for a Ride: The Pakistan Poverty Reduction Strategy Paper.* Islamabad: ActionAid, 2001.

Griffin, Keith. "Financing Development Plans in Pakistan." *Pakistan Development Review* 5 (1965): 610–20.

Haqqani, Hussain. *Pakistan: Between Mosque and Military.* Washington DC: Carnegie Endowment for International Peace, 2005.

Harvey, David. *The New Imperialism.* New York: Oxford University Press, 2003.

Hashmi, Bilal. "Dragon Seed: Military in the State." In *Pakistan: The Unstable State*, edited by Hassan Gardezi and Jamil Rashid. Lahore: Vanguard Books, 1983.

Jalal, Ayesha. *The State of Martial Rule: The Origins of Pakistan's Political Economy of Defence.* Cambridge: Cambridge University Press, 1990.

———. "The State and Political Privilege in Pakistan." In *The Politics of Social Transformation in Afghanistan, Iran and Pakistan*, edited by Ali Banuazizi and Myron Weiner. Syracuse: Syracuse University Press, 1994.

Kizilbash, Masood H. "Sale of National Assets." *DAWN.* April 16, 2007.

Kux, Dennis. *The United States and Pakistan 1947–2000: Disenchanted Allies.* Washington DC: Woodrow Wilson Center Press, 2001.

LaPorte, Robert, Jr. *Power and Privilege: Influence and Decision-making in Pakistan.* Berkeley and Los Angeles: University of California Press, 1975.

Lohalekar, Devidas B. *U.S. Arms to Pakistan: A Study in Alliance Relationship.* New Delhi: Ashish Publishing House, 1991.

Nayak, Pandav. *Pakistan: Political Economy of a Developing State.* New Delhi: Patriot Publishers, 1992.

Noman, Omar. *Pakistan: Political and Economic History since 1947.* London: Kegan Paul International, 1988.

Rashid, Jamil. "Pakistan in the Debt Trap." In *Pakistan: The Unstable State*, edited by Hassan Gardezi and Jamil Rashid. Lahore: Vanguard Books, 1983.

Rizvi, Hasan-Askari. *Military, State, and Society in Pakistan*. Basingstoke, UK: Macmillan, 2000.

Shafqat, Saeed. *Civil-Military Relations in Pakistan: From Zulfikar Ali Bhutto to Benazir Bhutto*. Boulder, CO: Westview Press, 1997.

Waseem, Mohammad. *Politics and the State in Pakistan*. Islamabad: National Institute of Historical and Cultural Research, 1994.

White, Lawrence J. *Industrial Concentration and Political Power in Pakistan*. Princeton, NJ: Princeton University Press, 1974.

Zaidi, S. Akbar. *Issues in Pakistan's Economy*. Oxford: Oxford University Press, 2005(a).

———. "Who Benefits from U.S. Aid to Pakistan." *Economic and Political Weekly* 46/32 (2011).

4

Insecurity Breeds Insecurity

ABID QAIYUM SULERI

The developmental challenges facing Pakistan are diverse and both chronic as well as acute. Some of these challenges will have short- to medium-term impact on Pakistan's development scene, while others will continue to affect the country's development in the longer run. But no matter what the nature and type of these challenges, there seems to be one common strand among all of them: Most of them have their origin in the policies that Pakistan has pursued over the last six decades. In other words, these challenges are "policy led."

My first hypothesis is that these challenges can be avoided, provided the right set of policies and actions is adopted and followed. Despite the fact that on the face of it, "the right set of policies and actions" sounds vague, in the literature on human development, broad parameters for such policies do exist. For example, Alkire suggests that one of the prerequisites for a right set of policies and actions is to follow a paradigm of people-centric development that should result in increased human security (2003).

In Pakistan's case, prolonged military rule and the country's peculiar geopolitical situation have led to the adoption of a security paradigm that has always driven policies and practices in all fields of national life. This security paradigm, however, remains confined to achieving "state security"—mainly through military means—and does not include other dimensions of security.[1]

It may be argued that following a state security paradigm in itself is not an altogether flawed approach. After all, this paradigm is what the existing organizational mandate and mechanism of the United Nations system is mainly based upon. The United Nations Charter states the maintenance of "international peace and security" as the main objective of the organization and obliges all members to "take collective measures for the prevention and removal of threat to the peace, and for the suppression of acts of aggression or breach of the peace" (The UN Charter, Article 1). I can buy into this argument, but what matters to me is the realization that state security cannot be achieved without achieving human security (Alkire 2003; Newman 2001).[2]

In fact, there are four interconnected levels of security: individual (human) security, national (state) security, regional security, and global security. Their interconnectedness makes it difficult to address the security of the state if security at one of the other levels has been compromised (Suleri 2010b).

My second hypothesis is that while successive governments in Pakistan have tried to achieve national, regional, and global security, they have always neglected individual security, which presents the biggest hurdle to the creation of effective policy responses to various developmental challenges facing the country.

Global security is also called cumulative or collective security, and therefore it is a global concern. This type of security usually falls under the purview of the United Nations and is frequently based on traditional state security assumptions. We have seen the international community (read: the West) joining hands and resources to tackle any issue that in its perception may jeopardize global security. In the ongoing war on terrorism, for example, the international security apparatus, the United Nations Security Council, authorized North Atlantic Treaty Organization (NATO) forces to take action and ensure that elements threatening global security are eliminated (Begum 2009). Pakistan, too, is playing its part in achieving global security. After September 11, 2001, it was asked to choose between "us" (those who wanted to curb terrorism) and "against us" (terrorist forces who had challenged global security), and then–military president of Pakistan, General Pervez Musharraf, opted to be an ally of the United States (Musharraf 2006).

Similarly, Pakistan always has striven to be involved in regional security mechanisms in order to ensure its national security as well as the security of the larger region of which it is a part. It joined various regional accords and networks such as the Baghdad Pact (CENTO) and the Manila Pact (the Southeast Asia Treaty Organization or SEATO) as early as the first decade of its creation. Since the 1980s it has been one of the leading members of the South Asian Association for Regional Cooperation (SAARC). Additionally, it has engaged with all its neighbors in various economic, trade, and other agreements. On the military side, Pakistan has fought three wars with India, ostensibly to challenge its eastern neighbor's ambition to become a regional hegemon. Pakistan also fought a decade-long proxy war against the Soviet Union on Afghan soil during General Zia ul Haq's era. Its current role in the war on terrorism and its eagerness to remain a part of any solution to the war in Afghanistan are manifestations of its desire to remain a relevant player in regional security and its willingness to pay the human, economic, and social costs for that. Here it is pertinent to mention that according to some conservative estimates, the total economic costs of defense and security of Pakistan have increased from US$6 billion in 2007–8 to US$10 billion in 2009–10 (SPDC 2010). Thus global security and regional security both seem to be high-priority policy issues for Pakistan.

The third and most important level of security that Pakistan's civil and military establishment always has tried to achieve is security at the national level. Almost all of the country's rulers have tried to attain national security through military means. All four of the military governments in Pakistan took over power in the name of protecting national security interests. The establishment not only determines national security interests but also determines who is working for or against those interests.[3] The establishment's stakes in national security are so high that at times it has portrayed even democratically elected prime ministers as national security threats (Bhutto 2008). For example, Prime Minister Nawaz Sharif claimed that the establishment had never shared with him the plan to go on the offensive against India on the Kargil front (the Kargil conflict brought Pakistan and India to the verge of nuclear war in 1999) (Bhutto 2008).

As mentioned earlier, I believe human/individual security has been ignored in Pakistan in the country's quest to attain national, regional, and global security. At times, human/individual security even has been perceived as a threat to national security. As a result, the state has worked actively to curb human/individual freedoms that guarantee people's right to free expression when their safety and security is endangered; their right to earn a livelihood to secure their incomes; and their right to form associations and join political parties in order to secure their political, cultural, and social rights. More often than not, the state has suspended these rights in the name of national security (*Time* 2007).[4] This mindset has also strengthened (in terms of both human and financial resources) the military and paramilitary institutions, because they are considered vital for safeguarding national security interests. This explains why there has never been a reduction in Pakistan's military expenditure, even when the country faced an acute financial crunch. Pakistan's leaders of all political and ideological stripes have—in their rhetoric as well as actions—reaffirmed time and again that they will meet the country's defense and security requirements, even if it means drastically cutting the money allocated for poverty alleviation, social-sector development, and food security (*The Economist* 2008).[5] This resolve has worked in the sense that Pakistan has a huge military machine with an active nuclear weapons program.

This success, however, has been achieved at a cost: ensuring human/individual security has never become a priority in Pakistan. Neglect of human/individual security is evident from the country's current account expenditure (Suleri 2010a). The country's current account expenditures can be classified using four "Ds"—debt repayment, defense-related expenditures, day-to-day administration costs, and development-related expenditures.

The Government of Pakistan would like to maintain its credit rating, which means it cannot default on its debts; debt repayment has to happen. The country has to spend huge amounts of money to achieve its global, regional, and national security goals. Expenditure related to defense and security, therefore, cannot be curtailed. Similarly, the entire administrative machinery will come to a halt if the government does not spend money on its day-to-day running. This expenditure has ended up consuming a major slice of the national income pie because the current political situation has necessitated coalition governments at the federal and provincial levels with every partner in the ruling coalition demanding and getting cabinet slots. This situation has resulted in cabinets becoming bigger than necessary and a massive increase in the expense of running the departments linked to each cabinet portfolio. The end result is that the government allocates more money for its administrative expenses with each passing year.

The only type of expenditure that seems flexible is public-sector development expenditure (Suleri 2011a). Thus, every time there is a fiscal problem (mainly due to overspending on the first three Ds), the size of the public-sector development program (or PSDP, which includes expenditures on public infrastructure development and provision of basic services such as health, education, drinking water, sanitation, disaster preparedness, and communication) is slashed.

We saw this happen in 2008–9 when the size of the federal PSDP had to be reduced from Rs. 337 (US$5.61) billion to Rs. 210 (US$3.5) billion because Pakistan could not convince the "friends of the democratic Pakistan forum" to provide it financial assistance. It happened again in 2009–10 when the federal PSDP had to be slashed from Rs. 421 (US$6) billion to Rs. 300 (US$ 4.2) billion because expected budgetary support from the Kerry-Lugar-Burman law never materialized. The size of the federal PSDP was yet again reduced from Rs. 280 (US$3.5) billion to Rs. 140 (US$1.75) billion in 2010–11 because the Government of Pakistan had to divert funds to flood rehabilitation. While allocations for the PSDP have suffered downward revisions for all these years, the budgeted expenditures on debt repayment, defense, and day-to-day administration have increased.

Here it is pertinent to mention that the PSDP is perceived to be a lubricant for the growth engine (Planning Commission of Pakistan 2011) and a guarantor of individual (read: human) securities through social-sector development (Qazi 2011). The effectiveness of a successful PSDP, in fact, can be gauged from reduced human/individual insecurities. What happens when spending on public-sector development is curtailed? It curbs human development and gives rise to economic, financial, and even social insecurities among the members of the society. These human/individual insecurities are further aggravated in unusual times like those that Pakistan is currently enduring.

The current coalition government, led by the Pakistan Peoples Party (PPP), took power in February 2008, when the world was facing three "F" crises: food, fuel, and fiscal (Wasti 2011). However, Pakistan was facing five "F" crises: fiscal, fuel, food, frontier (the war on terrorism across and around its western frontier), and functional democracy (the crisis in its political and administrative structure) (Suleri 2010b). In 2010, a sixth "F"—fragility of climate in the form of deadly floods—was added to the list of challenges being faced by Pakistan (World Bank 2010). There has been no let up in the intensity of all these "F" crises since 2008, partially because it is difficult to address these crises while ignoring any single of them (Suleri and Haq 2010; Khalid 2011).

In other words, all of these crises are interconnected, and their cumulative effect is much stronger than their respective individual effects. As mentioned earlier, this complex situation further aggravates individual insecurities. In the absence of an effective social safety net and in the presence of huge income inequalities, individuals with insecurities resort to extraordinary behaviors. Some of these behaviors, as reported in the Pakistani media, include violent and destructive protests for basic amenities such as the uninterrupted supply of electricity, natural gas, and water (see *Dawn News* 2011a; 2011b; 2011c); resorting to industrial actions (which may turn violent) (*Dawn News* 2011b); organ trade and putting children on sale (Robertson 2009); engaging in various criminal activities (theft, burglary, robbery, kidnapping for ransom, among others); and forcing women to engage in prostitution and children into child labor (*IRIN News* 2010). In the worst cases, some people commit suicide and/or kill all their family members (*IRIN News* 2010), while a few fall prey to the jihadi propaganda of militant groups and become suicide bombers or militant fighters. All these behaviors not only promote intolerance and violence, but they also lead to sociopolitical instability. Due to Pakistan's peculiar geostrategic situation, any sociopolitical instability has the potential to create a situation in which regional or global players may want to intervene.

However, this is but one aspect of human/individual insecurity. In the absence of strong social safety nets and in the presence of huge income inequalities, perception of individual marginalization, social vulnerability, social exclusion, and various forms of poverty may lead to social conflict and contestation over scarce resources when individual insecurities take on a collective identity—whether ethnicity, creed, gender, class, or region (Stewart et al. 2005; Suleri 2011b). This type of social instability may erode the basic societal fabric when it turns violent. The evidence that this is already taking place in today's Pakistan is there for everyone to see in the cases of urban violence in Karachi (Suleri 2011b) and the militant nationalist movement in Balochistan (Wirsing 2008; Suleri, Shahbaz, and Khwaja 2010).

As mentioned earlier, sociopolitical instability leading to violence threatens not only national security but also regional (and at times global) security. The international community gets concerned that a state with nuclear assets has limited control or no writ over its violent domestic groups (Kerr and Nikitin 2011). As a result, global and regional forces start doubting the state's capability to protect its nuclear weapons (Kerr and Nikitin 2011). This leads to regional and global interference in Pakistan, which in turn provides a solid excuse and rationale for enhanced national security measures (and increased spending on them, too).

As a matter of fact, Pakistan's development challenges present a classic example of the maxim that insecurity in any form breeds other forms of insecurities. Let us take the state of food security in Pakistan as an entry point to see how compromised security at one level compromises security at each of the other levels (see Figures 4–1 and 4–2).

A report jointly released by the United Nations' World Food Program (WFP) and the Sustainable Development Policy Institute (SDPI), a Pakistan-based independent think tank, observed that the state of food security in Pakistan has deteriorated since 2003 (Suleri and Haq 2010). The report reveals that the conditions for food security are inadequate in 61 percent of districts in Pakistan (80 out of 131). This percentage is a sharp increase from 2003, when conditions for food security were inadequate in only 45 percent of the country's districts (54 out of 120) (WFP/SDPI 2004). In terms of population, almost half of the people living in Pakistan (48.6 percent) are food insecure (without access to sufficient food for active and healthy life at all times) (WFP/SDPI 2004).

The report found circumstantial evidence that most of the food insecure regions are also the most conflict-prone and violent areas of the country. The Federally Administered Tribal Areas (FATA)—the theater for the war against terrorism—has the highest percentage of food insecure population (67.7 percent), followed by Balochistan (61.2 percent), and Khyber Pakhtunkhwa (56.2 percent), the latter two hobbled by religious and ethnic militancy, respectively.

Figure 4–1. Food Security Situation in 2003

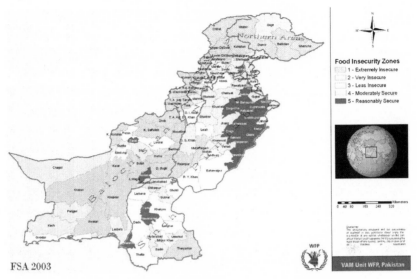

Source: WFP/SDPI. State of Rural Food Insecurity in Pakistan 2003. Islamabad: World Food Program and Sustainable Development Policy Institute, 2004.

Figure 4–2. Food Security Situation in 2009

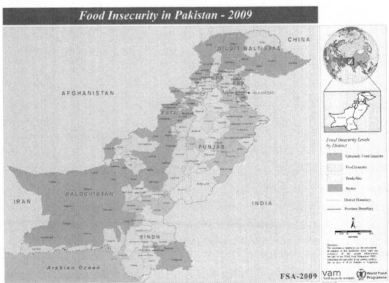

Source: Abid Qaiyum Suleri and Sahib Haq. State of Food Security in Pakistan 2009. Islamabad: World Food Program, Swiss Agency for Development and Cooperation, and Sustainable Development Policy Institute, 2010.

The population with the smallest percentage of food insecure people (23.6 percent) is in Islamabad, which is also perhaps the most peaceful place in the country. Among districts, Dera Bugti—which is otherwise known for being the seat of Pakistan's first natural gas reservoirs and as the hometown of Balochistan's influential nationalist family, the Bugtis—has the highest percentage of food insecure people (82.4 percent) (Suleri and Haq 2010).

Balochistan has the greatest number of districts with the worst instances of food insecurity. In fact, of the twenty districts in Pakistan with the worst instances of food insecurity, ten are from Balochistan, five are from FATA, three are from Khyber Pakhtunkhwa, and there is one each from Gilgit-Baltistan and Sindh. The number of districts from Balochistan in this category has doubled since 2003. Out of Balochistan's 29 districts, 26 do not meet the conditions for being food secure. None of the districts of Khyber Pakhtunkhwa, FATA, or Balochistan could even fall in the category of being considered reasonably food secure, as per the study. The three worst food insecure districts in Punjab, which is comparatively a food secure province, are in South Punjab (Rajanpur, Muzafargarrh, Dera Ghazi Khan). It is not a coincidence that there are echoes of Talibanization in southern Punjab.

Most of the above-mentioned districts are known for being extremely insecure and unsafe for different reasons. For the last decade, the war on terrorism has been fought (and continues to be fought) on Pakistani soil in both FATA and Khyber Pakhtunkhwa. North Waziristan, South Waziristan, Upper Dir, Orakzai, and Kohistan are the battlefields between the government and the Tehrik-e-Taliban Pakistan on the one hand and the Afghan Taliban and international forces on the other. Some of these areas face regular strikes by American drones and others have recently come under attack from the Taliban residing in Afghanistan. Insurgency by various nationalist groups (mainly due to the unequal distribution of resources) against the federal (and in some cases also the provincial) government and the military have been raging in some parts of Balochistan for the last several years. Balochistan is also rife with various ethnic conflicts (between the Baloch and the Pakhtuns and between the Baloch and the Punjabis) and sectarian ones (between the Shias and the Sunnis). Similarly, armed tribal conflicts are a routine in areas of upper Sindh, which also figures high on the food insecurity list. The perception of marginalization in South Punjab is so strong that the current PPP-led government has established a parliamentary commission to initiate spadework for the creation of a separate province for South Punjab.

Interpolating the maps of food insecure districts (Figures 4–1 and 4–2) and those that are physically unsafe and insecure (Figure 4–3) highlights the relationship between food insecurity and physical insecurity. However, due to the multidimensionality of both the violent conflicts in these areas

Figure 4–3. Number of Terrorist Attacks in Pakistan in 2010

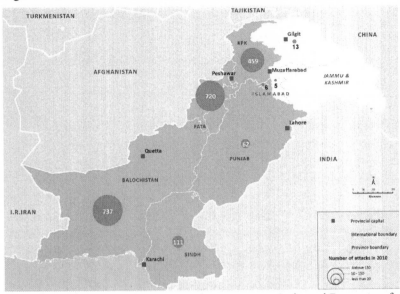

Source: SDPI/UNODC. Examining the Dimension, Scale, and Dynamics of the Illegal Economy: A Study of Pakistan in the Region. *Islamabad. Sustainable Development Policy Institute and the UN Office on Drugs and Crime, 2011.*

and the other reasons for food insecurity, it is difficult to establish a linear relationship between the two. Although there is no empirical evidence to prove that food insecurity is the only cause of militancy, violence, and conflict in the above-mentioned parts of Pakistan (or vice versa), it is an established fact that the relationship between violence, conflict and food insecurity is reciprocal, creating a vicious cycle that continues challenging the transition to sustainable development (Suleri 2010b; SPDC 2010).

Now let us have a look at another challenge that faced Pakistan in 2010 and 2011: floods in upper Khyber Pakhtunkhwa, South Punjab, upper Sindh, and adjacent districts of Balochistan in 2010, and floods in Sindh in 2011 (see Figure 4–4).

Flood-affected districts in 2010, according to the Office of Coordination of Humanitarian Assistance (OCHA) (2010), included Upper Dir, Lower Dir, Kohistan, and Mardan in Khyber Pakhtunkhwa; Dera Ghazi Khan, Rajanpur, Bhakkar, and Muzaffargarh in Punjab; Musa Khel and Jhal Maghsi in Balochistan; and Kashmore-Kandhkot, Shikarpur, and Jaccobabad in Sindh. All of these districts have extremely poor conditions for food security, and they are each beset by violent conflicts of various natures that pose serious physical security problems for their residents. They are also vulnerable to external or

Figure 4–4. Map of Flood-Affected Districts of Pakistan

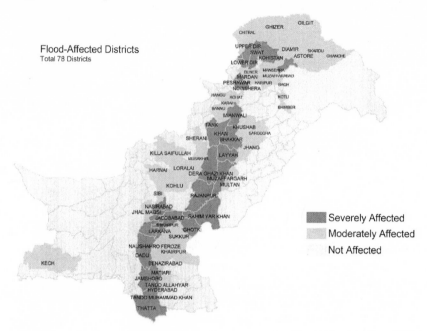

By ignoring the human dimension of security the state has failed to address one major factor that perpetuates violence, conflict, and physical

internal shocks, such as seasonal variations or extreme weather. Floods in 2011 were clearly the result of flawed policies and practices turning an unavoidable weather extreme into an avoidable human disaster. In fact, had there been enough attention to repair the irrigation infrastructure and drain outfalls in Sindh, the floods of 2011 could have been avoided (Suleri 2012).

The reason for mentioning the flood is to highlight that conditions for human/individual security in terms of security of livelihood, security of life, protection from diseases, and the guaranteed availability of basic amenities like education, water, sanitation, and housing have deteriorated over time in many parts of Pakistan. But at the same time, the state's security paradigm remains fixated on ensuring national, regional, and global security. In fact, the state has, unsuccessfully, tried to use the national security paradigm to overcome violence and conflict in the troubled parts of the country through enhanced military presence, increased expenditure on sophisticated weapons (arms imports increased in Pakistan from US$158 million in 2000 to US$1.14 billion in 2008), and rising allocations of money for paramilitary forces and police (defense expenditures in Pakistan increased from US$3.83 billion in 2000 to US$5.03 billion in 2009) (SPDC 2010).

By ignoring the human dimension of security the state has failed to address one major factor that perpetuates violence, conflict, and physical insecurity. Reduced access to food, as the SDPI study has shown, poor provision of basic amenities like health, education, and sanitation, along with decreasing economic opportunities, have mostly resulted from the state's failure to allocate resources for social-sector development plans and PSDP, which, as shown earlier, have seen massive budget cuts over the last several years.

As stated in the beginning, it is the state's policies that revolve around national, regional, and global security which need to change for an increased expenditure on human/individual security (for example, through public-sector development programs and effective social protection policies) to eradicate one of the major factors for insecurity, conflict, and violence in the country. It is not by continuing to increase expenditures on defense and security that Pakistan will become secure. It is instead allocating financial resource to ensuring the human dimension of security that will help reduce the intensity and the frequency of these conflicts, leading to a reduced requirement to spend money on defense and security and thus starting a virtuous cycle of security breeding security.

Notes

1. For a rigorous analysis of the changing security paradigm, see Gasteyger 1999 and Florini and Simmons 1998.

2. The objective of human security is to create political, economic, social, cultural, and environmental conditions in which people live, knowing that their vital rights and freedoms are secure.

3. The *establishment* is a term used commonly for the powerful military-dominated oligarchy in Pakistan. This group of individuals, while not exclusively military, is considered a key decision maker in major policy decisions ranging from buying and producing strategic weapons to writing the defense budget and using intelligence agencies in Pakistan and abroad (*The Guardian* 2007).

4. Individual security and individual rights are two distinct concepts and should not be confused.

5. Zulfiqar Ali Bhutto: "If India builds the bomb, we will eat grass or leaves, even go hungry, but we will get one of our own. We have no other choice" (October 15, 1965).

Reference List

Alkire, S. "A Conceptual Framework for Human Security." CRISE (Centre for Research on Inequality, Human Security, and Ethnicity) working paper 2. Oxford, UK: University of Oxford , 2003.

Begum, Imrana. "The War on Terrorism and NATO's Role in Afghanistan." *Journal of European Studies* 25/1 (2009): 49–71.

Bhutto, Benazir. *Reconciliation: Islam, Democracy, and the West.* London: Simon and Schuster, 2008.

Dawn News. "Tail-End Farmers Protest Water Shortage." June 19, 2011[a]. Available online.

————. "Increased Loadshedding, Outages Spark Violent Protest." July 18, 2011[b]. Available online.

————. "Power Riots Engulf More Cities, Towns in Punjab." October 4, 2011[c]. Available online.

The Economist. "The Spider's Stratagem." January 3, 2008. Available online.

Florini, Ann, and P. J. Simmons. "The New Security Thinking: A Review of the North American Literature." In *Project on World Security.* New York: Rockefeller Brothers Fund, 1998.

Gasteyger, Curt. "Old and New Dimensions of International Security." In *Towards the 21st Century: Trends in Post-Cold War International Security Policy,* edited by Kurt R. Spillmann and Andreas Wenger, 69–108. Bern, Germany: Peter Lang, 1999.

IRIN News. "Pakistan: Sold into Sex Work." April 25, 2010. Available online.

Khalid, R. "Climate Change: Threat Multiplier to National, Human Security." *The News.* June 21, 2011. Available online.

Kerr, P. K., and M. B. Nikitin. *Pakistan's Nuclear Weapons: Proliferation and Security Issues.* Washington DC: Congressional Research Service, 2011. Available online.

Musharaff, Pervez. *In the Line of Fire.* London: Simon and Schuster, 2006.

Newman, Edward. "Human Security and Constructivism." *International Studies Perspectives* 2 (2001): 239–51.

Planning Commission of Pakistan. *Analytical Review of the PSDP Portfolio.* Islamabad: Government of Pakistan, 2011.

Qazi, M. S. "The Quest for Sustainable Economic Growth." *The News.* June 6, 2011. Available online.

Robertson, Nic. "Man Must Choose Between Selling Kidney or Child." *CNN World.* July 16, 2009. Available online.

SDPI/UNODC. *Examining the Dimension, Scale, and Dynamics of the Illegal Economy: A Study of Pakistan in the Region.* Islamabad: Sustainable Development Policy Institute and the UN Office on Drugs and Crime, 2011.

SPDC (Social Policy and Development Center). *Social Development in Pakistan, Annual Review 2008–09: Social Impact of the Security Crisis.* Karachi: SPDC, 2010.

Stewart, Frances, Manuel Barron, Graham Brown, and Marcia Hartwell. *Social Exclusion and Conflict: Analysis and Policy Implications.* Oxford, UK: Centre for Research on Inequality, Human Security, and Ethnicity, 2005. Available online.

Suleri, Abid Q. "Fiscal Fire Fighting." *The News.* June 8, 2010[a]. Available online.

————. "The Social Dimensions of Food Insecurity in Pakistan." In *Hunger Pains: Pakistan's Food Insecurity,* edited by Michael Kugelman and Robert Hathaway, 78–85. Washington DC: Woodrow Wilson International Center for Scholars, 2010[b].

————. "Challenges Ahead." *The News.* February 6, 2011[a]. Available online.

————. "Baggage of History." *The News.* September 4, 2011[b]. Available online.

————. "Get Ready, It's Monsoon Time." *The News.* July 22, 2012. Available online.

Suleri, Abid Qaiyum, and Sahib Haq. *State of Food Security in Pakistan 2009.* Islamabad: World Food Program, Swiss Agency for Development and Cooperation, and Sustainable Development Policy Institute, 2010.

Suleri, Abid Q., Babar Shahbaz, and Meezan Z. Khwaja. "Natural Resources: Blessing or Curse?" SDPI working paper series 115. Islamabad: Sustainable Development Policy Institute, 2010.

Time. "Pakistan's State of Emergency." November 8, 2007. Available online.

Wasti, S. "Overview of the Economy." In *Pakistan Economic Survey 2010–11.* Available online.

WFP/SDPI. *State of Rural Food Insecurity in Pakistan 2003.* Islamabad: World Food Program and Sustainable Development Policy Institute, 2004.

Wirsing, Robert G. *Baloch Nationalism and the Geopolitics of Energy Resources: The Changing Context of Separatism in Pakistan.* Honolulu: Asia-Pacific Center for Security Studies, 2008. Available online.

World Bank. *Pakistan Floods (2010) Damage and Needs Assessment.* Washington DC: World Bank, 2010. Available online.

Part Two

CHALLENGES OF INFRASTRUCTURAL TRANSFORMATION

5

What Must Be Changed in Pakistan's Legal System, But How to Succeed?

AITZAZ AHSAN

The legal system and what needs to be changed in the legal system has continued to challenge humanity since the most ancient of times. This issue has been debated since the time of the Greek philosophers; even before that, the Hindu philosophers in the subcontinent were conflicted about what the law should be, what the ideal state of law and legal norms is, and how to structure legal norms in society.

Pakistan derives much of its legal and constitutional structures from the British Commonwealth tradition of relying on common law. Doctrinal personal faith, particularly Islamic or Hindu law or edicts, applies regarding succession, inheritance, marriage, and divorce. Certain Christian precepts apply to Christians. However, by and large, the overall structure is derived from common law based on certain fundamental principles of due process; an independent judiciary; certain fundamental rights inherent in citizenship of a state (in this case, the State of Pakistan), such as no one can be condemned unheard and everyone has the right to an audience in a court before a judgment is passed against that person. There are rules and processes in law that determine how notices are to be issued and how parties have to be notified that there is a proceeding against them pending in a court. While a great deal of time is spent carrying out processes, actual "due process" is a necessary concomitant of justice. There is also the fundamental principle of a fair trial, which is now embodied in Article 10–A of Pakistan's Constitution, pursuant to the Eighteenth Amendment, which others in this volume are addressing.

These are some of the fundamental principles that are enshrined in our legal system, and our legal system is based on these concepts. How the legal system actually works is another matter. How laws are enforced and put into practice or applied may be a different story. However, these five fundamental principles are shared, espoused, and embraced by Pakistani citizens from Khyber to Karachi, from Wagah to Quetta: independent judges; the right to a fair trial; equality before the law; due process of law; and the right to appeal an original sentence in an appellate forum. These, broadly, are the principles that are the foundations of our system, which the Pakistani citizenry embraces despite experiencing the delays of the legal system, the vagaries of law, the inconsistencies in the application of law, and the corruption of law enforcers. Our citizenry came out to fight for these principles. They expect their judges to observe the very highest standards.

It is a mischaracterization of Pakistani state and society to style and characterize us as Arabs or Middle Eastern. No Arab country has independent judges. Our people have a history of coming out on behalf of the judiciary and for the judicial process, as they did between 2007 and 2009, when the present chief justice of Pakistan, Iftikhar Muhammad Chaudhry, was deposed by a military dictator. Millions of people came out to stand up for the concept of an independent judiciary. It was not a power struggle. Every Thursday, all over the country, lawyers, civil society, and political activists came out and marched throughout the summer and winter months. For two long and brutal years, every Thursday was a "Tahrir Square" (the Cairo locale where protests had been held during the Arab Spring) in every town and hamlet across Pakistan, across the length and breadth of the country. People peacefully marched the streets and assembled in town squares in the pursuit of mere concepts: the rule of law, of due process, of equality before law, of civil liberties, of habeas corpus, of an independent and empowered judiciary. They were, most appropriately, led by the black-suit-and-tie-clad members of the bars of Pakistan.

No one was demonstrating for personal gain or to come into power. I was one of the people in the forefront; it was not my objective to grasp power or attain a political office. I was just one of the many who believed in the people of Pakistan and the dreams of the people of Pakistan, and that what they wanted were independent judges, a just and equitable due process, the rule of law, equality before the law, and fair trials.

Now does a judicial system governed by these concepts exist in contemporary Pakistan? That is a different question. The answer is no, it does not. In 2010, I concluded a case in the Supreme Court of Pakistan that had been initiated in 1946. I have another client, ninety-six years old, who has been petitioning for the last forty-eight years. We are only now finally at the closure of her case at the Supreme Court, but there are still delays.

Delays in our legal system are indeed the first and foremost impediment to citizens obtaining justice in Pakistan. Delays are no doubt a problem universal to all legal systems. Charles Dickens was so frustrated that he went so far as to say that "the law is an ass." He may have been speaking of the state of the legal process in nineteenth-century Britain, but we in the twenty-first century have a particularly exaggerated and painful distortion in our system. It is not abnormal for it to take ten to twenty years for the court to reach the final determination of a matter. In some lucky situations cases are determined "quickly," taking only five years. The first obvious flaw in our legal system that we have to address, therefore, is delay in the process of imparting justice, because justice delayed is justice denied.

Some points cannot be avoided; some reform needs to be legislated. There need to be limits on lawyers obtaining adjournments. This facility is abused and wastes time and public funds. It should be restricted in two respects: (1) the period of the adjournment; and (2) the number of adjournments that one lawyer/one party can obtain for every stage of a proceeding. Then there should be closure. In addition, heavy costs should accompany delays and adjournments.

However, delays and adjournments cannot be addressed until we invest more in the legal system. We need to have more and better-trained judicial officers, especially judges at the lowest subordinate court levels. When increasing the numbers of judges, we need to ensure the quality does not fall, or else we will have achieved nothing. We have been able to provide modern technological aids and computers to some judges under the Asian Development Bank's Access to Justice Program, but it is necessary to make more resources available, include many more judges, and expand this kind of training program.

Pakistan also requires police reforms. The police are a key part of the prosecution arm of the legal process in the criminal justice system. In addition to police reforms, Pakistan needs to ensure police accountability, and the police need to remain subordinate and accountable to judges when trials are being conducted.

The Eighteenth Amendment includes two major developments affecting Pakistan's legal system: Article 10–A and Article 19–A. Article 10–A provides, as a fundamental right, the right to a fair trial. This article does nothing new. This right was enshrined and implicit in Article 4 of the 1973 Constitution, which says that no one shall be dealt with except in accordance with the law. While the guarantee of a fair trial was implicit in the earlier article, Article 10–A addresses it more specifically, providing an important reassurance, and upgrades it into a inalienable right. Article 19–A of the

Eighteenth Amendment ensures access to information. This information must be available to both parties in a suit, the plaintiff and the defendant, thereby leveling the playing field, to some extent, and contributing to the ultimate outcome of better justice.

However, the problem with the Eighteenth Amendment occurs on a broader level. It was passed unanimously without debate. It was first discussed by twenty-nine MNAs (members of the National Assembly) and senators. These members of Parliament held exclusive in-camera proceedings over a period of about three months. What they decided was then brought onto the floor of the National Assembly, and within half a day, it was adopted unanimously. It was then adopted by the Senate, unanimously, within half a day as well. There were celebrations held all over the country because Pakistan had unanimously adopted the Eighteenth Amendment and what a good thing unanimity was. However, without debate, there are so many lacunas, so many corners and edges that need to be rounded off, and so many matters to raise, for example, the question of where federal employees go when their departments are devolved. Where does the budget for these now-devolved ministries (which now operate at the provincial, not the federal, level) come from and go to? These matters—involving hundreds if not thousands of such petitions—will go to the courts in the next ten years. When they are contested in the courts, the executive branch will inevitably complain that the courts are transgressing on its territory.

But what is it that has transformed the courts into activists? Such matters were not even raised by the executive or legislative branches of Pakistan's government when the Eighteenth Amendment was being considered, so they will need to defer to the courts to get these matters resolved. Thus, although laws may be reformed, in order to ensure the highest principles of fair play it may be that speedy proceedings in the legal system still cannot be ensured.

There is a duality in Pakistan's legal system that hampers justice. We abide by both common law and *sharia* law at the same time. *Sharia* law actually applies only in a limited field (to certain specified offenses and personal law), while the common law is applicable more generally. Reference to and reliance upon *sharia* precepts, however, are becoming wider practices, even though the principles of evidence as well as the standards of proof are different in the two systems. Often, therefore, there is some confusion and contention between the two systems on questions of their applicability. Their coexistence can be characterized sometimes as opposites, but always as unfriendly neighbors.

Common law precepts are more refined and more finely tuned to the realities of the contemporary world. These have also been interpreted and applied by enlightened modern-day judges delivering judgments with detailed reasons, and they are subject to a hierarchical structure of appeals and oversight. The opinion of the highest appellate forum in this hierarchy prevails and is obeyed by all.

But the question is not which of the two is better. The issue is with their interaction. And despite the fact that the precepts of the *sharia* are quite clear and precise, often too precise, there is an absence of consensus on their interpretation. The problem is with those who arrogate unto themselves the sole authority to interpret it—the viciously divided Islamic clergy or the Ulema. Within every Muslim state there is a multiplicity of Islamic sects, and hence, Ulema with different and opposing views. Each set of Ulema asserts that its interpretation of the precepts is the *only* correct interpretation. Not only does each, therefore, assume to itself alone the sole authority to lay down the law with vigor and often violence, but each also denies to any other its own right to interpret the *sharia*. There is very little room for coexistence, let alone agreement. The former circumstance prevails only because of the coercive power of the state, but therein lies the dilemma— it is unwilling and often unable to choose between rival sects.

The uneasy coexistence of principles derived from common law and the precepts of the *sharia* is indeed one major cause of the inefficient application of laws in Pakistan. It often creates confusion in the selection of the most appropriate principle applicable on a given set of *justiciable* (liable to trial in a court of justice) facts. However, Pakistan's problem is not only the identification of the applicable precept; even when the relevant precept is specifically identified, the system confronts another debilitating challenge: enforcement.

There is an enormous deficiency in the enforcement of laws, and even more so in an *equal* enforcement of laws. Parliaments may currently legislate the best laws ever devised in human history. Judges may place the most enlightened and modern interpretations upon these statutes. However, if they are not effectively enforced, they will remain *non est,* essentially nonexistent. The state needs to show more "guts and grit" in enforcement than it presently does.

But enforcement, too, is only one aspect. There has to be more. There has to be, most important, *uniform* enforcement. Unless laws are uniformly enforced, there will be no respect for them. The elite must be, and must be seen to be, subject to the same set of laws as the general populace. As long as a "VIP culture of exemptions and indemnities" exists, and as long as selective impunity and immunity survive, there will be no true implementation of the law. As long as certain people are able to walk through security screenings without being frisked because they are members of the "elite"—such as high government functionaries, military officers, members of Parliament, judges, politicians, or senior bureaucrats—there will remain a problem with our system. One often sees the ordinary citizens of Pakistan being made to stand in line as members of the elite whisk past them. In every walk of life, in every area of activity, this is the norm. Ordinary citizens wait as the elite move ahead, whether in selection for government jobs, contracts, or benefits. There is always discrimination. There is a palpable advantage in being a member of, or being associated by friendship with, the elite by either interest or blood.

People learn from the example of the elite that there is a premium on avoiding the law. Our elite gain benefits by avoiding the law. It is not a shining precedent, but it becomes a precedent for others to follow whenever opportunity allows. Followed, it can lead to anarchy and the breakdown of civil society. That is what we are confronted with now. There must, therefore, be strict and uniform application of law. Thus, there is a need to discard such discriminatory indemnity laws as the so-called National Reconciliation Ordinance of 2007, which exempts corrupt holders of public office of all guilt and liability if the crime was committed between certain dates. Charges of the misappropriation of billions in public funds were accordingly discharged by a single stroke of a military commander's pen.

I want, however, to conclude on a positive note. We can make our legal system viable, responsive, and capable of addressing any obstacles in Pakistan's future only when we rid ourselves of a culture of impunity and immunity. This nation can then work wonders. I see this in what I call "the random sample of three hundred." This is a random sample of men and women, drawn from all classes, regions, professions, persuasions, and creeds. It can be taken any day at any international airport in Pakistan.

Five times a day, three hundred people—a random sample—go to the Lahore Airport to board international flights. They throw around their luggage with abandon and little care for any other. They zigzag their carts. They reach over one another's shoulders to grab for boarding passes with better seats. They jostle one another, attempting to be the first to get onto the flight. Yet three hours later, these three hundred people land in Abu Dhabi or Dubai, and they all disembark in a straight line. They are the same people who left Pakistan; however, they arrive elsewhere transformed. Five times a day—three hundred people five times a day, fifteen hundred people a day—they are my random sample. It is irrelevant to speak of them as elite or common, or as policemen, farmers, landlords, soldiers, civil servants, industrialists, or industrial workers. These three hundred people are a random sample, and the system determines their responses.

Instead of having a system that requires all this pushing and jostling to get anywhere, we need a system bereft of impunity and immunity. All the indemnity laws that now exist in Pakistan, including the National Reconciliation Ordinance, are quite odd in the sociopolitical sense. How politics and society coexist in Pakistan is demonstrated in their everyday manifestations in a VIP culture.

But we do see pockets of life where people have been forced to discard the VIP culture. The three hundred boarding an aircraft to travel abroad are not the only example. There is another that shines out and that temporarily transforms a much larger proportion of the populace. This is on the Peshawar to Lahore motorway. Here, law enforcement has been effective and uniform. Here, there is no VIP culture. Nobody is seen changing lanes without flashing indicators, and no one exceeds the speed limit. Every vehicle on the motorway follows the rules and obeys the traffic laws. Why? Because everyone—yes, everyone—who does not follow the rules gets a ticket regardless of his or her station in life.

What Pakistan needs is a systemic change resulting in the uniform enforcement of law on everyone. Then all the issues I have mentioned—including equality before the law, the rule of law, independence of judges, the right to a fair trial, the right to a hearing—all these principles and wonderful concepts already embedded in our legal system will come into proper play.

Pakistan does not need to restructure its existing laws as much as it needs to restructure the values of society so the laws that exist apply to everyone equally. How passionately the people of Pakistan embrace the dream of the rule of law is evident from the massive crowds that were attracted to the Rule of Law movement led by the lawyers from 2007 to 2009.

Rule of law and equality before the law give citizens a genuine stake in the affairs and well-being of the state. Otherwise they perceive themselves as outcasts, as people "left out in the cold." And such people may become willing recruits for ideologues such as the Taliban.

Pakistan is the theater of an intense and brutal war. Its population is the population in the theater of war. This population, equipped with the equal application of law and due process, can itself be the most effective and nonviolent "weapon" in the war (or more appropriately, the "means to win the war"). Pakistan cannot afford to leave its hitherto benign "weapon" out in the cold, unattended, for any extremist to take control of. Success will depend on the enforcement of existing laws more than on any changes that may be introduced in them.

6

Political Impediments
to Development

HASAN ASKARI RIZVI

Pakistan is facing a difficult internal situation mainly because of a faltering economy and an increasingly dysfunctional political system that threatens its long-term viability as a coherent and stable political entity. The slowing of economic growth is accompanied by a growing budgetary deficit; corruption, and misuse of state resources to serve partisan and personal interests; mismanagement of public-sector enterprises; and a persistent energy crisis. The internal crisis is accentuated by double-digit inflation, increasing unemployment, and the deteriorating law-and-order situation in the face of religious extremism and terrorism.

One can talk of considerable progress in some sectors of the economy, especially agriculture, and of the federal government's efforts to provide financial assistance to the poorest of the poor. However, economic inequities have increased, and there is a noticeable neglect of socioeconomic justice, adversely affecting human or societal security for the common folks. As is the case in many developing countries, it is easy to find "some oasis of affluence and security" in Pakistan. However, poverty, dispossession, and the sociopolitical alienation "of a huge absolute number of people in all walks of life"[1] have created a strong potential for social turmoil, religious and cultural intolerance, and violence.

These are not insurmountable problems. Their solutions are suggested from time to time by Pakistani and other experts. Pakistan's official circles include economic and financial experts who have a good understanding of the country's economic and political predicament. They offer some strategies and options to cope with the current crises in Pakistan.

The dilemma is not the failure to identify the solutions but rather developing consensus on them, their prioritization, and how to implement them. It is the problem of politics and political determination to implement difficult but relevant strategies. The political context and the disposition of the political leaders are not helpful to pursuing these problems in a dispassionate and professional manner. The political and societal scene is dominated by the short-sighted compulsion and highly partisan disposition of the leaders and the parties and by endemic corruption that neutralizes the capacity and will of the political governments to address directly the problems that threaten the Pakistani state and society. They cannot develop a broadly shared understanding on ways and means to address these problems and stay the course.

Major Obstacles to Development

Politics in Pakistan is detrimental to socioeconomic development and human welfare for three major reasons. First, the political parties do not function as an effective political machine for interest articulation and aggregation or for evolving options for coping with the problems faced by the people. They lack a clear vision of the future and talk in general and vague terms about "the welfare of the people" or make unrealistic promises that can hardly be fulfilled. For example, the opposition parties promise to bring down the prices of essential commodities and eradicate corruption, two popular issues in Pakistani politics. However, no political party or leader outlines the practical steps and measures for reducing the prices or completely eradicating corruption. They never have a plan of action but simply talk of coping with socioeconomic problems if they come to power. The poverty of ideas and vision prevents them from challenging deprivation and underdevelopment head on.

Second, ethnic, linguistic, regional, and religious-sectarian fault lines have fragmented the political process. The political forces are divided, and the political parties suffer from factionalism and internal conflict that weaken their capacity to pursue a coherent policy. Most energies of leadership are spent on balancing different factions and accommodating their demands in order to keep them happy. Local rivalries also produce internal dissension and conflict. All of this has implications for the working of political parties and their leadership style. Often leaders spend a great deal of time managing internal rivalries and conflicts, leaving little time for serious thinking on policy matters.

Third, the political leaders and parties spend a lot of time and energy in polemical exchanges with their political adversaries. Their discourse is marked by opposition for the sake of opposition. All political parties have some leaders who are known for mudslinging at their political rivals, engaging in political exchanges in derogatory language, and resorting to personal attacks rather than debating policy issues. The political parties and leaders are more interested in engaging in a blame game, trading charges and counter charges. Confrontation often degenerates into questioning each other's patriotism; the political rivals are often described as anti-state and as security risks who should be restrained from engaging in politics. This confrontational environment leaves little scope for a dispassionate and down-to-earth discourse on the problems that afflict the economy and sociopolitical order.

Pakistan's political leaders are their own worst adversaries. They undermine one another's reputation and adversely affect the prospects of democracy with their personalized politics and unnecessary confrontation. If Pakistan's politics is damaging to socioeconomic development and political institutions and processes are not fully functional, the major blame has to be shared among the political leaders.

Nature and Dynamics of Party Politics

Pakistan began its independent life in August 1947 with one dominant party, the Muslim League, which had led the independence movement and assumed the mantle of leadership at the time of independence. Other political parties were weak and enjoyed limited support. With the passage of time the Muslim League lost its dominant position because of a crisis of leadership after the demise of Mohammed Ali Jinnah, who had led the party to independence. It also declined because of internal incoherence and factionalism and failure to offer an inspiring program for the future. Formulating the constitution was unnecessarily delayed. It took almost nineteen months after attaining independence to pass the Objectives' Resolution (August 1947–March 1949) for the constitution. Another seven years were spent framing the first constitution for Pakistan (March 1956). That constitution was scrapped in October 1958, when the military assumed power by displacing the civilian government.

Several political parties, set up by those who were members of or associated with the Muslim League, came into the political field. Others with no links to the Muslim League also established political parties. These political parties suffered the same ailments that afflicted the Muslim League, including internal disharmony and factionalism, a support base limited mainly to a region or a province and no nationwide support, a highly partisan worldview that equated the party's interest with the national interest, and a strength in criticism of political rivals and weakness in offering a practical plan of action for addressing the socioeconomic and political problems.

The political parties lack internal democracy and have an oligarchic authority pattern, dominated by the leader and the leader's close associates. Some political parties are so closely associated with the leader that his or her exit is likely to fragment the party. Internal elections are a formality, because they are neither open nor competitive. If a political party tries to experiment with an open and freely competitive election, the party tends to factionalize because the competing leaders engage in charges and counter charges on election-related issues, such as the enrollment of new members, flaws in the electoral process, and intimidation and fraud. Quite often the group that loses the party election either challenges the winner, which intensifies factionalism, or quits the party to set up a new group or party.

Over the years this pattern of party politics has not changed much, although two political parties, the PML(N) and the PPP, have been dominating politics since 1988. These two political parties endeavor to function within an all-Pakistan framework, and they enjoy varying degrees of nationwide support. Most others have a regional, ethnic, and narrow support base. Islamic parties have their peculiar appeal to religiously conservative and orthodox people. Most Islamic parties are closely identified with a specific Islamic fiqh or denomination, restricting the appeal to the followers of that specific religious denomination.

Political parties are supposed to evolve political and social networks that cut across ethnic, linguistic, regional, religious, and other divides and that promote political attachments and identities that are nationwide. They bring people into a nationwide political and social framework that overarches their other identities; those identities continue to exist, but their political appeal is reduced. The political parties in Pakistan hardly play such a role. Consequently, politics in Pakistan is highly divisive and fragmentary. It has not contributed to promoting political harmony and coherence. Political alliances are temporary arrangements for achieving immediate power interests. One commentator argues that

> there are a few political parties that could be described as aggregative and comprehensive cutting across social-economic, ethnic and regional cleavages. . . . The political parties like the PPP and different factions of the PML, especially the PML(N) and PMLQ [Pakistan Mulsim League–Quaid-i-Azam], are catch-all parties that endeavor to build support in all provinces and among various ethnic and regional groups. . . . However, most other political parties have localized or religion-based or ethnic dispositions.[2]

This type of politics leaves little room for dispassionate and serious efforts to address socioeconomic problems. The focus of the political leadership is on sustaining its support and causing problems for its adversaries. Opposition for the sake of opposition is so common that the government spends most of its energy maintaining its survival, and the opposition gives more attention to pulling down the government.[3] Politics has become nothing more than a power struggle devoid of any consideration of its negative implications for the economy, internal security, societal harmony, and the welfare of the common people.

Constitutional and Political Discontinuity

Pakistan's political dilemmas can be traced to constitutional and political breakdown and restrictions on political activities that have stifled the natural growth of a participatory political process. Two broad categories of discontinuities have marred Pakistani politics and turned them into an obstacle to socioeconomic development and human security: problems in creating a durable constitution; and the implications of military takeover for political continuity and maturation of the political process.

Pakistan experimented with different constitutional formulas over the years either by framing a new constitution or by introducing far-reaching changes in the current constitution to accommodate the priorities of the dominant elite. In the first decade of independence the two constituent assemblies took a long time to frame the first constitution because the members diverged sharply on the basic constitutional features. The major political factors discussed in the previous section of this chapter made it extremely difficult for the first constituent assembly (1947–54) to agree on the basic features of constitutional arrangements. For example, the assembly spent an unnecessarily long time coming to agreement on the representation of different provinces and administrative units in the National Assembly.

The most perplexing problem was the representation of East Pakistan (now Bangladesh) in Parliament. East Pakistan was defined as one administrative unit, but it had a larger population than West Pakistan, which comprised several provinces and administrative units. The assembly also diverged on the powers of the two houses of Parliament. After long wrangling the members agreed to equal representation of East and West Pakistan in the national legislature, which was to have one chamber only.

The nature of the federal system was another perplexing issue. The conflict was over the distribution of power between the federal government and the provinces. The demand for greater provincial autonomy for East Pakistan, the Northwest Frontier Province (now Khyber Pakhtunkhwa), and Sindh was resisted by the dominant political elite, hailing mainly from the Punjab, and by the Muslim League leaders. The trends toward centralization manifested in the integration of various provinces and administrative units in West Pakistan into one integrated province in 1955, causing much resentment in the political circles of the smaller provinces and administrative units. The federal government rejected these objections as threats to national unity.

The third constitutional issue that fractured Pakistani politics in the first decade of independence was the issue of a national language. The controversy was related to Bengali political and societal leaders' demand that Bengali be made the national language, whereas the ruling Muslim League favored Urdu. In 1954, after a lot of bitterness and conflict on the language issue, the constituent assembly agreed to recognize both Bengali and Urdu as national languages of Pakistan.

The fourth issue is related to the question of whether or not Pakistan should have a joint electorate or separate electorate. After years of deliberations the National Assembly decided in 1956 in favor of a joint electorate for East Pakistan and a separate electorate for West Pakistan. This decision was changed in 1957, when a joint electorate was enforced throughout Pakistan. In 1979, General Zia ul-Haq's military government introduced a separate electorate in order to win over the orthodox Islamist leaders and parties. In 2002, Pakistan returned to a joint electorate under the military government of General Pervez Musharraf.

The fifth issue that delayed the constitution pertained to the number of chambers in Parliament. All federal systems have parliaments with two chambers. Initially, Pakistan's political leaders proposed a two-house Parliament. However, it was decided in 1955 to have a unicameral Parliament, with seats divided equally between East Pakistan and West Pakistan. The unicameral system was replaced with a bicameral legislature in the 1973 Constitution.

The sixth constitutional issue also pertained to the system of governance, and was whether Pakistan should have a presidential system or a parliamentary system. There was a general understanding in political circles during the immediate aftermath of independence that Pakistan would adopt a parliamentary democratic system. However, after the establishment of the first military rule in October 1958, the official circles favored the presidential system, which was incorporated in the 1962 Constitution. The 1973 Constitution returned the country to a parliamentary democracy.

Discontinuities were also caused by four military takeovers—in October 1958, March 1969, July 1977, and October 1999—that placed varying degrees of restrictions on civilian political activities. The first two military regimes of Ayub Khan and Yahya Khan scrapped the existing constitutions (the 1956 Constitution and the 1962 Constitution). Ayub Khan introduced a presidential system with centralization of power. Yahya Khan announced the broad features of a new constitution, but his military government collapsed soon afterward because of the abysmal performance of the Pakistan military in the 1971 India-Pakistan war, which caused the separation of East Pakistan.

General Zia ul Haq and General Pervez Mushrarraf suspended the 1973 Constitution and later revived it after introducing far-reaching changes to protect the political interests of their military regimes. Zia ul Haq made such changes to the constitution in 1981 and 1985, and Pervez Musharraf engaged in constitutional manipulation in 2002. Both coopted a section of the political elite and excluded those who contested their legitimacy in order to "civilianize" military rule and ensure the continuity of key personnel and policies from military rule to post–military rule period. They also restricted the role of political parties by placing them under various restrictions. Military rule not only caused constitutional breakdown and political discontinuity but also denied civilian institutions, processes, and personnel the ability to learn democratic politics through experience. The lack of continuity did not permit the political institutions and processes pass through a maturation process that ensures stability and conflict management through legal-rational institutional arrangements.

Repeated military rule enabled the armed forces to acquire such a salience in the state system and the society that it dominated the foreign policy and security affairs and emerged as an important player in the national economy. The civilian governments from 1988 to1999 and from 2008 to 2012 faced the challenging task of balancing the pressures of democratic politics while avoiding alienating the top brass of the military. The implications of these two considerations conflicted periodically, making the task of political management for civilian leaders a complex affair.[4]

The post-military civilian arrangements have suffered from a democracy deficit and faltered in addressing the issues of public welfare and development. The civilian political leaders lack self-confidence in dealing with the military because their energies are spent pulling together the party and political links after long years of military rule. Political parties and leaders are so divided that they engage perpetually in mutual bickering and unrestrained power struggles, enabling the military and bureaucracy to exploit their internal contradictions. Their mutual conflicts make it extremely difficult for them to assert their primacy over the bureaucracy and the military. They are also unable to pursue socioeconomic development and public welfare, which causes alienation of the common people, especially among those between the ages of sixteen and thirty, who constitute a substantial part of the population.

This trend of weak political leadership and the ascendancy of the bureaucracy and the military began within a couple of years following independence but were accelerated after the first coup in October 1958. The civilian struggle to stay afloat in a political domain suffering from military pressure continues unabated. Philip Odenburg argues that

> the periods of procedural democracy have been deeply flawed by the lack of electoral mandates and a constitutional framework in the first period (1947–58), the misuse of executive power in the second (1972–77), and the military's behind-the-scenes authority in the third (1988–99). . . . Pakistan's democratic institutions, when they were allowed to exist, were too often window-dressing for the civil and military bureaucracy that wielded real power, unchecked by the courts.[5]

Islam, National Identity, and Nation-Building

The issues surrounding the relationship between Islam and the constitutional and political systems of Pakistan have baffled political and societal leaders. The problems, including operationalization of the teaching and principles of Islam in terms of political institutions and processes in the context of the modern nation state, continue to haunt Pakistan. The failure to resolve these issues has made it difficult to articulate Pakistani national identity and what it means to be a Pakistani. How should Pakistanis define their national identity and relationship with the state?

The Muslim League invoked Islam as a mark of identity and an instrument for political mobilization in the last ten years before independence. There was a broad-based understanding in the immediate aftermath of independence that the state and the political system would have some relationship with Islam. However, the precise nature of this relationship was not fully articulated by the Muslim League. Should Pakistan be a religion-dominated Islamic state or a Muslim state in which Muslims constitute an overwhelming majority? The other key issues that remained inconclusive include whether Pakistan should be viewed as an ideological state or a state with an ideology and what the role and position of non-Muslims in an Islamic state should be. The Muslim League had not worked on the details of the constitutional system that was adopted after independence. It invoked Islam for political mobilization and talked of Islamic history, culture, and civilization in order to emphasize a separate Muslim identity and to demand a separate homeland for the Muslims of British India for the protection and advancement of their identity, rights, and interests.

The debate about what constitutes an Islamic state and what the major responsibilities of an Islamic state are was one of the factors delaying framing the constitution. This controversy did not end after the passage of the constitution in 1956. Political leaders like Mohammed Ali Jinnah and others envisaged Pakistan as a modern democratic state that derived its ethical basis from Islam. They viewed the teachings and principles of Islam as a source of inspiration for the framers of constitution rather than viewing the teachings and principles of Islam as forming the substance of the law and the constitution. The religious leaders talked of creating a religious political order based strictly on a puritanical, literalist view of Islamic teachings and practices as they existed in the earliest period of Islam. They advocated a highly orthodox and conservative view of Islam for creating punitive, regulative, and extractive arrangements that gave an inbuilt advantage to them in the state system.[6]

Pakistan's various constitutions adopted a liberal and modern democratic system of governance with some stipulations emphasizing Pakistan's identification with Islam. It was not until the ascendancy to power of General Zia ul Haq in 1977 that the Pakistani state accommodated the perspectives of orthodox and conservative religious leaders and used its apparatus to enforce their Islamic perspectives in the society. This accentuated Islamic-sectarian conflict, weakened internal harmony, and gave reason to question the legitimacy of state processes to those who did not share the official state perspective on Islam.

The controversy over the role of Islam in the political system and how to articulate Pakistani identity continues to cause political and social conflict in the society. The unresolved issues include the tension between territorial Pakistani nationalism and Islamic universal community; the content and nature of Islamic orientations; whether Pakistan should be an Islamic-ideological state or a Muslim-majority state with an ideology; secular-Pakistani identity versus the state's identification with Islam; whether the state should enforce Islam by decrees; and who will decide the Islamic character of laws and state actions. Other contentious issues relate to the rights and status of religious minorities and the status and role of women. Farzana Shaikh rightly identifies the dilemmas of the relationship between Islam and the state and how to define Pakistani identity:

Despite broad (if uneasy) acceptance that Pakistan meant (and continues to mean) different things to different people, its multiple meanings have invariably frustrated the cohesion of a national community that is anchored in, and is still widely judged to be representative of, an undifferentiated religious community. Indeed, the burden of its presumed status as the bearer of a religiously informed "communal consensus" has compounded the uncertainties attached to Pakistan's national identity.[7]

These issues continue to dominate the political discourse and have led to a tendency on the part of people with strong religious views to question the legitimacy of the state system if it does not conform to their vision of an Islamic system. This breeds disharmony and conflict and diverts the attention of the policymakers from addressing the key issues of economic and social development.

Religious Extremism and Militancy

Pakistan's capacity to pursue socioeconomic development has been greatly compromised by the growth of Islamic orthodoxy, extremism, and militancy. The tradition of religious tolerance and sociocultural pluralism gradually eroded in the 1980s and later, when the military government of General Zia ul Haq used the state apparatus and resources to promote Islamic orthodoxy and militancy. This strategy was adopted by the military government to mobilize support from the orthodox religious circles in order to undercut the support of those who challenged General Zia ul Haq's rule. This also enabled him to mobilize international support for his government when the United States and other Western countries sought his government's cooperation to build up Afghan-Islamic resistance to challenge the Soviet military intervention in Afghanistan (1979–89). A host of armed Islamic groups that included Afghans, Pakistanis, and Muslims from several Islamic countries was established to fight the Soviets in Afghanistan. Even after the death of General Zia ul Haq in August 1988, Islamic militancy continued to be supported by the Pakistani military for pursuing Pakistan's foreign policy agendas in Afghanistan and Indian-administered Kashmir.

The rise of religious orthodoxy and militancy led to an attenuation of religious and cultural tolerance and intensified internal conflict and violence. These trends "not only imposed pressures on religious minorities but have also accentuated interdenominational conflicts among Muslims. There is less patience for religious and cultural divergence, and self-styled vigilantes threaten those who do not share their religious perspective."[8]

In addition to Islamic political parties that take part in the electoral process but represent religious orthodoxy and conservatism, there are four broad categories of Islamic militant entities. They challenge the primacy of the Pakistani state and want to overwhelm it in order to impose their religious-political agenda based on their vision of Islam.

The first category includes a large number of ultra-conservative Islamic clergy who are literalist in their interpretation of religious texts. They are based in mosques and Islamic seminaries and question the legitimacy of the existing political and legal order and reject modern democracy. However, they are unable to agree among themselves on an alternative political and economic order. They preach and teach religious orthodoxy based on their Islamic denominational group, rejecting the interpretation of the Qur'an and the Sunnah by other Islamic denominational groups. They create a mindset that is Islamic-sectarian and supports militancy.

Second, there are militant Islamic groups and their breakaway factions that use extreme violence and intimidation, including public execution, to enforce their Islamic-political agenda. Their views are derived from a narrow and bigoted understanding of Islamic teachings combined with tribal or local traditions. Most of these groups are based in Afghanistan or in Pakistan's tribal areas and want to establish an Islamic state system of their choice in Afghanistan, Pakistan, or both. The Tehrik-e-Taliban Pakistan (TTP) is the biggest umbrella organization for several militant Islamic groups based in Pakistan's tribal areas.

Third, some of the highly conservative militant groups focus on dislodging Indian rule in Kashmir. They view Kashmir as an Islamic land under the occupation of a non-Muslim state, India. They are based in the Pakistani mainland or in Pakistan-administrated Kashmir.

Fourth, a host of Pakistani-based militant groups identify with a particular Islamic denomination or sect. They have a strong Islamic-sectarian orientation and reject all other Islamic denominational groups. Their narrow and bigoted Islamic sectarian disposition causes violent conflicts in Pakistan. In the past the fault lines were the Wahhabis/Deobandis and the Shias. Now, the conflict between the Wahhabis/Deobandis and the followers of Barelvi Islamic traditions has become more pronounced. All this causes internal conflict and increased threat of violence. Most mosques and public prayer places are now heavily guarded by police or armed volunteers to secure them against armed assault from rival sectarian groups.

The TTP and other militant groups based in the tribal areas and the Islamic-sectarian groups based in mainland Pakistan have increased their violent activities in mainland Pakistan since 2007. They have targeted official civilian and military buildings and personnel as well as ordinary people in public places, especially in markets, religious places, and shrines in different cities by using suicide and roadside bombings. The city of

Peshawar experienced more violence from militant Islamic groups than any other city in Pakistan from October to December 2009. Such violent incidents peaked in 2009–10. The year 2011 saw a considerable decline in such incidents and deaths.

Most of these groups have developed strong societal support by invoking Islamic-denominational networks, seminaries, and mosques. Growing anti-Americanism has also enabled these groups to mobilize support. In the Punjab these groups also leveraged anti-India sentiments to mobilize support. Their societal linkages and support networks make it extremely difficult for the federal government to control these groups. Their sympathizers are sitting in civilian and military establishments.

The troubled law-and-order situation, especially violence and growing personal insecurity, has discouraged foreign investors from investing in Pakistan. Pakistani business and industrial groups are hesitant to make new long-term investments. Some of these groups shifted their investments to the Persian Gulf region during 2007–11. As there are no signs of improvement in internal security, Pakistan's economy has little chance of recovery in the near future.

Civilian Governance and Development Problems Since 2008

The assumption of power by elected civilian governments at the federal level and in the provinces in March 2008 (after the February general elections) engendered some hope that they may be able to contain religious extremism and militancy, improve the internal security situation, and salvage the troubled economy.

There are some important achievements by the civilian elected political order. The political parties in Parliament cooperated with one another to enact the Eighteenth and Nineteenth constitutional amendments (April 2010 and January 2011, respectively). The amendments strengthened the constitution's parliamentary and democratic character, which had been diluted by General Pervez Musharraf's military government. The unanimity among the federal and provincial governments on the Seventh National Finance Commission Award (December 2009) was a rare achievement that evolved a formula for dividing the revenue between the federal government and the provinces. It also announced the package of socioeconomic reforms for Balochistan under the title Agaz-i-Haqooq-i-Balochistan (November 2009) and abandoned the construction of new military cantonments in Balochistan, as demanded by the major political parties from that province. Other important welfare measures were the Benazir Income Support Fund and related programs designed to give financial help to the poorest families in all provinces, and the reinstatement of people who were removed from their jobs by the PML(N) government in the 1990s. The Army decided to increase the recruitment of Baloch youth to the Army and launched educational projects in Balochistan. The military, backed by the civilian government, was successful in dislodging the Taliban from Swat/Malakand, where it had virtually taken over and was planning to expand its control to other areas. The military operation in April-July 2009 retrieved the Swat/Malakand area. By the end of 2009 the military had taken control of most of South Waziristan. Since then, the military has engaged in counterterrorism in five tribal areas (Bajaur, Khyber, Mohmand, Orakzai, and Kuram), but it has not, so far, conclusively overwhelmed the Taliban and other militant groups in these areas.

However, the elected governments at the federal and provincial levels have demonstrated limited capacity to address effectively various domestic threats to Pakistani state and society. These governments faltered in governance and political management and thus could not control religious and cultural intolerance, internal insecurity, and terrorism. Other challenges not addressed adequately include the budget deficit, inflation, price hikes, periodic shortages of essential food items, and acute electricity and gas shortages. There are serious complaints of corruption and nepotism against the official circles. The internal law-and-order situation poses a serious challenge in Balochistan, where Baloch dissident groups periodically resort to violence in Baloch districts against government installations and personnel, power transmission lines and gas pipelines, their political opponents, and people hailing from other provinces, especially the Punjab. Karachi also experiences violence and killings from time to time. However, the most serious threat is the faltering economy, which the civilian governments have failed to salvage, forcing them to rely heavily on external financial support (loans[9] and grants) and foreign remittances by overseas Pakistanis to their families. The provincial and federal governments are also relying heavily on borrowing from local Pakistani banks. The major obstacle to tackling these problems in a satisfactory manner is the nature of politics in Pakistan. The political parties and leaders pursue their partisan interests in such a manner that they pay little, if any, attention to the challenges that threaten Pakistan's future as a functioning state capable of fulfilling its primary obligations to its citizenry.

All political parties subscribe to democracy and constitutionalism, but their political management does not always reflect this commitment. Political parties and their leaders are so divided and immersed in their partisan agendas that they cannot take up any social, political, or economic issue on its own merit. The objective is to serve the narrow party interest and put pressure on political adversaries. Constitutional and legal institutions and processes are treated as instruments for advancing party interests. If the institutions and processes do not help to achieve the party's partisan objectives, the political leaders bypass them and adopt extra-parliamentary methods.

The political leaders' idiom of politics and methods are nondemocratic. They often use rude and un-parliamentary discourse and resort to personalized comments or mudslinging against their political adversaries. If they cannot get their agenda fulfilled through Parliament, they are not hesitant to engage in street agitation. For every major political party the Parliament and democratic processes are relevant only to the extent that they contribute to achieving partisan interests.

The PPP wants to hold on to power at the federal level and in Sindh by all means possible, including building partnerships based on expediency with different political parties. The major opposition party, the PML(N), devotes itself to embarrassing the PPP government or making incessant attempts to pull it down. Politics thus turns into a limitless power struggle rather than a political exercise for serving the people by addressing their socioeconomic problems.

The PML(N) has periodically engaged in street agitation in support of its political demands rather than using the Parliament for that purpose. In the last week of February 2009, when the Supreme Court disqualified Shahbaz Sharif, chief minister of the Punjab, from membership in the provincial assembly, he lost his office and the federal government imposed the governor's rule. The PML(N) decided to go to the street to protest against the governor's rule, combining it with a demand for restoration of Justice Iftikhar Muhammad Chaudary as the chief justice of the Supreme Court. During these days Nawaz Sharif publicly encouraged civil servants to defy the government.

In 2011–12, the PML(N) launched twin street protests to force the federal government to quit and remove President Asif Ali Zardari from his office. The most popular slogan in the PML(N)'s public rallies was "Go, Zardari, go." The PML(N) leadership did not invoke Parliament to remove the federal government and Zardari because it did not have sufficient votes in the National Assembly to move a vote of no-confidence against the prime minister. Similarly, the PML(N) did not have the two-thirds majority in both houses needed to impeach the president. It therefore decided to hold public meetings and stage protest marches to paralyze the federal government, accusing the federal government and President Zardari of corruption and the misuse of state patronage and resources to advance personal and partisan interests.

The PML(N) street protests did not involve any issue of public welfare. It was a power struggle in the tradition of the 1988–99 period, when these two political parties engaged in a brute struggle for power. As at that earlier period of civilian rule, the PML(N) argued that the removal of the federal government was the only way to address the problems of the state and its citizens.

During these years all major political parties had to share the blame for Pakistan's socioeconomic predicament and the troubled law-and-order situation because they were in power either at the federal level or in the provinces. The federal government comprised the PPP, the Muttahida Qaumi Movement (MQM), the Awami National Party (ANP), and the PMLQ. The PPP was a partner with the MQM in Sindh and part of a multiparty coalition in Balochistan. In Khyber Pakhtunkhwa the PPP shared power with the ANP. The Punjab was ruled exclusively by the PML(N). Such a sharing of power among political parties was unprecedented in Pakistan's political history. If governance and political management by the federal coalition government led by the PPP was poor and if it mismanaged public welfare and economic development, the performance of the PML(N) government in the Punjab was equally disappointing. Complaints about poor governance, the troubled law-and-order situation, and related societal problems were common in the Punjab.

The PML(N) leaders were focusing on what they described as corruption and mismanagement by the federal government and President Asif Ali Zardari in their street protests, hoping that this would cause the collapse of the federal government. They also hoped that as the federal government was discredited in the streets, the Supreme Court might order some punitive action against it on account of corruption and poor governance, including the removal of some senior government officials for noncompliance with its orders. They expressed the hope that the military alone or in collaboration with the Supreme Court might remove the federal government. Some opposition leaders floated the idea of establishing an interim government of professionals and technocrats in place of the federal government under an order of the Supreme Court that would be enforced by the military. The opposition parties supported the removal of Prime Minister Yousaf Raza Gilani by the Supreme Court on the charge of contempt of court in June 2012. They wanted the Supreme Court and the military to remove the PPP-led federal government altogether.

The PPP counteracted such campaigns by highlighting what it described as the misdeeds of PML(N)'s leaders, Nawaz and Shahbaz Sharif, and how the building up of their industrial and financial empires synchronized with their years in power under the military government of General Zia ul Haq and later.

Some political parties offered themselves as alternatives to the PPP and the PML(N). Imran Khan projected his Pakistan-i-Tehrik-i-Insaf (PTI) as an alternative to the PPP and the PML(N); its top leadership was convinced that it could sweep aside the two major political parties in the next general elections. The Jamaat-i-Islami also viewed itself as a credible replacement for the two major parties. The political idiom and discourse of the PTI and the Jamaat-i-Islami was no different from the political idiom of the PPP and the PML(N). They engaged in polemical political exchanges, often blaming the major political parties for the ills of the Pakistani state and society. The MQM and the PMLQ also used foul language against their political adversaries. On October 13, 2011, the PML(N) and the MQM members were involved in a brawl in the National Assembly; other members intervened to save it from turning into a major physical clash.

The political leaders and parties did not hesitate to violate democratic norms to pursue their partisan power agendas. The ruling party wanted to hold on to power at any cost. The opposition left no stone unturned to pull down the government. All political leaders were strong in their verbal commitment to democracy, but they violated democratic norms in letter and spirit at the operational level. One commentator rightly pointed out that the elected governments "did not adhere to the required democratic principles in their conduct of affairs. And similarly, the opposition also played an important role in destabilizing the elected government, ultimately eroding the democratic process."[10]

The key point missing in the ongoing political wrangling in 2012 is that no political party has made a serious effort to address the major problems afflicting Pakistan state and society. Nor have any parties offered a workable plan of action for coping effectively with the troubled economy, terrorism and internal insecurity, price hikes, power and gas shortages, and economic and political inequities.

The political parties and leaders find it difficult to think beyond their narrow party interests. Their highly partisan politics undermine the prospects of socioeconomic development. They do not adopt a professional and nonpartisan disposition for reviewing the imperatives of socioeconomic development and equality of opportunities.

The official Pakistani reports on socioeconomic development, released in October 2011, show that the percentage of households living in poverty has increased to 40 percent. The United Nations Development Program report ranks Pakistan 145 among 187 countries in the Human Development Index.[11] The *Daily Express* (Lahore) reported on November 27, 2011, that the Punjab government received forty-two thousand applications for ninety jobs of junior clerk and mail despatcher. The rising youth unemployment makes them vulnerable to extremism. Add to this situation the fact that foreign direct investment in Pakistan has shown a considerable decline in 2009–12, due mainly to the deteriorating law-and-order situation, especially terrorism and street crime, serious power shortages, and the absence of an investment-friendly environment. These trends are inimical to social and economic development and threaten democracy, amicable resolution of societal conflicts, and the electoral process.

Concluding Observation

All political leaders and parties in Pakistan make repeated commitments to the eradication of poverty and unemployment and the promotion of socioeconomic development and a secure future for the common people. However, Pakistani governments have not been successful in fulfilling these promises. The major problem is not the identification of the ailments that trouble Pakistani state and society. The real difficulty is the way that political leaders and parties manage political and societal affairs. Their priorities are dominated by narrow partisan interests and power politics. The development issues and considerations are often subordinated to the overall political concerns of each party. A requisite democratic politics that is responsive to the needs and aspiration of the people is missing. The political leaders and parties lack a singular commitment to development and social justice issues in a nonpartisan and professional manner.

Politics in Pakistan is a major obstacle to pursuing development goals in an earnest manner. The disposition of the political leaders and the way they pursue their partisan interests leave little space for a dispassionate and shared approach to address the development issues in a manner that will benefit ordinary people, and there is a widespread perception in the society that the socioeconomic situation is not moving toward a positive and human-friendly direction. Several factors have contributed to anti-development politics. These include failure to evolve a sustainable agreement on the operational norms of the polity, inconclusive articulation of the relationship between Islam and the state, problems of political parties and divisive and non-aggregative politics, constitutional and political discontinuities by military intervention, an overall democracy deficit, and especially the absence of regular and noncontroversial elections.

Despite the return to elected civilian rule in 2008, the federal and provincial governments have generally faltered in governance and political management. The disposition of the political parties and leaders in government or in opposition is so parochial that they cannot take up development and societal welfare issues in a mutually agreed upon and professional manner.

Since the government wants to hold on to power at any cost, the opposition is bent on pulling down the government by all possible parliamentary and extra-parliamentary methods. The idiom and discourse of politics is non-democratic, and the political leaders trade charges and counter charges on each and every policy measure. They are unable to work together to salvage the faltering economy, improve the law-and-order situation, and especially check the growing religious and cultural intolerance and terrorism.

The incessantly confrontational politics and brute power struggles divert the attention of policymakers from the key issues of economic and social development. If the present political trends continue, Pakistan may turn into a nonperforming state with little operational capacity to fulfill its primary obligations to its citizenry. Much depends on whether the civilian political leaders can rise above their narrow partisan interests and use their leadership and organizational skills for promoting internal security and stability, social and political coherence, and socioeconomic development.

Notes

1. Mahbubul Haq, Human Development Centre, *Human Development in South Asia 2005: Human Security in South Asia* (Karachi: Oxford University Press, 2005).

2. Hasan Askari Rizvi, "Political Parties and Fragmented Democracy," in *Pakistan: Reality, Denial, and the Complexity of Its State*, ed. Heinrich Böll Foundation, 66–82 (Berlin: Heinrich Böll Stiftung, 2009), 81.

3. Safdar Mahmood, *Pakistan: Political Roots and Development, 1947–1999* (Karachi: Oxford University Press, 2000).

4. For a review of military rule and its impact on civilian politics, see Lawrence Ziring, *Pakistan in the Twentieth Century: A Political History* (Karachi: Oxford University Press, 1997).

5. Philip Oldenburg, *India, Pakistan, and Democracy* (New York: Routledge, 2010).

6. For different visions of Islamic teachings and constitution making, see Shaukat Ali, *Pakistan: A Religio-Political Study* (Islamabad: National Institute of Historical and Cultural Research, 1997).

7. Farzana Shaikh, *Making Sense of Pakistan* (New York: Columbia University Press, 2009).

8. Hasan Askari Rizvi, "At the Brink," in *The Future of Pakistan*, ed. Stephen P. Cohen, et al., 182–98 (Washington DC: The Brookings Institution, 2011), 188.

9. The State Bank of Pakistan reported that, on September 30, 2011, Pakistan's external debt and liabilities amounted to US$61.835 billion (*Pakistan Today* [Lahore], November 28, 2011), see "Profit" section.

10. Zafar Iqbal, "Elitist Political Culture and the Perils of Democracy in Pakistan," in *Pakistan: From the Rhetoric of Democracy to the Rise of Militancy*, ed. Ravi Kalia, 138–59 (London: Routledge, 2011), 138; see also Frederic Grare, "Pakistan's Pursuit of Democracy," in ibid., 160–76.

11. *Pakistan Today* (Lahore), November 30, 2011, see "Profit" section.

7

Reforming Pakistan's Bureaucracy

Will the Eighteenth Amendment Help?

SAEED SHAFQAT

Democratic and military rulers alike must rely on bureaucracy to implement policies. However, in post-colonial societies, they are equally enthusiastic to subordinate bureaucracy, bend its "steel frame" and sparingly work on attitudinal change. In Pakistan's case both the democratic and military rulers have attempted to subordinate bureaucracy through purges and reform. Have these patterns led to a change in the attitude, behavior, and performance of the bureaucrat and the structure of civil services in Pakistan? Policy analysts and political pundits are now debating what impact the Eighteenth Amendment will have on the civil services of Pakistan. The outcome of that process remains to be seen, but it will certainly affect Pakistan's development prospects. The question is, will it be a positive or negative impact?

This chapter is divided into four parts. First, it provides a brief overview of the origins and evolution of the civil service in Pakistan. Second, it briefly reviews and evaluates the reports of four commissions (from 1972 to 2009) set up by the Government of Pakistan concerning civil service effectiveness. Two reports were produced under democratic regimes and two under military regimes. Each report and its findings and recommendations is understood, interpreted, and evaluated in the context of three essential factors: the prevailing sociopolitical environment, the regime type, and the ruler's imperative. Third, this chapter explores why reform efforts have focused solely on the higher, federal bureaucracy and not that existing within the provincial governments. Finally, it assesses how the recently implemented Eighteenth Amendment is reshaping federation-province relations and the role and structure of civil services in the country. I argue that both democratic and military rulers' reform efforts have been to subordinate the bureaucracy rather than change behavior, improve service delivery and citizen welfare, or enhance professional skills, managerial capacity, and public accountability. Consequently, politicization, institutional decline, preoccupation with survival, and preserving the status quo have become pervasive in the civil services of Pakistan and deepened the crisis of governance.

Historical Overview

Colonial rule has been a potent force in influencing the political culture and bureaucratic and political institutions of Pakistan. During 150 years of colonial rule, the British Raj laid the foundations of strong centralized and effective bureaucratic institutions, in which elected public officials and parliamentary institutions had a limited role. It is understandable that the British built centralized bureaucratic institutions for revenue collection, intimidation, and control over colonized people. A number of scholarly writings recognize that Pakistan inherited "strong bureaucratic institutions" and "weak representative institutions."[1] It needs to be emphasized at the outset that the British did not create the Indian Civil Service (ICS) with the view that they would have political bosses. They constructed an administrative structure that was not to be controlled politically by the "natives." Therefore, those who joined the ICS had considerable autonomy and discretion in performing their functions. These officers were expected to rule, uphold, and enforce the laws that the British had devised and developed to govern the local Indians. Colonial rulers were careful not to ignore the cultural sensitivities of the various regions of India. Therefore, each province had its own tradition of administration.

In Punjab, the British adopted a paternalistic model of administration. This model developed into the dominant mode of governance in areas that came to constitute contemporary Pakistan. The Raj carried out their social engineering by reinforcing the influence of the elite class who were already powerful in the traditional order and rural structure of the Punjab, such as tribal leaders and feudal landowners. The sources of this paternalistic model can be traced from the 1860s. When Indians began to compete and join the ICS and perform administrative functions with the same autonomy as British officials, local political interference was kept minimal. These factors gave the officer in the field considerable autonomy to make decisions regarding developmental work. Therefore, invariably, keeping in view the broad policy goals, the district officer simply used discretionary powers to conduct the business of the government within the broad framework provided by the Raj's rules and laws. This practice continued in post-independence Pakistan.

During the Raj, through their bureaucracy, the British provided patronage to landlords and religious and tribal elders by providing land grants, titles, pensions, and other rewards in order to coopt them to ensure political stability. Thus, colonial rule laid the foundations of patron-client relationships.[2] In the post-independence period, this patron-client relationship between the bureaucrat and the local elites acquired new meaning and salience in the rural setting of the districts. As the electoral process gained more legitimacy, it reinforced further the patron-client relationship and the political culture of factionalism prevalent in rural Pakistan. The bureaucrat became and was perceived to be the guarantor of security, provider of patronage, and protector of the influence and power of the local elites.[3] Thus, a culture of politics and representation that could have allowed the evolution and development of political parties did not emerge. Patronage and reward distribution were monopolized by the bureaucrat and not by the political party. Therefore, for landlord families in the rural power structure, it became imperative to have one family member be a part of government to provide patronage, extend influence, and ensure security. This paternalistic pattern was reinforced by the military regimes through local bodies' ordinances (Basic Democracies Ordinance 1959, Local Government Ordinance 1979, and Local Government Ordinance 2001). The Eighteenth Amendment recognizes local government as a third tier of the federal structure and therefore offers political parties an opportunity to break the traditional monopoly of bureaucracy by electing public officials at the local level—thus empowering the citizen and enhancing the credentials of party representatives at the local level to legislate and govern.

From 1947 to 1971 the military governed, the bureaucracy ruled, and the political parties and their leadership dithered. During this period the military-bureaucracy nexus gained momentum and consolidated its hold on key policymaking institutions in the country. However, it was the elite service—the Civil Service of Pakistan (CSP)—that dominated the positions of policy and decision making in the country. The collapse of Pakistan in 1971 was followed by the weakening of both the civil and military bureaucratic institutions in the country.[4] After the breakup of Pakistan, political leadership and political parties briefly emerged as powerful actors, asserting their control in shaping public policy and decision making at the highest levels of government. The Pakistan Peoples Party (PPP) under Zulfiqar Ali Bhutto assumed power and sent a clear message to both the military, by purging twenty-nine officers above the rank of brigadier, and the bureaucracy, by dismissing thirteen hundred civil service officers. Therefore, the push for civil service reform occurred under the popular perception and reality that real power was in the hands of the bureaucrats and that this demanded structural and behavioral change. The drivers of the civil service reform effort were motivated by the belief that the people could be empowered only by cutting the bureaucracy to size and by establishing the supremacy of the elected officials over the nonelected officials.[5] Thus, the politics of civil service reform is driven by considerations of subordinating bureaucracy and establishing the supremacy of the political and occasionally calling for change in the attitude of bureaucrats. However, in the process, governance reform, ensuring effective implementation and improving delivery of services has remained marginalized.

Content and Context of Civil Services Reform

For purposes of brevity, conceptual clarity, and historical sequencing, the four reports on bureaucratic reform under analysis here (1973 Civil Service Reforms, Anwar ul Haq Commission Report, Fakhar Imam Report, and Ishrat Hussain Report) are divided into two broad periods: 1972–2001 and 2001–9. During this span of time three salient trends in reform efforts in Pakistan can be identified. First, reform has primarily focused on reforming the federal government (that is, not the provincial governments) and its structures. Second, the 1973 and the 2001–2 Local Government Ordinance reforms (one under a democratic regime and the other under military rule) were radical departures from the existing philosophy and operational rules of governance. Therefore, both had deep impacts on the character, composition, orientation, and outlook of the higher civil services. Third, the 2007 National Commission Government Reform (NCGR) appeared to have a broader mandate to review the process of governance at the federal, provincial, and local levels, but its focus remained on civil services and not issues of governance.

Why did that happen? Has that in any way changed the direction of reform efforts? Did these reform efforts improve governance, delivery of services, or empower people? This last question remains critical and is later examined in conjunction with the current reforms resulting from the implementation of the Eighteenth Amendment.

Assessing and Evaluating Civil Service Reforms

This section reviews and evaluates the findings of four commissions set up by the Government of Pakistan between 1972 and 2009 and their reports. Each report's findings and recommendations must be understood, interpreted, and evaluated in the context of three essential factors: the prevailing sociopolitical environment, the regime type (democratic or military), and the ruler's imperative.

The broad thrust of these reforms has not been reorganization, rejuvenation, and "reinvention" of the entire government machinery; instead, the primary focus has been on reforming one major segment of the federal government—the Higher Civil Services of Pakistan—the assumption being that both in perception and reality power resides there. Political reforms (for example, reform of political parties, representative government, and their linkages with the administrative machinery of the country) have remained peripheral. Therefore, another important component of government reform, defining the role of and relationship between the political and administrative components of government, has been neither considered important nor addressed adequately in these reports.

First Phase: 1973–2001

During this phase three significant reforms were formulated and two were partially implemented. As noted above, the distinguishing feature of this phase is that the reforms' primary attention is on the federal government and on the dispersal of power from the higher civil services. In the rural power structure the political class (landlords/tribal chiefs) was overawed by the role of bureaucracy, which operated through a paternalistic model, and therefore its primary target was curbing the authority of ICS/CSP cadre. Thus, central/federal civil services emerged as key targets of reform and purges. Little attention was paid to streamlining provincial cadres, and departments and to making room for strengthening provincial autonomy, nor did these reform efforts suggest measures for improving delivery of services, empowering citizens, or providing remedies that promote citizen welfare. The primary thrust remained de-concentration of power at the highest echelons.

Democratic Regime: Civil Service Reforms Under Zulfiqar Ali Bhutto

The 1973 reforms were conceived and designed in haste. The sociopolitical environment was rife with discontent. The bureaucracy was discredited because of agitation and protests in the urban centers and the breakup of the Pakistani state in 1971.[6] The PPP and its leadership had assumed power through popular vote. Therefore, the ruler's imperative was to establish a superordinate-subordinate relationship between the elected public officials and the administration.[7] The 1973 reforms struck at the very core of the elitist edifice of Pakistani bureaucracy, the CSP, which had maintained supremacy through constitutional protection, a cadre system, and exclusivity of training. The 1973 reforms disrupted this by including the unification of the grading structure, abolition of classes among civil servants, promotions in horizontal movement, job evaluation, induction of private-sector individuals in specified fields, and a Common Training Program (CTP) for all federal services. Bhutto sought more than simple subordination of the bureaucracy; he ventured at changing the processes and structure through which the civil servants acquired norms of behavior. He conveyed the impression that behavioral change among civil servants could be achieved by changing the patterns of training, saying:

> We are going to give the highest priority to training. Correct training plays a critical role in promoting efficiency, reforming the attitude of officials and inculcating a better sense of public service and probity in them. Training institutions can become a major catalyst of change and reform in the hands of government.

The lofty ideals that Bhutto promised to introduce through training remained rhetoric and could not be developed into training policy as the situation demanded. The Administrative Reforms Policy announcement raised the expectation that reformed curriculum and course programs would be developed urgently. However, little innovation or imagination was used to create an appropriate training institution. In haste, International Hotel on the Mall and parts of the old CSP Academy were turned initially into grounds for all CSS (Central Superior Services) trainees; later the Finance Services Academy was turned into the Academy for Administrative Training (now called the Civil Services Academy). In short, an adequate and desirable infrastructure was not created to inculcate new patterns of behavior and structural changes in the services, and so only transitory arrangements for training were made. Civil service training, instead of gaining the salience and importance that Bhutto said he wanted to give to the new type of training institutions, remained elusive. Training instructions that emerged were ill conceived and weakly organized. Thus, the initial four years of the CTP were chaotic. Despite these limitations, the old pattern of exclusive training for ICS/CSP cadre was broken, and a foundation for a new kind of training institution, in which all CSS would participate, was laid. Faced with this fait accompli, the senior bureaucrats, particularly after the overthrow of Zulifikar Ali Bhutto's government (1977), reluctantly began to accept the reality of an inadequate but new training institution. During the 1980s and beyond, gradually, through trial, experimentation, and halfhearted attempts, the new training institutions acquired a degree of continuity and stability. Thus, the training program that emerged in the post-reform period has been inclusive, striving to integrate and give a sense of direction and coherence to all the CSS. Whether or not training at the Civil Services Academy has brought any significant change in modifying the attitude and behavior of bureaucracy toward citizens or given greater coherence to the CSS needs further research,

Important and innovative initiatives through private-sector induction or lateral entry, given the commensurate lack of transparency and violation of principles of merit and professionalism in the process, became politicized, resented, and resisted by the bureaucracy, and failed to gain legitimacy among stakeholders.[8] While workers lost the constitutionally granted security of service that was previously the rule, the reforms importantly established the supremacy of political leaders over the policy process and somewhat diminished the role of the bureaucracy. However, the negative implications of the reform loom larger: disregard for merit and appointment through political connections; dismissal of civil servants without due legal process; unwarranted political interference in postings and transfers, making the bureaucracy docile and subservient to politicians; and subversion of the personal and institutional integrity of the civil services.

These reforms also alluded to empowering citizens through local government, but they did not develop more than a blueprint for doing this. These reform efforts also show serious gaps not only on how to improve the functioning of federal, provincial, and local governments, but also in suggesting ways to facilitate interdepartmental coordination, reorganization of individual departments, and streamlining distinct needs (for example, human resource management, management performance, capacity building, and improving the delivery of services).

Sociopolitical Environment and Ruler's Imperative: Anwar ul Haq Commission Report (1978–79)

General Zia ul Haq, as the military ruler of the country, was bitterly opposed to the regime of Zulfiqar Ali Bhutto, whom he had deposed, and he was committed to reverse and defuse Bhutto's reformist policies. To reestablish the CSP and restore its confidence, he appointed Anwar ul Haq, a former member of the CSP, to head a new commission on civil service reform.[9] The resultant report is a critique and reassessment of the 1973 reforms. It recognizes that the restructuring done by the Bhutto reforms could not be dismantled, but it also elaborates how, through improvisation, the damaged glory of the CSP could be restored. Under the military regime the ruler's imperative was to mend fences with the higher echelons of bureaucracy. Therefore, the report made a case for restoring constitutional guarantees at the federal level for the higher cadres, allowing selective lateral entry, revitalizing training, respecting merit, and empowering public service commissions to ensure that recruitment is based on merit. It also recommended fixing tenures of chairmen and members of the federal and provincial public service commissions. The important contribution of the report was that it expanded the reform domain to provincial and local government. The guidelines provided in this report continue to resonate well with the higher echelons of bureaucracy, particularly the District Management Group (DMG).

Based on its guiding principles of effective accountability, equality of opportunity, professionalism, security of service, power and authority decentralization, and continuous review and modernization of the government organization, the commission also made several recommendations specifically for the provinces. It made recommendations regarding local and district governments and provincial relations that reassured the higher bureaucracy as well as provincial political leadership. It retained deputy commissioners as the linchpin of the provincial administrative system. Local governments were restricted to the administration of justice (for example, minor criminal and civil cases); provisions of small industries; education below university level; health and veterinary services; administration of local police; modernization of agriculture, forestry and fishery fields, and construction; maintenance of roads and irrigation channels; and management of food rationing, population planning, social welfare, and community development programs. Elected officials (for example, chairmen of the district councils) were reduced to auxiliary roles.

A less noticed but important contribution was that the report gave attention to gender issues at a time when the military regime was least receptive to them. The report recommended correcting the prevailing male-female imbalance by catering to women's training needs, providing female trainers, including women in the selection process, making part-time jobs available to women, and allowing the transfer of spouses in the event of a woman's transfer.

The ensuing report, the *Fakhar Imam (1999) Report of the Commission on Administrative Restructuring on Re-Engineering of the Federal Government Organization*, endeavors to lay out a framework for an administrative restructuring of the federal government and its communication linkages with the provincial governments. This commission was constituted under Prime Minister Nawaz Sharif's Pakistan Muslim League government.

The very composition of this commission clearly indicates that the political leadership and the ruling party took a serious look at governance issues facing the country and aimed to review and reform the structure of the administrative setup in Pakistan. As in earlier endeavors, the primary focus was on the administrative structure of the federal government and not on the provincial government.

The commission's agenda was administrative restructuring, but the "Terms of Reference" were enlarged to include a civil service reforms package. When it comes to the question of federal-provincial relationships, the commission recommends transfer of power to the provincial governments in some specified areas, but at the same time, favors maintenance of the federal government's interference in the provinces. Ironically, it recommends that the prime minister personally oversee the process of restructuring and reengineering civil service reforms and the government. This report suffers from limitations and myopia similar to those in the 1973 reforms, notably of establishing superordinate-subordinate relations with the bureaucracy, a nightmarish enterprise without first consolidating representative institutions and institutionalizing the political party system.

It made salient recommendations that could streamline provincial departments regarding reorganization and transfer of bureaucrats from federal to provincial departments. It recommended that those ministries on the "concurrent list,"[10] where the federal government's role was confined to coordinating and obtaining foreign assistance, might be appropriately provincialized through consultation with the respective provincial government for smooth transfer. The list appropriately included the Ministries of Environment, Forestry, Agriculture, and Livestock; Health; Education; Local Government and Rural Development; Social Welfare Development; Population; Welfare; and Special Education. In 2011, per the Eighteenth Amendment of the Constitution, nearly all of these ministries have been devolved to the provinces. In addition, the Ministries of Culture, Tourism, Sports, Youth, and Women also stand devolved.

Ishrat Hussain Report, National Commission on Government Reform (2007)

The NCGR Report, like the earlier *Report of the Commission on Administrative Restructuring on Re-Engineering of the Federal Government Organization*, focuses extensively on the federal government, though it also provides considerable support and insight on provincial and district government reform.[11] Constituted under the government of Pervez Musharraf, this commission attempted to integrate local, provincial, and federal tiers of the civil services.

The report proposes four tiers of services: All Pakistan Service (Grades 17–22 Occupational Groups, Grades 20–22 National Executive Service), Federal Civil Service (Grades 17–22), Provincial Civil Service (Grades

17–22), and District Civil Service (Grades 1–16). Further, it suggests combining the District Management Group (PMG) and the Police Service of Pakistan and renaming the new entity the Pakistan Administrative Service (PAS). It transforms current and future positions in the federal and the provincial Secretariats Group into the National Executive Service (NES) for Grades 20–22 with recruitment being made directly through the Federal Public Service Commission. The NES would consist of four specialized cadres: finance and economic management; social sector management; regulatory management; and general management. It also groups together the positions of tehsil/town municipal officers (Grade 17), executive and district revenue officers, district planning officers, district finance officers, district coordination officers, and other relevant positions at the level of the provincial and federal government under the PAS and shares them with the DMG. The Provincial Civil Services shall consist of five components: Provincial Management Service (PMS); Provincial Executive Service (PES) and Provincial Technical Services; cadres such as irrigation, communications, education, health, police, and so forth; Provincial Judicial Service (PJS); and subordinate employees (Grades 1–16).

The PMS would fill in the positions at the tehsil (county), district, and provincial government levels, all of which are of a general nature, such as a tehsil municipal officer (TMO), deputy district officer (DDO), executive district officer (EDO), and district officer (DO) in revenue, finance, planning, and community development departments. The PES would be constituted on the lines of the National Executive Service.

At the district level, district cadres (posts 1–16) may be constituted only for the departments in which there is minimal critical strength and a viable progression structure. Teachers and health workers are to be appointed on a contractual basis, and the post of district coordination officer would be redesignated district chief operations officer.

The report addresses the relationship between the federal and provincial governments by outlining a multi-year development plan for the provinces and delineating the responsibilities to be undertaken by the district governments. It formulates an overall provincial policing plan, while asking district police officers to develop district policing plans within this framework. It also establishes the overall procedures for financial management and reporting and personnel management to be adhered to by local administrations. With regard to personnel management, it develops procedures and processes for arbitration and review of employment disputes. Finally, it ensures the establishment and effective functioning of the District Public Safety Commission, Zila Mohtasab (district ombudsman), Musalahati (consultative) committees, monitoring committees, and others under the Local Government Ordinance.

The report also strengthens the institutional infrastructure, expands the scope of in-service training opportunities for the majority of officers working outside the cadre services, and upgrades the quality of training institutions. The Provincial Management Academies would expand their activities for the training of their newly inducted generalist officers under the same guidelines as the federal government. As the majority of the officers of these governments and district governments are in the field of education, health, police, agriculture, engineering, and municipal services, the professional training of these officers was proposed to be made mandatory and linked to their promotion.

All training institutions should be autonomous bodies with their own boards of directors consisting of eminent persons in their fields. The board should enjoy the financial, administrative, and operational powers to manage the training institutions in an effective manner. The report gives two options: first (O-I) is to establish a centralized training division under Services and General Administration that will be responsible for accessing training needs, tracking the training needs of officers, advising the training institutions, and coordinating all public-sector training institutions. The second (O-II) is to establish a decentralized training system in which each department in the provincial government is responsible for training officers under its control.

To strengthen the monitoring and oversight functions of the provincial governments, the Board of Revenue should post limited staff in regional headquarters and assign these staff members the powers to inspect eight to ten district governments each year in order to ensure that the policies, standards, rules, and regulations are being observed. They will invoke the participation of potential beneficiaries and, by reflecting the priorities of the communities, attract their participation in the implementation and monitoring of the projects. Instead of provincial or federal governments, local governments are provided with funds to engineer and execute their own development projects.

The four reports demonstrate a broad consensus on retaining and reinvigorating the three essential elements of regulating the behavior and conduct of bureaucrats through merit-based recruitment by strengthening federal and provincial public service commissions and upgrading the respective recruitment systems by developing job specifications. The reports also advocate the importance of continuing training, but there are few suggestions about how to enhance training academies and needs. Finally, there is little attention paid in the reports to on-the-job training, and it is left to the bureaucracy to develop its own on-the-job training procedures.

Generational Shifts in Bureaucracy

Following the breakup of Pakistan, the democratization of the state affected recruitment, training, and development in the civil services. The years following 1971 were tumultuous, to say the least. In light of the 1973 reforms, the first group of trainees endured a very difficult training period—in fact, during the first five CTPs, there was almost no training because there was serious resistance to the very idea of the CTP. Those who were introducing changes were neither skilled enough nor fully prepared but, more important, they lacked the vision to redirect the character, the orientation, and the value structure of the services from the colonial mode to a focus on the welfare of the people. The transformation from a paternal to a transparent, open, and welfare-centric bureaucracy could not be inculcated in this way. Instead, the CTP training was to downgrade the CSP and treat all as equal. For example, all service positions did not receive equal training with only the CSP, police, and foreign services receiving combined training. Also, members of the CSP were the only ones sent abroad for education—so from their point of view the very concept of common training was degrading.

The first five batches of CTP recruits did not receive adequate training as the modules, facilities, and directing staffs were poorly equipped. Ironically, for the first two batches of CTP recruits, the director continued to be a CSP officer, and for the next few years officers of the Audit and Accounts Services and Education headed the departments. The CSP, suffering from benign neglect, never really owned the new DMG. This neglect did not allow the bonds of service that were previously the hallmark of the CSP to develop. The first generation of CTP *wallas* (graduates) gained maturity and could aspire to positions of joint secretary and beyond in the late 1990s, but such promotions gained momentum only around 2001 and 2002 when the Local Government Ordinance (LGO 2001) was being launched. However, by then former employees of the CSP were on the last leg of their service journey, and by 2007 most would retire. The Local Government Ordinance created a sense of unity among the retiring CSPs and the ascending DMG cadres. The two reluctantly banded together to fight the assault on the powerful office of the deputy commissioner, which the LGO aimed to disrupt and dismantle. Despite this attack, the architects of the LGO could not anticipate that within the provincial government (particularly in the Provincial Secretariat), the DMG *wallas* were emerging as a formidable force. Effective enforcement of the LGO could not happen if they were not neutralized.

Despite the resultant frustration, demoralization, and erosion of power, the LGO also served as a catalyst for the DMGs and ignited a sense of unity, allowing them to venture slowly and methodically to reconnect with the political leadership in the provinces. The year 2004 marked the ascendancy of the DMG *wallas* at both the provincial and federal levels. Five years later, in 2009, the first three batches of the DMG were retiring.

The second generation (1978–88) of CTP *wallas* entered the service in the post-1978 period. This generation, serving during the regime of General Zia ul Haq (1977–88), underwent training during Zia's Islamization program, which occurred during this period. The Civil Services Academy revised its curriculum to include Islamic studies. The conduct of training as well as the overall environment induced changes in attitudes and conduct, and the very notion of public service was expected to conform to Islamic rituals and symbolism. During this period great effort was made to change the image, conduct, and behavior of the Pakistani bureaucracy. A visible manifestation was the new dress code instituted for civil servants; the model civil servant changed from someone who wore Western garb to someone who wore the local *shalwar kameez* (long shirt and baggy pants) and was expected to pray in the office.

This generation of officers gained maturity and attained policymaking positions at the federal level in the last phase of General Musharraf's rule. By 2006, they were ready to replace the CSP. The rise of this generation also coincided with the emergence of a civilian and democratic regime in the country. Currently, this is the generation that is at the helm of leadership at the federal and provincial levels.

The third generation (1988–99) entered the civil service in the post-Zia period. During the decade of 1988–99, the country underwent a phase of political liberalization accompanied, however, by resistance to the ideas of liberalism. Once again, the civil services were compelled to adapt to a dramatically changed political environment. This generation now serves at the middle tier of government. For this generation, the post-9/11 environment opened up new opportunities for training, particularly at universities in the United States and U.K. The U.S. Educational Foundation of Pakistan and the British Chevening programs, providing scholarship for master's degrees abroad, offer a unique opportunity to the members of higher civil services— particularly for this generation—to compete for and secure scholarships. In the decade since 2002, approximately two hundred civil servants have availed themselves of these opportunities.

Two contradictory trends emerged during this period. First, the LGO 2001 had a demoralizing effect on the DMG; while serving as a morale booster for the police, other services remained largely indifferent to its existence. Second, as the post-9/11 environment gave new salience to governance and security, improving the skills and human resource capacity of the Pakistani bureaucracy became a local and global priority. It also coincided with another important development whereby the federal government conceded that donors could directly approach the provinces for development projects, which included civil service reform and building the capacity of provincial governments.

This generation appears to be the most dynamic, highly qualified, and vigorous in moving toward project management; significant numbers of these officers have also eventually chosen to opt out of government service. Decisions to opt out of government service have produced a crisis of retention. A significant number of officers from this generation have taken extended leave or left government service to join the World Bank, the Asian Development Bank, USAID, DFID, UNDP, and other international organizations. The resultant shortage of well-educated, competent, motivated, and professionally qualified officers at the mid-career level has emerged as a serious challenge for Pakistan's bureaucracy.

The most recent generation of government civil servants (2000–2010) entered the bureaucracy at a time when a "reversal" of Pakistan's transition to democracy (1999) had begun. This generation acquired training under critical political conditions. The 2001 LGO's immediate and most visible impact was that the police emerged as the preferred service of the new entrants, and the DMG was relegated to a secondary preference. This separated merit from the CSP/DMG and demolished the mystique of the district/deputy commissioner. In addition, in the wake of the infamous 9/11 World Trade Center attacks, policing, intelligence gathering, and law and order gained global salience. A combination of local and global circumstances encouraged this generation increasingly to opt for police service. New entrants joining the civil services began to see more promising career prospects in the police service as compared to other services. Therefore, an unanticipated consequence of the LGO 2001 has been the opening up and expansion of the number of police officers and administrators in Pakistan's districts. While the office of deputy commissioner was eliminated, the positions of district coordination officer, district revenue officer, and others created new vacancies for the DMG. Similarly, the division of the police into investigation, administration, and other areas multiplied openings for new entrants in this service. Thus, by default and not necessarily by design, the DMG and police *wallas* have emerged as the primary beneficiaries of the LGO 2001. This is the generation currently working in the field and holding positions in the districts or as deputy secretaries in the Provincial Secretariats. However, the overall impact of recent reforms, generational shifts, and foreign training opportunities has been that retaining qualified and professionally competent bureaucrats in government service has become a serious challenge.

Civil Services Reform, Constitutional Architecture, and the Eighteenth Amendment

While the focus of the various commissions and reports was the federal civil service, each report in a marginal way built connections across federal, provincial, and local governments. The reports also take into consideration the issue of provincial autonomy and building the capacity of provincial civil service, but both issues remained peripheral in analysis and possible improvements. Thus, provincial autonomy and improving governance emerged as critical constitutional and policy concerns under General Musharraf's regime (1999–2008). Under his rule three decisions—first, the LGO 2001; second, the Seventeenth Constitutional Amendment; and third, the Provisional Constitutional Order on Judges and eventual removal of the chief justice of the Supreme Court of Pakistan—widened the gulf between the federation and the provinces. To curb such excesses and restore balance between the federation and federating units, the Eighteenth Amendment has recently emerged as a landmark piece of legislation that could bring a paradigm shift in Pakistan's mode of governance and constitutional architecture.

The Eighteenth Amendment has been promulgated as a legislative tool to facilitate a power-sharing mechanism. On President Asif Ali Zardari's initiative, in April 2009, the National Assembly and the Senate of Pakistan adopted all-party motions. In pursuance of these motions the speaker of the National Assembly established a Parliamentary Committee (with twenty-six members) comprising all political parties represented in the two Houses. The committee elected Senator Mian Raza Rabbani of the Pakistan Peoples Party Parliamentarians as chairperson of the committee; it held seventy-seven meetings over a period of one year and adopted ninety-seven amendments to the Constitution of 1973. The Houses passed the Eighteenth Amendment Bill in June 2010. The major thrust of the Eighteenth Amendment has been evolving power-sharing mechanisms and enhancing provincial autonomy. Arend Lijphart, a leading exponent of federalism, argues that such a mechanism, when formulating a constitutional design for a federal system, "denotes the participation of representatives of all significant communal groups in political decision making, especially at the executive level."[12] Therefore, I assert that the Eighteenth Amendment has implications beyond the domain of provincial legislatures. It is having an impact on the very structure of the federal and provincial civil services.

Before we discuss the nuances of these implications, we must examine the political system and the existing institutional arrangements within it. Over the years, despite serious hiccups, the aspiration to maximize provincial autonomy within the ambit of the federal system continued to persist. The Eighth and Seventeenth Amendments (the first seven amendments also need to be kept in mind) undermined the very spirit and foundations of the 1973 Constitution. The Eighteenth Amendment is an attempt by the democratically elected government to rescue and resurrect the federal spirit and revive the principle of provincial autonomy as embodied in the 1973 Constitution.

To better understand the nuances of the legislative relationship between the federation and the provinces in their present structural form, we need to view it in a general historical context (tracing it back to the Government of India Act, 1935) and then pay particular attention to the effects of the Eighth and Seventeenth Amendments, which necessitated the Eighteenth Amendment. For example, the Eighth Amendment altered Article 48 to give the president power to act at his sole discretion and to ensure that the validity of any action thus performed cannot be questioned on any grounds whatsoever. This should be read with the insertion of Article 58(2)(b), under the aegis of the same amendment, which gave the president discretionary powers to dissolve the National Assembly. This power was removed by the Thirteenth Amendment but reinstated by President Pervez Musharraf through passage of the Seventeenth Amendment. In a restorative attempt, the Eighteenth Amendment again took this power away from the president.

Alterations were made to Article 90 by the Eighth Amendment that vested all executive authority of the federation in the president (powers very similar to those exercised by the governor general under the 1935 Act). The president was to exercise these powers either directly or through subordinate officers. The Eighteenth Amendment has subsequently reversed this. Executive authority of the federation is now exercised by the federal government in the name of the president (the federal government is not limited to the president but extends to the prime minister and the federal ministers).

Discretionary powers were granted to the president under the Eighth Amendment with respect to the appointment of the prime minister under Article 91. Furthermore, the prime minister held office "during the pleasure of the president." The Eighteenth Amendment, though, makes the post of the prime minister electable by the members of the National Assembly—not by the president—thereby ensuring a more democratic process. The Eighth Amendment had brought the appointment of provincial governors (under Article 101) uncannily close to how it was first conceived in the 1935 Act;

the Eighteenth Amendment, in an attempt to devolve some of the powers away from the center, has awarded advisory powers to the prime minister in this regard.

After passage of the Eighth Amendment, a provincial governor had considerable powers with respect to the dissolution of the Provincial Assembly (again similar to the 1935 Act), and under Article 105 the governor could appoint a caretaker government at his discretion. Following the Eighteenth Amendment, the governor is required to act "on and in accordance" with the advice of the provincial cabinet and the chief minister. The power to dissolve the Provincial Assembly by a governor was concretized by the Eighth Amendment and later by the Seventeenth Amendment (Article 112). This discretion has been since curtailed by the Eighteenth Amendment.

Article 270A not only inserted the name of General Zia ul Haq in Pakistan's constitution, but also used the constitution as an engine of retrospective validation for all previous military orders while granting the general the right to exercise this power in the future as well. The Eighteenth Amendment has removed General Zia ul Haq's name from the constitution. The Seventeenth Amendment was drafted along similar lines as the Eighth Amendment and expanded the powers of President Musharraf. For example, it inserted two extra clauses in Article 41, which describes the powers of the president and deems him to be elected if there is a referendum passed in his favor. The Eighteenth Amendment has deleted this undemocratic clause. This is a pertinent and important change because through the Eighth and Seventeenth Amendment the federal bureaucracy was brought under the president, while the Eighteenth Amendment brings it back to the prime minister. The assumption is that elected governments are accountable to the electorate and conscious of citizen welfare; therefore, bureaucracy would not only implement government's policies efficiently but be equally responsive to public needs. However, this assumption does not hold up in Pakistani reality, where military interventions undermine the rule of law and bureaucrats' neutrality and politicians' attempts to subordinate bureaucracy promote politicization—and that breeds misgovernance.

Pakistan's colonial history left undeniable imprints on the constitutional, political, and administrative architecture of the whole system of government. It was manifest through constant interference with the democratic machinery by the military, but more important, through the grammar of the 1956 and 1962 Constitutions. The current constitution, drafted in 1973, has also had a rather tumultuous past. Persistent praetorian interventions robbed the government/constitution of its initially intended parliamentary form and lent it presidential characteristics, especially through the aegis of the Eighth and the Seventeenth Amendments.

A presidential form of government, while being just as democratically inclined as its parliamentary counterparts, does have certain inherent problems that make it less attractive to and, more important, impractical for post-colonial societies like Pakistan. These issues include "frequent executive [and] legislative stalemates," stemming from the fact that all power vests in the center with the office of the president and "the rigidity of presidential terms of office." Conversely, parliamentary forms of government have more potential for power sharing as they have a cabinet which "offers the optimal setting for forming a broad power-sharing executive," and they do not have presidential elections, which introduce "a strong element of zero sum game into democratic politics with rules that tend toward a 'winner-take-all' outcome."[13] An additional advantage of such a structure is that minorities get a proportional share of the "pie" as opposed to being relegated to a voiceless periphery.

Conclusion

This chapter has attempted to contextualize the deterioration in bureaucratic conduct within the broader parameters of colonial history, reformist efforts, the sociopolitical environment, and the imperatives of democratic and military rulers, particularly in the last four decades. Pakistan's bureaucracy has lost its pre-1971 coherence and elitist character; it has become fragmented, dysfunctional, dispirited, and politicized. The Eighteenth Amendment offers an opportunity for redefining the politician-bureaucrat relationship by relying on a rule-based, merit-driven, and professionally trained bureaucracy. This can best be understood and pursued by examining the power-sharing spirit that the amendment invokes between the federation and the provinces. This power-sharing spirit does not evoke an equally supportive response from the federal bureaucracy because it implies curtailing the bureaucracy's power and allowing provinces more say in matters of financial allocation, resource management, and self-governance.

The most conspicuous contribution of the Eighteenth Amendment toward restoration of the originally intended form of government is found in the alterations it makes to Articles 141 through 144, whereby the concurrent list is abolished and the provinces now have autonomy to determine their own internal affairs. Furthermore, under Article 140A, considerable powers have been devolved to the provinces with respect to local governments, which also have an increased level of autonomy now. The provinces have been given ownership of their own resources, paving the way for financial self-sufficiency and augmentation of their provincial autonomy. It is this broad thrust of the Eighteenth Amendment that has created a legal framework paving the way for enhancing provincial autonomy. However, a combination of factors—incompetent federal government, the so-called Establishment (military, bureaucracy, a group of politicians)—is creating hurdles in the implementation of Eighteenth Amendment.

The Eighteenth Amendment is not only responsible for reducing the provinces' dependence on the center but has also been instrumental in creating an environment conducive to power sharing, the other fundamental tenet of federalism. For instance, it has galvanized the Council of Common Interests (CCI) into action (Article 153 to be read with Articles 154 to 156). This measure will have a twofold effect. First, it will reinforce the parity of provinces with respect to matters that the federation still retains (through the Federal Legislative List). Second, it puts all provinces on equal footing—irrespective of their geographical, economic, and other disproportionalities—by ensuring their presence in CCI.

Power sharing is further facilitated by the Eighteenth Amendment through the aegis of the National Finance Commission award process, which has rearranged the annual fiscal structure of the distribution of financial resources among the provinces by the federal government. This has not only assuaged previous grievances lodged against certain provinces for usurping the lion's share of funds to the detriment of others, but it has also increased the sense of ownership of the smaller provinces while promoting a consensus of power sharing.

In addition to these specific examples, the general tenor of the Eighteenth Amendment is to ameliorate the power-retentive effects of the previous amendments and to minimize the feeling of distrust that the provinces have been harboring for one another in the absence of any form of power sharing and autonomy from the center. This is obvious from the fact that the chief ministers of all the provinces have been granted consultative powers with respect to any decision that is made by the center pertaining to their respective provinces. Enhancing provincial autonomy and empowering chief ministers implies power sharing between the federation and federating units, and that also furthers the principle of political supremacy over bureaucracy. However, that does not automatically lead to better accountability of provincial bureaucracy or improvement in delivery of services to the people. This is a major inadequacy of the Eighteenth Amendment and puts onus on provincial leadership to build the capacity of provincial bureaucracies and also monitor their performance on delivery of services.

A distinguishing feature of post-colonial states is that they are often a conglomerate of military and bureaucratic institutions that not only assume a dominant role at the federal level, but also, owing to a powerful historical tradition, can mediate with the political classes. Pakistan is no exception, though its case has been exceptional, in the sense that despite displaying a consistency with post-colonial institutional practices, the military has invariably adopted a more overtly disruptive role in democratic and electoral processes as compared to the bureaucracy. Civil society, on the other hand, has consistently displayed a rather vigorous preference for a "democratic parliamentary system and through popular mass movements demonstrated disapproval of military dictatorships."[14] This situation is not unique to Pakistan; political systems in a large number of post-colonial countries have exhibited strong democratic aspirations yet are saddled with a deficit insofar as the rule of law is concerned due to the fragility of pro-democratic groups and political parties.[15] However, this popular aspiration for democracy, coupled with several acquisitions of power by democratically elected governments, has not been able to achieve the requisite concretization it should have by now, primarily due to the ineptitude of the elected political leadership. Thus, mismanagement, politicized bureaucracy, corruption, and disrespect for the rule of law and merit have deepened the crisis of governance in Pakistan.

Theoretically, the legal and political framework that the Eighteenth Amendment offers in redefining federation-province relations augurs well for building the capacities of provincial bureaucracies and improving delivery of services along with provinces taking ownership over decision making. As noted above, incompetence of politicians and resistance from higher echelons of military and bureaucracy could hamper effective implementation of the Eighteenth Amendment. To counter these moves and to take advantage of what the Eighteenth Amendment offers to provinces, the provincial governments could take several steps: first, streamline and strengthen their provincial public service commissions for recruitment of provincial cadres; second, modernize and upgrade provincial services training academies; third, award postings and transfers based on merit and institute three-year tenures; fourth, link pay with performance and the delivery of services; fifth, for citizen empowerment and effective local government, explore possibilities of district service; sixth, minimize political interference in the workings of provincial bureaucracy to improve governance; and finally, strengthen and streamline provincial legislative committees for adoption of comprehensive, judicious, and pro-public welfare laws. The Eighteenth Amendment is a step in the right direction to develop mechanisms for not only power sharing but also building blocks for democratic governance and developing pro-poor policy choices. However, ensuring its success will depend upon concerted action and partnership among political parties, the bureaucracy, and civil society.

Notes

1. Ayesha Jalal, *Democracy and Authoritarianism in South Asia: A Comparative and Historical Perspective* (Lahore: Sang-e-Meel Publications, 1995), 9–28; and Khalid B. Sayeed, *The Political System of Pakistan* (Boston: Houghton Mifflin, 1967), 12–28.

2. D. A. Low, ed., *The Political Inheritance of Pakistan* (London: Macmillan, 1991). Several articles in this book provide informative analysis of and insight on the history, culture, and colonial modes of governance in the areas that constitute contemporary Pakistan.

3. Robert Laporte, *Power and Privilege: Influence and Decision Making in Pakistan* (Berkeley and Los Angeles: University of California Press, 1975); and Saeed Shafqat, *Political System of Pakistan and Public Policy* (Lahore: Progressive Publishers, 1989), 137–50.

4. Charles Kennedy, *Bureaucracy in Pakistan* (Karachi: Oxford University Press, 1987).

5. Andrew Wilder, "The Politics of Civil Service Reform in Pakistan," *Journal of International Affairs* 63/1 (Fall/Winter 2009): 19–37.

6. Z. A. Bhutto, *Civil Services Reforms* (1973), 1–45.

7. Saeed Shafqat, *Civil-Military Relations in Pakistan: From Zulfikar Ali Bhutto to Benazir Bhutto* (Boulder, CO: Westview Press, 1997), 57–65.

8. Saeed Shafqat, "Pakistani Bureaucracy: Crisis of Governance and Prospects of Reform," *The Pakistan Development Review* 38/4, Part II (Winter 1999): 995–1017.

9. Anwar ul Haq, *Report of the Civil Services Commission (1978–1979)* (1979), 1–287.

10. The 1973 Constitution of Pakistan had two lists—federal and concurrent. The Eighteenth Amendment abolished this.

11. Ishrat Hussain, *Report of the National Commission for Government Reforms*, www.ncgr.gov.pk.

12. Arend Lijphart, "Constitutional Design for Divided Societies," *Journal of Democracy* 15/2 (April 2004): 100.

13. Ibid., 102.

14. Saeed Shafqat, "Democracy in Pakistan: Value Change and Challenges of Institution Building," *The Pakistan Development Review* 37/4 Part II (Winter 1998): 281.

15. Ibid.

Part Three

CHALLENGES
OF HUMAN SECURITY

8

Social Protection

Extending Exclusion or Ending Exclusion?

Saba Gul Khattak

Though many constitutions ascribe to the ideals of a welfare state, the state in the developing world today has few resources to extend adequate social services to an expanding population. This situation is compounded by the challenges of a neo-liberal international economic order that has translated into the lifting of subsidies and increased (largely indirect) taxation. Such measures have exacerbated inequalities as the poor pay disproportionately without receiving meaningful benefits from an impoverished state. Over time, public-sector capacities have weakened and the systematic decline in the state's ability to protect citizens has raised concerns on the left and the right about poverty and vulnerability and the need to address them effectively.

Debates on social protection have received considerable attention in recent years due to the intensification of poverty. While the concept of poverty has been extensively debated, there is general agreement today that it is not only a material condition; it extends to the denial of human capabilities and dignity. Poverty numbers and trends are a deeply political issue as they reflect the state's ability to ensure citizens' well-being. Therefore,

This chapter has benefited significantly from my intense involvement in the writing of the chapter on social protection for the (now abandoned) Tenth Five-Year Plan of the Planning Commission in 2010, from interaction at workshops on social protection with various experts and government representatives for developing a social protection framework for Pakistan, and colleagues at the Planning Commission. I am especially grateful to Salma Omar, Stephen Kidd, Kaiser Bengali, and Najumuddin Najmi for their intellectual input, and to M. S. Kazmi and Abdul Jamil for their support.

how a state institutes measures to extend social protection to the poor and vulnerable groups is critical.

Social protection consists of programs in social assistance and social insurance. The term is often used interchangeably with social security and social safety nets though these are a subset of social protection. The main conceptual difference between social protection, social security, and social safety nets is that the former two are rights-based[1] and the latter is philosophically based in instrumentalist reasoning[2] that accompanied market liberalization. There are also critical differences among the three concepts: social protection pertains to investments in human capital that are both a practical and strategic response for overcoming intergenerational poverty and vulnerability.[3] Social security, promoted by the International Labour Organization (ILO) in the 1970s, aimed to protect formal-sector workers through unemployment insurance, retirement income, disability income, access to health care, education, and other payments to their dependants. As the informal sector dominates the economic structure of developing countries, large segments of workers remain unprotected by social security systems. Social safety nets, promoted by the World Bank in the 1990s, primarily consist of non-contributory, need-based, cash-transfer programs aimed at the poor to enable them "to manage risk." Safety nets also include microcredit, school stipends, and food and nutrition programs. The logic is that instead of generalized subsidies, the poor would be identified and protected through targeted safety nets—the only problem was that too many slipped through the nets. As "band-aid" social safety net–style measures failed to address or even dent poverty in any way, the arguments in favor of social protection policies to ensure a minimum level of decent employment, education, and health as rights coalesced. Globally, the ILO has pushed the concept of a minimum social protection floor that translates into integrated strategies for providing access to essential social services and income security for all.[4]

The Pakistan Context: Dual Trends and Multiple Institutions

This section discusses the calculation of poverty numbers and approaches to combating poverty reflected in Pakistan's Constitution (1973) and subsequent policies. It describes the major institutions and initiatives of different governments and asserts that duplication and limited coverage continue to be key challenges in Pakistan's social protection landscape.

Across the 1990s, poverty increased from 26.1 percent in 1990 to 34.5 percent in 2000–2001. However, poverty dropped more than ten percentage points to 23.9 percent by 2004–5 and thereafter consistently decreased to 23 percent in 2005–6 and 19 percent in 2007 (the latter was retracted by the government amid wide questioning). Change in poverty is correlated with change in per capita GDP growth; though there was growth, yet the pace of change in poverty headcount ratios could not undergo such drastic changes. Many economists[5] and institutions such as the Social Policy Development Center (SPDC) questioned the nature and impact of economic growth on poverty, asserting that much of the growth had taken place in the financial sector and that it had not led to increased employment.[6]

Though no poverty numbers are available after 2006, the Economic Survey of Pakistan[7] 2008–9 acknowledged that the level of poverty according to various exogenous sources ranges "from 22.3 percent of the population in 2005–06 to between 30–35 percent in 2008–09."[8] This translates into approximately 52 million persons (out of a population of approximately 176 million) below the poverty line, if we take the 30 percent conservative estimate.

What has been the Pakistani government's response to poverty? Below I discuss the conceptual, policy, and institutional solutions that have materialized over the last twenty years or so.

There is a two-pronged view of providing welfare services to the vulnerable: the first holds that it can be addressed through private initiatives, such as private philanthropy and charity; the second holds the state responsible for such initiatives through public-financed programs. Both are reflected in the constitution, which ensures social assistance (charity approach) through Article 38 (Sub-sections a–d), which holds the state responsible for the "well-being of people" and the provision of "basic necessities of life" to the indigent and the disadvantaged, and which promotes a rights-based social insurance approach by holding the state responsible for "social security by compulsory social insurance." The rights approach is further supplemented by Pakistan's international commitments and agreements.[9] In addition, pressures upon the state to define and implement its commitments are reflected through the creation of several taskforces and commissions over the last two decades:

- Commission on Social Security 1993
- Task Force on Social Security 1994
- Task Force on Pensions 1996
- Task Force on Labour Welfare Levies 2000
- Social Protection Strategy 2007 (draft) prepared by CRPRID

Most policies to fight poverty came in tandem with the introduction of structural adjustment policies (1988) and the Poverty Reduction Strategy Papers (PRSP I and II) initiated in 2001 and finalized in 2003.[10] Structural adjustment policies decreased state subsidies and employment, on the one hand, and introduced the social action programs (discussed later in the chapter) to mitigate negative impacts upon the poor, on the other hand. The PRSP was intended to increase economic growth and reduce poverty (not eliminate it) through pro-poor policies and programs.[11] The PRSP II (2007–8) made available a greater percentage of funds for poverty alleviation (from 0.6 percent of GDP to almost 1 percent of GDP) in the form of safety nets (poverty reduction is one of the nine pillars of the PRSP program).

Given that poverty numbers and measures to arrest and reverse poverty are both moral and political concerns, different governments create their own flagship institutions for implementation of social protection programs. They reflect the dual approaches (rights and charity) toward addressing poverty and vulnerability. For example, the exclusive rights-based social insurance approach through contributions was in vogue in the 1970s, when most social security institutions, such as the Workers Welfare Fund (1971) and Employees Old Age Benefits Institution (1976), were established. Similarly, the charity/social assistance approach is visible in the creation of the Zakat and Ushr departments in 1980 by the Zia ul Haq regime, which argued that *zakat* was ordained by religion and that it was an Islamic state's responsibility to deduct and distribute *zakat* among the deserving.[12] Furthermore, a mix of both charity and rights approaches are reflected in the workings of institutions created subsequently. The Pakistan Bait ul Mal (PBM), created by the Nawaz Sharif government in 1993, had an overlapping mandate with *zakat* (funding for life-threatening illnesses, orphanages, funds for wheelchairs for disabled persons, food support program), while other initiatives such as school stipends for child laborers were inspired by the human development approach. In 1994, the Ministry of Social Welfare was formed; its primary mandate was to alleviate poverty and promote social progress. It focused on children, people with disability, and special education. By 1999 the Pakistan Poverty Alleviation Fund (PPAF) was created to address poverty through microfinance (discussed later in the section). Finally, the formation of the Benazir Income Support Program (BISP) and its significantly high allocations indicate the current government's priorities: targeted income support exclusively for women in the household alongside food support programs that were previously administered by the PBM.

How have different programs of social security and social assistance served the poor of Pakistan? (See the following text box for summarized version.) In terms of direct cash transfers from Zakat[13] and Bait ul Mal,[14] the two largest government programs before BISP was introduced, approximately three-four million people of the estimated fifty-two million below the poverty line had received some form of assistance in 2009–10. Specifically, Zakat assisted

Social Insurance Programs in Pakistan (Contributory)

Workers Welfare Fund (1971): Finances housing projects and welfare measures such as education scholarships, training, "re-skilling," apprenticeship, marriage grants, and death grants. It had approximately 18,000 beneficiaries in 2009–10 and 22,127 beneficiaries in 2010–11.

Employees Old-Age Benefits Institution (1976): Includes old-age pension, invalidity pension, survivors' pension, and old-age grants. It spent Rs. 93 million on 409,254 beneficiaries in 2010–11.

Social Assistance Programs in Pakistan (Non-Contributory)

Zakat (1980): Collected by the federal government through banks; provides assistance to the needy, indigent, poor, orphans, widows, and handicapped. Schemes include Guzara allowance, educational stipends, health care, social welfare, Eid grants and marriage grants. There were 1.1 million beneficiaries in 2010–11.

Pakistan Bait ul Mal (PBM 1992): Placed with the Ministry of Social Welfare (formed in 1994), which developed the first National Social Welfare Policy that focused on vulnerable groups. PBM undertakes a variety of individual assistance programs by providing grants to individuals for a variety of purposes such as providing child support for schooling, dowries, and health expenses; it runs orphanages and centers for rehabilitation of child labor, and provides food and non-food items to internally displaced persons. There were 2.1 million beneficiaries of its interventions in 2009–10.

Benazir Income Support Program (2008–9): Provides cash transfers of Rs. 1,000 per month to a woman of a qualifying household that has less than Rs. 6,000 per month income. It launched programs for setting small businesses *(Waseela e Haq)*, *Waseela e Rozgar* (skill development) and *Waseela e Sehat* for health insurance of Rs. 100,000 to families. Beneficiaries: 3.4 million families

1.1 million persons in 2010–11, while PBM assisted 2.1 million persons through its interventions in 2009–10. Moreover, the funds available to these programs indicate a falling trend in terms of people's contributions to *zakat* and shrinking allocations to PBM.[15] BISP currently provides Rs. 1,000 per month to 3.4 million families. Social security programs have provided even more sparse coverage; only 3.9 million workers received assistance from the Workers Welfare Fund, and 409,254 from the Employees Old Age Benefits

Institution in 2010–11. Other programs, such as government-subsidized microfinance schemes financed through government-sponsored microcredit institutions,[16] have benefited a limited number of the poor, largely because microfinance schemes benefit those who are already above the poverty line. For example, the PPAF, designed to promote economic activity among the poor living in the less developed areas, failed to fulfill its mandate because it primarily provided funds for microfinance to NGOs[17] in the better-off districts—a policy that does not help the poor directly because they cannot take advantage of microfinance schemes.

Clearly, Pakistan's safety net and social security programs reach out to only a fraction of those who, by the definitions of the programs, should be entitled to benefits. Also, the beneficiary numbers probably overrepresent them, as many are one-time recipients of, for example, cooked food or a marriage grant. In addition, the nature of assistance is such that it can only partially tackle the deep-rooted poverty people face. Pakistan's diverse institutions and programs reflect a hotchpotch of conceptual approaches without sustainability, while a large number of Pakistanis continue to live in poverty and the vulnerable fall into poverty.

Challenges: A Social Protection Policy and Implementation

This section looks at the political and institutional challenges of developing a social protection policy as well as lack of an enabling policy environment. It looks at provincial and institutional turf issues as well as lack of a research-based approach to policymaking.

Despite long years of consistent preoccupation with anti-poverty measures, there is no stated policy on social protection in Pakistan. The Draft Social Protection Strategy (2007) was developed in the light of the PRSP under the Center for Poverty Reduction and Income Distribution (CPRID) housed at the Planning Commission during the Musharraf era (1999–2007), but the new government declined to own the policy, arguing that the new challenges of international economic recession and low economic growth required a new approach. Although the Planning Commission attempted to lead the process of developing a social protection policy with active input from provincial governments, this process also stalled due to institutional turf battles. In addition, in the Punjab, the Chief Minister's Taskforce on Social Protection also attempted to streamline social protection initiatives but could not succeed and was quietly disbanded in 2011.

Consensus on a social protection policy requires horizontal coordination across federal institutions, vertical coordination with provincial initiatives, and an institutional umbrella under which the government can assimilate diverse social protection programs. This has been proposed for a number of years, but issues of institutional autonomy and control block attempts at coordination while different institutions push different uncoordinated remedies to tackle poverty and vulnerability. There is seldom any rigorous analysis and debate about the underlying assumptions that inform different policy options.

A range of social protection measures and the methodologies for implementation needs to be analyzed rigorously and backed by reliable data. Often, programs are initiated without prior research, whereby the most optimal options are sidetracked. For example, BISP, Pakistan's main social safety program, identifies the poor through a proxy means test (PMT) administered through the poverty scorecard[18] to verify the poorest of the poor in a "scientific" manner for cash transfers. Previously, elected representatives (MNAs and MPAs) identified the poor, but this system of targeting was considered unscientific and politically motivated, hence unacceptable to the World Bank.[19] Any research would have shown that the PMT method of identifying the poor was/is inappropriate for a populous country like Pakistan as it comes with high overheads due to household visits. In addition, inclusion and exclusion errors are significant;[20] it appears there was little difference between the politician-led targeting with no overheads and the "scientific" targeting with high overheads.[21] The government admits that it has no funds to update the data regularly. This implies that those who qualify for the BISP transfers will remain program beneficiaries even if they "graduate" out of poverty; while many who fall into poverty some years from now would be ineligible simply because the survey may not be updated.

The trend that every change of government elicits a new federally driven program has continued. BISP, the most recent (2008) federal initiative, runs side by side with Zakat, PBM, and initiatives of the Ministry of Social Welfare and Special Education (before its devolution), and PPAF. BISP has thus repeated the past pattern: creation of new institutional setups in the presence of old ones. Although social protection was the mandate of the Ministry of Social Welfare, capacity problems in the ministry were typically cited as the reason for placing social protection in the newly created BISP. Instead of relying upon existing mechanisms after reforming them, it is now standard practice in Pakistan to enact new institutions and legislation. It is all too easy for various multilateral and bilateral donors to assert that the existing institutions are either corrupt or inept or both, therefore justifying creation of parallel institutions. This defeats any impetus for good governance or efficiency. The inept institutions continue as white elephants while new ones slowly slide into political illegitimacy and economic oblivion after a change in government.

Ownership issues also play a critical role in the success and sustainability of programs. The federal government's technocratic, centralized, top-down programs have generally lacked ownership at the provincial and grassroots levels. Under the current democratic dispensation of a coalition government, lack of ownership of federal programs, especially in the Punjab, has become more acute. In particular, cash transfers are viewed as politically motivated programs for votes. Both the opposition and coalition partners are wary of such initiatives. They thus put in place their own parallel programs.[22] Over time, numerous small initiatives have accumulated that slowly bleed limited funds. For example, in 2009 the Chief Minister's Taskforce on Social Protection identified seventy-two small and large special initiatives in the Punjab alone.[23]

In the Pakistan context, economic policy failure to extend economic growth benefits to the poor and vulnerable underscore the need for comprehensive social protection through increased investments in human development. Many economists believe that investments in the productive rather than social sector result in economic growth while others believe that increased investment in social protection, especially during times of low economic growth, spurs and sustains economic growth. In the Pakistan context, such debates have barely informed economic and social policy.[24] Social protection is generally understood to be synonymous with social safety nets, and as such, its connection with sustaining high economic growth rates is barely examined in public forums.

The Eighteenth Constitutional Amendment,[25] introduced in April 2010, has resulted in additional challenges for social protection policy enunciation. Fifteen ministries, including the major social-sector ministries, such as education, health, population, social welfare, labor, women, culture, and youth, were devolved to the provinces. Theoretically, the devolved subjects are now the exclusive domain of provincial governments, yet the federal government's role continues. After provincial governments refused to take on accumulated liabilities of the population program and health projects, the Council of Common Interests decided that the federal government shall continue to fund these programs at 2010–11 levels.[26] Given that all projects were cut by 50 percent due to the diversion of funds to flood-affected areas, health and population budgets were frozen at highly reduced levels. In addition, fewer resources are available from the federal government after the National Finance Commission (NFC) Award (2010), meaning that it will be difficult for it to honor social-sector commitments.[27] Thus, Pakistan faces a difficult situation: it cannot curb population growth rates or provide health services on the basis of highly inadequate protected health and population program budgets.

Preexisting poverty, unreliable research and data, limited institutional capacity and growth, an uncertain political landscape coupled with low economic growth rates resulting in resource constraints make funding social protection programs a significant challenge. The fact that World Bank loans and Pakistani taxpayers' contributions directly fund social protection programs makes their continuity dependent upon loan renewals. Whether they will be prioritized for loans in the future is not only a political decision but also one of sound design and implementation of the programs that are accessible as a right by any citizen, and that can demonstrate maximum returns in terms of human security and development. Simple cash transfer programs will not motivate taxpayers to contribute toward social protection as they do not see themselves benefiting from these programs. This is all the more reason to ensure that the design of the social protection programs attracts taxpayers through the principle of universalism.

Social Sector Trends: The Case for Social Policy

"It is also important to recognize that the impact of economic growth on living standards is crucially dependent on the nature of the growth process (for instance, its sectoral composition and employment intensity) as well as of the public policies—particularly relating to basic education and healthcare—that are used to enable common people to share in the process of growth."[28]

Taking its cue from the quotation above, this section compares Pakistan's investments in education, health, and population welfare (social sector) with social protection allocations. It argues that it is important to invest in education and health because the state needs to give people their rights and because such investments shall yield relatively higher returns than investments in "band-aid" social safety nets that are paraded as social protection.

In the 1990s, improving people's access to health, education, population welfare, and water and sanitation were prioritized under the auspices of the structural adjustment policies that introduced the Social Action Programs (SAP-I in 1993–95 and SAP-II in 1996–2000). SAP-I was to raise Pakistan's social indicators so as to protect the poor from the negative effects of economic liberalization. However, SAP-I failed to improve Pakistan's Human Development Index ranking or effectively overcome the structural barriers to vulnerability.[29] Subsequently, the MDG (2000–2015) commitments included setting up institutional reporting and funding mechanisms to achieve social progress. Furthermore, the Fiscal Responsibility and Debt

Limitation Act of 2005 required that expenditures on social- and poverty-related spending would not be less than 4.5 percent of GDP in any given year.[30] Despite these measures the pace of improvements has been frustratingly slow as Pakistan has slipped to 145 on the Human Development Index (out of 187 countries) and is below the regional average.[31] According to the *Pakistan Millennium Development Goals Report 2010,* literacy rates have risen from 35 percent in 1990–91 to only 54 percent in 2009–10, and enrollment ratios rose from 46 percent in 1990 to 57 percent in 2009–10. The infant mortality rate remained 85 per 1,000 throughout the 1990s, and decreased to 72 per 1,000 in 2009–10 while immunized children aged up to twenty-three months were 75 percent of the population in 1990–91, compared to 78 percent in 2008–9. The fertility rate came down from 5.4 to 3.7 percent over almost two decades between 1990 and 2009, and the population growth rate has stayed between 2 and 2.6 percent adding approximately 3.5 million people a year.[32] Though multiple reasons explain the disappointing performance, urgent improvements in education, health, and population welfare interventions are a must for providing fundamental rights to citizens and thereby benefiting from the demographic dividend.

The Eighteenth Constitutional Amendment has declared education a universal right through Article 25a, which states that "the state shall provide free and compulsory education to all children of the age of five to sixteen years in such a manner as may be determined by law." The implementation of this right requires expanded budgets, improved access, and quality. Pakistan's education budget indicates a downward trend recently, shown in Table 8–1.

Education as a percentage of GDP has dropped from 2.4 percent between 2005 and 2007 to 1.8 percent between 2010 and 2011. It is clear that the current trends cannot ensure the implementation of education as a universal right to Pakistani children. What is striking about Table 8–1 is the fast-paced increase in the recurring budget compared to the development budget. We shall return to this later in the chapter.

In the area of health, Pakistan's budgets indicate a worse trend compared to education trends. Over the last decade, health expenditures account for approximately 0.5 percent of GDP (see Table 8–2).

Overall, the recurring budget accounts for a significant portion of the total expenditures, and it has expanded at a faster pace than the development budget, especially in education. This is largely attributable to the doubling of salaries and increments to match inflation. However, increases in recurring budgets are not complemented by performance improvements in education completion rates or health coverage. The issue of deep reform for quality services continues to plague Pakistan.

Table 8–1. Public-Sector Expenditure on Education (Rs. in billions)

Year	Development	Recurring	Total	Increase	% of GDP
2000–2001	08	68	76	–	1.6
2001–2	09	70	79	4%	1.9
2002–3	10	80	90	14%	1.7
2003–4	30	94	124	39%	2.20
2004–5	33	106	139	12%	2.12
2005–6	42	129	171	23%	2.40
2006–7	56	160	216	26%	2.42
2007–8	63	180	243	13%	2.49
2008–9	75	200	275	13%	2.10
2009–10	76	236	312	13%	2.05
2010–11	65	310	375	20%	1.8
2011–12	91	273*	364	–3%	–

*estimate

Source: *Government of Pakistan,* Economic Survey of Pakistan 2010–11 *(Islamabad: Ministry of Finance, 2010), Statistical Appendix, 6–7.*

Table 8–2. Public-Sector Expenditure on Health (Provincial and Federal) (Rs. in billions)

Fiscal Year	Development Expenditure	Recurring Expenditure	Total Expenditure	Percentage Change	Percentage of GDP
2000–2001	5.94	18.34	24.28	9.9	0.72
2001–2	6.69	18.72	25.41	4.7	0.59
2002–3	6.61	22.21	28.81	13.4	0.58
2003–4	8.50	24.31	32.81	13.8	0.57
2005–6	11.0	27.0	38.0	15.8	0.57
2006–7	16.0	24.0	40.0	5.3	0.51
2007–8	20.0	30.0	50.0	25	0.57
2008–9	27.0	32.67	60.0	20	0.57
2009–10	33.0	41.10	74.0	23	0.56
2010–11	38.0	41.0	79.0	7	0.54
2011–12	19.0	23.0	42.0	(–)47	0.23

Source: *Government of Pakistan,* Economic Survey of Pakistan 2010–11 *(Islamabad: Ministry of Finance, 2010), 142.*

Development funding in the social sector is often not about quality improvements. Many ministries integrated project staff salaries into the development budget instead of the recurring budget. For example, the government's Population Planning Program and the federal flagship People's Primary Health (Lady Health Workers—LHWs) Project suffered when the federal PSDP was reduced in 2010 because the PSDP could only partially cover salaries of the lady health workers.[33] Any development budget cuts mean that project implementation suffers, as staff salaries are protected. This implies that staff members cannot utilize their time effectively due to limited supply of, for example, vaccines or contraceptives. Overall, much of the government's social-sector investment is wasted when project implementation is delayed or partial; it also continues to be significantly below the minimum percentage of GDP required for the social sector.

Consistently insufficient social-sector allocations and releases and high rates of approval of new projects have prevented social-sector programs from operating smoothly[34] as they lead to time and cost overruns. An overall throw-forward of Rs. 3.1 trillion accumulated by 2011–12.[35] In addition, cuts in the federal PSDP for diverting funds to mitigate for natural disasters or security concerns have reduced social-sector allocations, thereby affecting service delivery.

Given that social safety nets are a major pillar of the PRSP, the government has invested in safety nets as a priority rather than in social-sector quality improvements per se. This has raised questions about how prudent it is to invest in safety nets instead of the social sector, where most expenditures account for salaries (recurrent budget) rather than investments in quality improvements and expansion to remote rural areas.

Table 8–3 provides a comparative picture of the federal government's social protection budget and its social-sector development budget in terms of three major streams: education, health, and population welfare. It demonstrates some of the lopsided priorities at the federal level, which has been the source of funding for a majority of social protection and social-sector programs until recently. It should be noted also that while economic growth rates slowed, population growth rates continued to be high, putting additional burden upon limited public-sector resources that could only partially fund social services.

We witness parallel trends in the post-2008 scenario that do not necessarily complement one another; the bulk of new investments consist of unconditional cash transfers, ensconced in "band-aid" approaches, to women, while social security and insurance account for a tiny number of eligible persons. State spending for charitable purposes also continues alongside food subsidies

Table 8–3. Federal Budget Social-Sector Development Budget and Social Protection Budget Comparison (in Rs. billions)

	2003–2004	2004–2005	2005–2006	2006–2007	2007–2008	2008–2009	2009–2010	2010–2011
Education[a]	30	33	42	56	63	75	76	65
Health[a]	8.5	11	16	20	27	33	38	19
Population[a]	3	2.5	4	4	4	4	5	4
Social Sector (dev) Total[a]	41.5	46.5	62	80	94	112	119	88
Social Protection Total[b]	15.8	16.9	16	21.7	21	35.8	53.7	119.3

[a] *Falls into social-sector category. Aside from education, health, and population, the social sector includes many other subjects (such as labor, women, culture, sports, youth, and tourism) that are omitted here as their budgets have been miniscule.*
[b] *Social Protection Programs include Zakat, PBM, PPAF, Microfinance, ESSI, EOGI, and BISP (post 2007–8).*

Source: Planning Commission of Pakistan, Pakistan Millennium Development Goals Report 2010 *(Center for Poverty Reduction and Social Policy Development, 2010).*

that do not benefit the poor exclusively—and in some cases benefit the rich more.[36] The conceptual framework, fundamentally welfarist, is problematic because it negates people's rights. There are a small proportion of programs that have a human development component. For example, education stipends for children under the PBM were instituted in fifteen districts of Pakistan; however, the conditional cash transfer amounts were small (Rs. 300 for one child and Rs. 600 for two or more children). Only a small percentage of the poor receive some form of assistance, while a large majority do not even receive the social services that the public sector is mandated to provide through the government's line departments. Overall, the scale is small and the impact insignificant in the overall context of Pakistan's poor.

While the trend of making conditional cash transfers has been initiated, it raises the thorny issue of discrimination against those who do not have access to government facilities due to the distance or absence of such facilities. There are anomalies in social-sector and social-protection policies; that is, shrinking public services do not reach the bulk of the population, especially in rural and remote areas, thereby exacerbating poverty and inequality, while significant amounts given as cash transfers/charity cannot rescue the poor from poverty.

Way Forward

This chapter argues that handouts through targeted social safety nets at the cost of decreasing investments in education, health, and population welfare have not paid off on either front—that of the social sector or of social safety nets. The latter offer too little to a tiny segment of the population, while the former requires deep reform and accountability. Piecemeal solutions amount to throwing money at problems; they cannot address poverty and human development. A comprehensive approach to social policy and social protection is required.

The current arrangements will only exacerbate poverty and exclusion rather than ending them. More specifically, development spending has been consistently slashed not only due to low economic growth rates but also due to diversion of funds for recurring natural calamities and significantly high investments in cash transfer programs. While the challenge of poverty is daunting, so is the inability of the PSDP to provide basic social services: education, health, water, and sanitation. Population growth projections indicate that the challenges shall expand.

A commitment to institutional reform and strengthening is needed for social protection. This entails reform of many institutions that duplicate one another's work so they can function more efficiently. It also means recognizing that the creation of new institutions as an attempt to "fix" the inadequacies of dysfunctional institutions does not constitute a solution. In fact, it exacerbates the problem. Thus, the regular institutions of government should be made to work instead of creating new ones. At the most, this may require an umbrella institution that can bring together different social protection programs and ensure that they are in sync. In a nutshell, the solution lies in governance reform.

Strengthening civil society capacities is also a key area for intervention. Given that the economic adjustment programs in their different permutations (from SAPs to PRSPs) have increased the number of poor and attempted to replace the state systematically with the market, the state alone cannot ensure that social protection be ideally implemented. Active engagement at every step of policy development and implementation by a diverse set of actors in civil society (such as journalists, intellectuals, activists, and independent experts) can complement responsible decision making in terms of available choices and options with the government for formulating and implementing transparent social protection.

Social protection should be systematically laid out as a comprehensive set of programs stemming from rights that the state provides its citizens. At present, in its disfigured form, it is heavily influenced by a welfarist "band-aid" approach, encapsulated by the social safety nets that provide a combination of conditional and unconditional cash transfers. These initiatives have not necessarily been about giving rights to the poor but about mitigating for the negative impacts upon the poor. Politicians support cash transfers (as extensions of the charity approach at state expense) as they attract voters. Shifting from the "band-aid" mindset to a systematic rights-based approach shall also attract voters. The need to provide services to the poor as a right in conjunction with the need to win elections is reflected in the recent legislation (Article 25a of the Constitution) that has made education a fundamental right for Pakistani children. Such an approach can help generate pressure from the grassroots level up; the demand from voters can compel political representatives to ensure the provision of quality schooling in their constituencies, while scarce public funds may enhance transparency in the provision of quality services rather than simple cash transfers.

A comprehensive social protection policy offers a way out: it advocates for increased investments in social services. A number of options can be explored without increased taxation or expensive targeted programs. Current spending can be utilized more effectively through universal schemes that do not involve sizable overheads or massive surveys, as in the case of PMT; eliminating duplication and obsolete programs by undertaking social audits; and setting aside a percentage for a social protection fund from revenues generated through natural and other resources. State policy needs to reach out to the middle class, which constitutes approximately 30 percent of the population. If this class is convinced to pay taxes through an assurance that they would be used expeditiously, and social protection benefits through universal programs would accrue to them also, it may indicate a way out.

Notes

1. Defined as an intrinsic good, which cannot be violated at the altar of expediency.

2. Defined as the set of means employed to achieve certain ends. In this context the ends to be achieved are not freedom from deprivation but the pursuit of economic growth and efficiency. For further elaboration see Amartya Sen, *Development as Freedom* (Oxford: Oxford University Press, 1999).

3. "Social protection includes labor market interventions (labor market regulations, programs and wage setting rules), social insurance programs (such as pensions, unemployment and family benefits, sick pay), social assistance (transfers in cash or kind, subsidies and workfare), and programs to assist especially vulnerable groups (disabled people, orphans and vulnerable children, etc.). The core conjecture is that well-designed and cost-effective Social

Protection is crucial for the achievement of all MDGs" (World Bank, "The Contribution of Social Protection to the Millennium Development Goals" [Washington DC: World Bank, August 2003], 3, available online).

4. The social protection floor initiative, adopted in 2009, is a global social policy approach. For details, see the ilo.org website.

5. The decreasing trends in poverty as claimed by the Musharraf regime (through analysis at the Center for Poverty Reduction and Income Distribution) were widely questioned for their veracity by 2007. For example, within the government, Pervez Tahir, the chief economist at the Planning Commission, resigned in 2006 due to grave differences of opinion over the data used for calculating reduced poverty. Kaiser Bengali highlighted that economic growth in the financial sector did not generate employment and therefore could not translate into the drastic decrease in poverty and vulnerability.

6. For example, see SPDC annual review, "Combating Poverty: Is Growth Sufficient?" (Karachi: SPDC, 2004).

7. "The CPRSPD [Centre for Poverty Reduction Social Policy Development] estimated a sharp decline in the headcount poverty ratio for 2007–8. However, these findings appear to contradict other assessments that were conducted subsequently and that better reflect global and domestic price developments after June 2008" (Government of Pakistan, *Economic Survey 2008–09* [Islamabad: Ministry of Finance, 2009],196).

8. Ibid., 197.

9. UN Convention on the Rights of Persons with Disabilities (CRPD); UN Convention on the Rights of the Child (UNCRC); ILO Convention concerning Equal Remuneration for Men and Women Workers for Work of Equal Value; Universal Declaration of Human Rights; UN Convention on the Elimination of All Forms of Discrimination Against Women (CEDAW); ILO Convention on the Abolition of Forced Labour; UN International Covenant on Economic, Social and Cultural Rights (ICESCR); ILO Convention on Discrimination in Employment and Occupation; ILO Convention on Minimum Wage; ILO Convention on the Worst Forms of Child Labour.

10. The major focus areas of the PRSPs were inclusive and sustained high economic growth; rehabilitation of flood-affected families; support for small and medium enterprises; facilitating expansion of microfinance facilities; people's works program; protecting the poor and vulnerable (social protection programs); enhancing pro-poor budgetary expenditures; skill development; and human resource development.

11. Thirty-five percent of the population was said to be below the poverty line in 2000–2001.

12. *Zakat* was deducted automatically from savings accounts of Muslim Sunnis. It was imposed by the state and could not be disbursed to non-Muslims. For a detailed analysis, see Imran Ashraf Toor and Abu Naasr, "Zakat as a Social Safety Net: Exploring the Impact of Household Welfare in Pakistan," *Pakistan Economic and Social Review* 42/1 and 2 (2004): 87–102.

13. *Zakat* scheme, introduced under the military dictator General Zia ul Haq (1977–88), requires that people pay 2.5 percent of their assets for the well-being of those who are destitute and below the poverty line. The funds were made available through government sponsored *Zakat* committees, and people could receive a subsistence allowance or receive funds for medical care, dowry, or education of children.

14. Bait ul Mal is a government-funded program that is used for various welfare schemes, such as helping orphans, child laborers, and people with disabilities, and for medical expenses of the needy.

15. Allocations to PBM have ranged between Rs. 5 billion in 2006–7 to Rs. 3 billion in 2007–8 and 2009–10, and Rs. 4 billion in 2011–12.

16. There are two million microfinance clients of eight microfinance banks, twelve NGOs, and nine microfinance institutions, according to the Pakistan Microfinance Network (presentation at the PM Secretariat in February 2012).

17. PPAF's mandate is to alleviate poverty through wholesale provision of funds for microcredit. A Planning Commission review entitled *Review of Pakistan Poverty Alleviation Program and National Rural Support Program* (April 2011) found that 62 percent of disbursements were confined to the twenty high economic and high social status districts of Pakistan, proving that loans could be returned only by the slightly better-off people rather than the poor. Furthermore, 63 percent of PPAF funding was disbursed to ten of ninety partner organizations.

18. The poverty scorecard uses a set of indicators with a focus on assets, highly correlated with poverty, to rank the household welfare status. The total score is a proxy of household social welfare.

19. The World Bank provided Pakistan a US$60 million Social Safety Nets Technical Assistance credit in 2009.

20. The World Bank's *Project Appraisal Document for a Social Safety Net Technical Assistance Project*, Report no. 47288–PK (2009), stated: "If the poorest 25 percent of population is set as the target group, the under-coverage rate is 52 percent and the leakage rate is 37 percent. This means 52 percent of the poor (the poorest 25 percent of population) will be excluded while 37 percent of beneficiaries are non-poor (or do not belong to the poorest 25 percent of population)" (87). For details, access the document online. However, Pakistani policymakers were desperate to obtain the loan and therefore overlooked the fine print. When this fact was pointed out, it elicited a negative reaction from both the World Bank and BISP.

21. A number of papers that cover the pros and cons of targeting are relevant: David Coady, Margaret Grosh, and John Hoddinot, *The Targeting of Transfers in Developing Countries: Review of Experience and Lessons* (Washington DC: World Bank, 2003); Amartya Sen, "The Political Economy of Targeting," in *Public Spending and the Poor: Theory and Evidence*, ed. Dominique Van De Walle and Kimberley Nead (London: Johns Hopkins University Press, 1995).

22. The *sasti roti* program (low-cost bread) in the Punjab, the Sindh Benazir Support Program, and the Bacha Khan Program in Khyber Pukhtunkhwa are examples of parallel initiatives at the provincial level that have run alongside the federal BISP and Pakistan Bait ul Mal.

23. This was stated at a stakeholder meeting jointly organized by the Planning Commission and Planning Board of Punjab in March 2010 in Lahore.

24. Some economists, notably Akmal Hussain, have written about inclusive economic growth consistently. See Akmal Hussain, *Battling Extremism: A Policy Framework for Growth through Poverty Reduction*. Working paper (Islamabad: Government of Pakistan Working Group on Poverty Reduction Strategy and Human Resource Development, 2009).

25. This amendment abolished the Concurrent Legislative List, consisting of forty-seven subjects that fell under both the federal and provincial governments' domain; by so doing, provinces acquired complete autonomy over subjects including social-sector policy and implementation.

26. For instance, in July 2010, the Ministries of Health, Education (including higher education) and Population had throw-forwards of Rs. 130 billion, Rs. 89 billion, and Rs. 32 billion, respectively. See Hafiz A. Pasha, Sakib Sherani, Zafar H. Ismail, Rizwan Sheik, Asif Iqbal, and Muhammad Imran, *Analysis/Review of PSDP, Phase-1 Report on Macro-Fiscal*

and Development Framework for the PSDP, unpublished report (Planning Commission of Pakistan, 2010).

27. The seventh NFC Award of 2010 gave greater fiscal autonomy to the provinces, increasing their share vis-à-vis the federal government from 48.75 percent to 56 percent in 2010–11 and to 57.5 percent in 2011–12. In actual terms it meant that Rs. 68 billion was transferred to the provinces from the federal government.

28. Jean Dreze and Amartya Sen, "Putting Growth in Its Place," *OutlookIndia* (November 14, 2011), 2.

29. SAP-I was closed when it showed scant results. The World Bank asserted that the program failed due to corruption in Pakistan, ignoring the fact that the policies that had added to poverty and vulnerability in the first place were not geared to poverty reduction.

30. Government of Pakistan, *Economic Survey of Pakistan 2010–11* (Islamabad: Ministry of Finance, 2010), xvi–xviii.

31. *UNDP Country Report-Pakistan: Human Development Indicators* (Islamabad: UNDP, 2012).

32. Planning Commission of Pakistan, *Pakistan Millennium Development Goals Report 2010* (Islamabad: Center for Poverty Reduction and Social Policy Development, 2010).

33. The total allocation for the project is set at Pak Rs. 8 billion in the PSDP; whereas, salaries alone amount to Rs.10 billion in addition to the costs of procuring medicines and other supplies such as registers, informational material, and paying for transport costs of LHWs, etc.

34. The PSDP shows a declining trend over the last two decades, from over 8.5 percent of the GDP in the early 1990s to only about 3 percent of the GDP currently (Pasha et al., *Analysis/Review of PSDP*, 1).

35. Ibid., 5.

36. For example, the government gives a wheat subsidy to flour mills. The mill owners benefit from the wheat support price because they can sell the subsidized wheat at higher market prices through under-the-counter methods.

9

"No American, No Gun, No BS"

Tourism, Terrorism, and the Eighteenth Amendment

JOHN MOCK

In August 2001, a young rock climber in Yosemite National Park told me his dream was to go to Pakistan for first ascents of big rock walls along the Baltoro Glacier. Pakistan was hot on the international climbing scene. Then came September 2001. Like most other tourists, I skipped Pakistan in 2002. In 2003, when I returned to see for myself what the situation was, Pakistani friends greeted me warmly and told me that tourists were "like someone both holy and noble," a rare and seemingly endangered species. But the "9/11 wars" took their toll on Pakistan. Violence increased, foreign governments issued travel warnings, and the overall environment for tourism deteriorated. By February 2011 the situation had become so tense that a European friend in Pakistan sent me an e-mail stating that whenever he went to a hotel or took a taxi, he had to first say, "No American, No Gun, No BS." The fallout from the Raymond Davis case meant that any foreigner in Pakistan was a subject of suspicion, and Americans were the most suspicious of foreigners.[1] The arc of international tourism in Pakistan has changed dramatically, and it is not easy to be a tourist in Pakistan today.

The war on terrorism in Pakistan and terrorism's war on Pakistan are the obvious factors in the steady erosion of Pakistan's tourism market.[2] But there are also important demographic and structural issues. Analyzing what Pakistan tourism actually is, why it exists, and how it figures in Pakistan's economy helps one understand the dilemmas facing Pakistan tourism as it charts a new direction under the Eighteenth Amendment to the constitution.

Pakistan Tourism—The Official Picture

Pakistan joined the United Nations World Tourism Organization (UNWTO) in 1976; it prepared its first national tourism policy in 1990 and its second in 2010.[3] Pakistan has a National Conservation Strategy that emphasizes the interdependence of tourism and conservation. In 2004, the Government of Pakistan gave tourism its own ministry. NGOs, scholars, and the private sector have identified and highlighted the tourism and ecotourism potential of Pakistan (Kreutzmann 1996; Mock and O'Neil 1996), discussed approaches to sustainability (Mock 1999; Lama and Sattar 2004), and published guidebooks (Mock and O'Neil 2002). There is an Ecotourism Society in Pakistan, and many Pakistan tour operators incorporate ecotourism principles into their offerings. In 2011, Himalayan Holidays (Pvt) Pakistan won the 2011 Responsible Tourism Award for its offerings in Kaghan and Astor.

The *National Tourism Policy 2010* accords well with the UNWTO statement on Millennium Development Goals: "to promote the development of responsible, sustainable and universally accessible tourism." The UNWTO highlights tourism as "a key to development, prosperity and well-being" (UNWTO 2010b). The scope of Pakistan's policy recognizes tourism's role in poverty alleviation, sustainable economic development, and promotion of regional harmony, and emphasizes the need to ensure environmental sustainability and active participation of all sectors. The policy encompasses the Millennium Development Goals of eradicating extreme poverty and hunger, ensuring environmental sustainability, and establishing a global partnership for development. Tourism in Pakistan, according to a December 2010 World Bank study, has the potential to increase employment, raise income, preserve bio-cultural assets, and diversify the economy. The foreword to the *National Tourism Policy 2010* glowingly describes Pakistan as "a land of adventure, nature, culture and history where every tourist has something to get himself entertained, enjoy, explore and experience." But the policy also recognizes that this potential has not been realized, and the World Bank report points to an "increasingly negative perception about Pakistan" as the main brake on any progress in the tourism sector.

The *National Tourism Policy 2010* and the Ministry's *Tourism in Pakistan–2009* cite statistics that show tourists are coming to Pakistan (see Table 9–1). From 2008 to 2009, according to the UNWTO's 2010 edition of *Tourism Highlights*, international arrivals to Pakistan actually increased 3.9 percent to almost 855,000, in contrast to a worldwide decline of 4.2 percent and a South Asia regional decline of 1.5 percent. And, although the

U.S. dollar value of tourism receipts declined a modest 1.2 percent, the Pakistan rupee value increased 15.6 percent.

But if Pakistan's tourism potential is "unrealized," then what is the source of the statistical expansion of tourism to Pakistan?

Table 9–1. Foreign Tourist Arrivals and Receipts for Pakistan, 2000–2009

Year	Arrivals[a] (thousands)	Percent Change over Previous Year	Receipts[b] (US$ millions)	Percent Change over Previous Year
2000	556.7	28.8	84.4	10.5
2001	499.7	−10.2	92.2	9.2
2002	498.7	−0.3	105.4	14.4
2003	500.9	0.6	135.6	28.6
2004	648.0	29.4	185.6	36.9
2005	798.3	23.2	185.3	−0.2
2006	898.4	12.5	260.1	40.4
2007	839.5	−6.6	276.1	6.2
2008	822.8	−2.0	243.5	−11.8
2009	854.9	3.9	240.6	−1.2

[a]FIA, Ministry of Interior   [b]State Bank of Pakistan

Who Are the Tourists?

Understanding who the tourists are is a first step in understanding tourism in Pakistan. However, defining a tourist is as difficult as describing what tourism is. The global tourism industry boasts that it contributes over US$1 trillion, which is about 5 percent annually, to worldwide economic activity. Hence, it is not surprising that the UNWTO offers a very broad definition of *tourism* as "the activities of persons traveling to and staying in places outside their usual environment for not more than one consecutive year for leisure, business and other purposes" and differentiates tourism along a topology of borders as inbound tourism, outbound tourism, and domestic tourism. Such typologies do little to elucidate what it is to be a tourist and to engage in tourist activities, nor do they readily differentiate between tourists and other "travelers" such as refugees or displaced persons (Salazar 2004, 86).

Given Pakistan's report of tourism growth during the recent global economic downturn, it is not surprising to see that the Ministry of Tourism adopted the UNWTO definition of *tourist* and distinguishes just two categories: foreign tourism (that is, inbound tourism) and domestic tourism. The Ministry of Tourism narrows the definition to exclude economic migrants "seeking gainful employment" or "following an occupation," but adds the interesting qualifier for foreign tourists that "all Overseas Pakistanis traveling on foreign passports whose usual place of residence is outside the country . . . fall within this definition." This revealing definition offers a new perspective of what it means to be a tourist in Pakistan. One can be a Pakistani yet still be a tourist in one's native country. The Ministry of Tourism definitions then turn to the economic aspect of Pakistanis as tourists in Pakistan, employing a typology of tourist activity delineated along economic lines into low-revenue tourists and high-revenue tourists—a typology worth quoting: "Tourists visiting friends and relatives (VFR) in Pakistan do not spend much on lodging and boarding and are described as low revenue tourists."

Foreign Tourists

The Ministry of Tourism reports that in 2009, 44.3 percent of all foreign tourists came from Europe, but that "a sizeable percentage were ethnic Pakistanis holding foreign passports visiting for VFR purposes" (Ministry of Tourism 2009, 7) and were classified as low-revenue tourists. Although the report does not explicitly state that the 19 percent of foreign tourists who came from the United States and Canada were also ethnically Pakistani, it is reasonable to assume they were. (Discussion later in this chapter about the destination of foreign tourists in Pakistan further supports this assumption.) These North American tourists would also stay with relatives and friends and not spend much on hotels or meals. An additional 21 percent of foreign tourists came from South Asia. These three areas generated almost 85 percent of Pakistan's foreign tourism in 2009, most of which is classified as low revenue.

Foreign tourists were 71 percent male and 55 percent age 16–40. The Ministry of Tourism reports that "more than three-quarters of foreign tourists visit Pakistan for family visits (56 percent) and business (21.4 percent)." The average foreign tourist in 2009 stayed about twenty-five days and spent US$11 per day. These statistics show that Pakistan's foreign tourists are quite different from foreign tourists elsewhere in the region and in the world. Tourists elsewhere typically seek destinations different from their everyday environment, making tourism "the business of 'difference' par excellence" (Salazar 2004, 85). Pakistan's foreign tourists are not very "foreign." Rather, they are overseas Pakistanis visiting friends and family and conducting business with associates in Pakistan. They tend to match Pakistani society, where mobility is higher for younger males.

Pakistanis Traveling Abroad

Outbound tourism is not part of Pakistan's official tourism typology. It receives only an oblique reference in a discussion of the "travel balance," that is, the earnings from incoming foreign tourism minus the "foreign exchange consumed by Pakistani nationals on religious travel for Umrah and Hajj" (Ministry of Tourism 2009, 19). In 2009 this was a negative balance of US$776.37 million. This religious travel clearly falls within the admittedly broad UNWTO definition of tourism, but in Pakistan, it is the Ministry of Religious Affairs that is responsible for pilgrimage outside Pakistan. In the rest of the Muslim world, including Saudi Arabia, religious travel is tourism, but not in Pakistan. Although inbound tourism and outbound (religious) tourism are linked economically, administratively, and structurally, they are kept separate in a sort of "sacred-secular" duality. In 2009, according to the Ministry of Religious Affairs and reported on the hajinformation.com website, there were about 160,000 Pakistani Hajj pilgrims[4] at a standard cost of Rs. 200,000 per person and 272,000 Pakistani Umrah pilgrims. These tourists are big business for Pakistan Hajj and Umrah operators. Travel, from whatever motivation, is an important engine for economic opportunity and heritage preservation.

Domestic Tourism

Pakistan's definition of *domestic tourism* is also quite broad, encompassing anyone away from home for more than one day but less than six months, excluding those traveling to earn money at their destination. This typology does not distinguish tourists from other internal migrants, such as persons displaced by natural disaster or security operations, or health and education migrants. Data on internal migration is patchy, outdated, and lacks analysis linking it to livelihood strategies, according to a report prepared by the Centre for Public Policy and Governance (CPPG 2011). Domestic tourism statistics for Pakistan interestingly appear to parallel the increased mobility of young Pakistanis noted by the CPPG report. In 2009, the Ministry of Tourism estimated 46 million domestic tourists, 54 times the number of foreign tourists, approximately equivalent to 25 percent of the population of Pakistan. They were predominantly male (72 percent) and between 16 and 40 years of age (55 percent). Twenty-one percent were students. The Ministry of Tourism does not offer any estimate of the economic activity generated by this internal movement. However, it records that 52 percent travel for "social calls," 76 percent travel by road, and 75 percent stay with friends or family. Only 16 percent stay in hotels or guest houses (Ministry of Tourism 2009, 20–21).

These tourists also fall into the category of low-revenue tourists. Their numbers are enormous: about half of the men in Pakistan and most of the men under forty. The effect is significant, even if no figures capture the actual economic impact. Yet are they actually tourists? The statistics seem to speak more to Pakistan internal migration, especially young male mobility, rather than describing recreational tourists traveling for leisure to attractive destinations or cultural centers. Analyzing this massive internal movement as tourism is likely not the best approach to understanding its motivations and its effects on socioeconomic, cultural, and political transformation in Pakistan. Yet the sheer scale of this mobility does show that Pakistanis are able and willing to move freely within the country. Deriving benefit from their movement through tourism requires mitigating security concerns along roads and at destinations, improving access, and strengthening infrastructure. Such steps would help not just tourism, but most other economic spheres in Pakistan.

Regional Tourism Comparisons

In the Asia Pacific Region, Pakistan received 0.5 percent of the total tourist arrivals and 0.2 percent of the total tourism receipts in 2009 (UNWTO 2010b). As a percentage of GDP, Pakistan tourism ranks among the lowest in the region, ranging between 0.7 percent and 0.5 percent of GDP (UNESCAP, §25) and at just 0.3 percent in 2009 (Ministry of Tourism). Although Pakistan's GDP has shown continual growth,[5] as has the GDP of other countries in the region, tourism receipts as a percentage of GDP have stagnated, which is in contrast to the rest of the region. Tourism in Pakistan is not the major industry it is in other countries, no matter how broadly and inclusively the government defines tourism. In 2009 it ranked number 19 among Pakistan's top twenty industries, just above carpets and rugs. Tables 9–2 and 9–3 offer regional comparisons.

Table 9–2. International Tourism Receipts (in US$ millions)

Area/Country	1998	1999	2000	2001	2002	2003	2004	2005	2006	2007
Bhutan	$8	$9	$10	$9	$8	$8	$13	$19	$24	$30
India	$2,949	$3,010	$3,718	$3,342	$3,300	$4,560	$6,307	$7,652	$8,927	$10,729
Indonesia	$4,255	$4,352	$4,975	$5,277	$5,797	$4,461	$5,226	$5,094	$4,890	$5,833
Malaysia	$3,237	$4,403	$5,873	$7,627	$8,084	$6,799	$9,183	$10,389	$12,355	$16,798
Maldives	$303	$314	$321	$327	$337	$402	$471	$287	$512	$586
Nepal	$248	$229	$219	$191	$134	$232	$260	$160	$157	$234
Pakistan	$556	$492	$551	$533	$562	$620	$765	$828	$919	$900
Sri Lanka	$369	$414	$388	$347	$594	$709	$808	$729	$733	$750
South / Southwest Asia	$12,318	$10,280	$13,570	$15,986	$18,502	$21,059	$25,893	$30,838	$31,632	$35,788
Southeast Asia	$23,457	$28,016	$30,469	$31,134	$32,987	$29,442	$37,852	$39,481	$49,803	$62,408

Source: UNESCAP (2010)

Table 9–3. International Tourism Receipts as Percentage of GDP

Area/Country	1998	1999	2000	2001	2002	2003	2004	2005	2006	2007
Bhutan	2.2%	2.2%	2.2%	1.9%	1.5%	1.3%	1.8%	2.3%	2.7%	2.4%
India	0.7%	0.7%	0.8%	0.7%	0.7%	0.8%	0.9%	0.9%	1.0%	0.9%
Indonesia	4.1%	2.8%	3.0%	3.3%	3.0%	1.9%	2.0%	1.8%	1.3%	1.3%
Malaysia	4.3%	5.4%	6.3%	8.2%	8.0%	6.2%	7.4%	7.5%	7.9%	9.0%
Maldives	56.1%	53.3%	51.4%	52.3%	52.6%	58.1%	60.7%	38.3%	55.9%	55.5%
Nepal	4.7%	3.9%	3.5%	3.1%	2.1%	3.3%	3.2%	1.7%	1.6%	1.9%
Pakistan	0.7%	0.6%	0.7%	0.7%	0.7%	0.6%	0.7%	0.6%	0.6%	0.5%
Sri Lanka	2.3%	2.6%	2.3%	2.2%	3.5%	3.8%	3.9%	3.0%	2.6%	2.3%
South / Southwest Asia	1.3%	1.1%	1.4%	1.7%	1.8%	1.7%	1.8%	1.8%	1.6%	1.5%
Southeast Asia	4.9%	5.0%	5.1%	5.4%	5.1%	4.1%	4.7%	4.4%	4.6%	4.8%

Source: UNESCAP (2010)

Pakistan Tourism Revisited

Drilling down into the statistics presented in the *National Tourism Policy 2010*, a more nuanced picture of Pakistan tourism emerges. Pakistani men, mostly under age forty, come to Pakistan or travel within Pakistan mostly to visit family and friends but also to conduct some business. They stay in homes in urban areas and do not spend much per day, usually going out to eat or doing some shopping. This is Pakistan's tourism market. It is a fairly steady market, because the exigencies of family and relationships within Pakistani society will always induce people to visit on important occasions whenever possible.

Pakistan tourism overall is motivated by familial, societal, and religious factors and carried out by Pakistani nationals or overseas Pakistanis, who are mostly younger males. It has a substantial financial component, and because it is motivated by a sense of duty and obligation, it is less susceptible to disruption from concerns about safety or security. This tourism, inbound, outbound, and domestic, is the core of Pakistan tourism.

This core is quantifiable and consistent, motivated by identifiable and measurable factors, and performed by a readily recognizable segment of the nation. The who, why, where, and how are discernible, but what is not evident is how tourism is being harnessed to benefit the nation in line with Millennium Development Goals.

Instead, we see tourism organized along insular lines of family, community, identity, and religion.[6] It occurs because society and religion require it. It is less affected by global politics and has little direct relevancy to Millennium Development Goals and to models of tourism that link conservation and development.

Pakistan employs a broad generic definition of tourism but has modified it to include overseas Pakistanis. This allows Pakistan to claim to be an active participant in the global tourism industry, while at the same time claiming that Pakistan's tourism potential is unrealized. Pakistan's spectacular mountain landscape and rich cultural heritage, viewed from the perspective of the global tourism industry, offer broad-based income-earning opportunities that could increase employment, diversify the economy, and preserve bio-cultural heritage. Yet the steps needed to realize this are not taken. Regulatory barriers hinder tourist entry and movement, inadequate infrastructure prevents reliable travel to tourist destinations, and the overall security perception is not attractive to tourists. Instead, Pakistan encourages overseas Pakistanis to visit as tourists. Pakistan, through its lack of action in promoting recreational leisure tourism by Western middle-class travelers who seek "difference," is signaling that it does not want that kind of tourist. Western governments, through travel warnings, signal that they do not want their citizens going to Pakistan as tourists.

Tourism and Remittances

In several important ways, the core of Pakistan tourism parallels Pakistan's overseas remittance pattern. As the following statistics show, they actually appear to be linked. This linkage, I suggest, offers an explanation for why Pakistan needs a steady flow of overseas Pakistanis arriving as tourists and is willing to forgo earnings that might come from Western recreational tourists.

Remittances play an important role in Pakistan's economy, contributing 4 percent of GDP annually since 2004 (Ahmed et al. 2011, 179). According to the State Bank of Pakistan, in 2010–11 the main sources of overseas remittances were:

- Saudi Arabia,
- the United Arab Emirates,
- the other Gulf Cooperation Council (GCC) member states (Bahrain, Kuwait, Oman, and Qatar),
- the United States,
- the U.K.,
- other European Union countries, and
- Canada.

Pakistanis working in the Persian Gulf region typically hold Pakistan passports. Pakistanis working in the United States, the U.K., the European Union, and Canada are more likely to hold non-Pakistan passports. As one recent study notes, "Pakistanis settled in western Europe and North America are important sources of remittances to Pakistan" (Ahmed 2011, 179). In 2009, 32 percent of overseas remittances came from Europe and 22 percent came from North America (Migration Policy Institute 2010). The pattern of remittances from Europe and North America matches the pattern of international tourist arrivals from Europe and North America. In 2009, 275,351 international tourists arrived from the U.K., representing 32 percent of all tourist arrivals. In the same year 117,465 arrived from the United States, representing 14 percent of all arrivals. Arrivals from Europe (including the U.K.) represented 44 percent of arrivals, and Canada represented 5 percent of all arrivals (Ministry of Tourism 2009). Overall, 63 percent of international tourists come from Europe and North America. These arrivals are not leisure tourists but rather are people of Pakistan origin visiting friends and relatives. When they cannot visit, they send remit-tances—55 percent of all foreign remittances—to Pakistan. As tourists, neither their numbers nor their economic effects are very significant—less than 0.5 percent GDP, barely enough foreign exchange to support Hajj and Umrah. But as senders of remittances, their effect is substantial, contributing more than 2 percent of GDP.

Another important aspect of remittances is that they "are stable . . . and tend to go up when the economy suffers recession as a result of financial crisis, natural disaster or political conflict" (Ahmed 2011, 176). Pakistan international tourism arrivals also appear relatively stable, despite major natural, financial, and political shocks.

These characteristics of remittances accord well with Pakistan's interna-tional tourism, which, I have argued, is at its core predominantly Pakistanis visiting friends and relatives. They also accord with Pakistan's divergence from regional and global tourism trends.

Pakistan and World Tourism

Pakistan's core tourism pattern is not typical of that throughout the world. The UNWTO reports that worldwide, 51 percent of tourism is for leisure, recreation, or vacation. In Pakistan the percentage of foreign tourists with this motivation is 14.7 percent. Worldwide the percentage visiting friends and relatives is 27 percent, but in Pakistan it is 56 percent. Pakistan tourism is mostly about VFR and social calls. The leisure segment of the international tourism trade is not visiting Pakistan. "Pakistan," notes the Ministry of Tour-ism, "is not a leisure tourist destination and very few tourists come to Pakistan to visit archaeological or historic sites, or for sports, study, or health" (2009). The (unintended?) irony of this statement is matched by a recent World Bank report on tourism which notes that "currently, cultural tourism in Pakistan does not seem to play a role proportionate to its richness" (World Bank, Asian Development Bank, and Government of Pakistan 2010, 56).

The foreword to the Ministry of Tourism's *National Tourism Policy 2010*, however, envisions a Pakistan tourism that could be something else: "Pakistan possesses splendid tourist attractions: lofty mountains, beautiful valleys, ancient civilizations, living oldest and modern cultures, natural tourist attractions, sacred places of worship of almost every religion, places of historical interest, virgin beaches, deserts, fertile plains and a lot more." Pakistan's tourist attractions are indeed splendid and unique and give Paki-stan a competitive advantage for high-revenue leisure tourists. But these attractions are not what motivate Pakistan's core tourism. Pakistan's inherent competitive advantage is not realized.

Cultural tourists visiting archeological and historic sites, adventure tourists visiting mountain regions, and ecotourists visiting Pakistan's wide range of ecological zones are economically desirable high-revenue tourists who provide direct economic input into local economies. As a case in point, the Ministry of Tourism estimates that more than half of the total income earned in the tourism sector is earned in mountain areas of Pakistan, where job opportunities are scarce (Ministry of Tourism 2009, 20). But neither Pakistan's six World Heritage Sites (Moenjodaro, Taxila, the Takht-i Bhai complex, Thatta, the Rohtas fort, and the fort and Shalamar Gardens in Lahore), nor Pakistan's spectacular mountain landscape (with ten of the world's twenty-five highest peaks) are by themselves enough to sustain high-value tourism. International tourism to Pakistan's cultural sites has dwindled despite World Heritage designation, and although Pakistan's mountain area, Gilgit-Baltistan, is relatively peaceful and secure, difficulty of access and the overall security perception have steadily eroded international tourist arrivals so that "only the most determined adventure tourist arrives" (World Bank, Asian Development Bank, and Government of Pakistan 2010, 53).

Regional Aspect of Adventure Tourism

The divergence of adventure tourists from the core of Pakistan tourism is readily observable in the figures for international tourists in Gilgit-Baltistan, the center of adventure tourism in Pakistan. In 2009, just under 8,000 international tourists visited Gilgit-Baltistan, of whom half were from China,[7] with the rest from Japan, the United States, Germany, the U.K., Korea, and Spain (Ministry of Tourism 2009, 50–52). Recall that 275,000 U.K. passport holders and 117,000 U.S. passport holders arrived in Pakistan that year. Those tourists did not visit Gilgit-Baltistan. The figures for Gilgit-Baltistan look more like a typical roster of international climber nationalities.[8]

But these "die-hard" fans of Pakistan are no longer coming. The number of mountain climbers visiting Pakistan declined 35 percent in 2008, 32 percent in 2009, and 34 percent in 2010, equaling the disastrous 2002 season (Ministry of Tourism 2009, xvi). Trekking saw a similar drastic decline. In 2002, to encourage high-revenue mountain tourists, Pakistan cut the fee for mountaineering expeditions in half and raised the height limit for peaks that could be climbed without a permit from 6,000 meters to 6,500 meters. These regulatory easings yielded an increase in mountain tourism. However, since 2008, numbers have declined despite continuation of the fee reduction and height increase. Tables 9–4 and 9–5 show Pakistan's mountaineering and trekking numbers.

Table 9–4. Pakistan Mountaineering

Year	Expedition Arrivals	Total Climbers
1994	50	393
1995	59	384
1996	56	408
1997	57	500
1998	50	320
1999	64	461
2000	59	351
2001	70	482
2002	27	n/a
2003	53	441
2004	58	603
2005	67	475
2006	78	n/a
2007	83	799
2008	78	521
2009	43	335
2010	27	234

Note: n/a = not available.
Source: Ministry of Tourism and Alpine Club of Pakistan (2006)

Table 9–5. Pakistan Trekking

Year	Trekking Parties	Total Trekkers
1994	128	697
1995	129	823
1996	166	912
1997	197	1102
1998	165	950
1999	184	803
2000	168	861
2001	244	1,318
2002	n/a	n/a
2003	n/a	n/a
2004	238	1,604
2005	251	1,443
2006	n/a	n/a
2007	n/a	n/a
2008	173	630
2009	134	470

Note: n/a = not available.
Source: Ministry of Tourism

For mountaineers and trekkers, the Baltoro Glacier, with seven of the world's twenty-five highest peaks, including K2, is an incomparable destination. Over 70 percent of all mountaineers and organized trekkers visiting Pakistan come to the Baltoro Glacier.[9] These are high-revenue tourists who generate employment. Trekking groups typically hire two to three porters per trekker,[10] plus a guide and cooks. Mountaineering expeditions typically hire eleven or more porters per climber, plus a guide and cooks (Mock and O'Neil 1996). These groups stay in hotels, travel on domestic flights, and hire local vehicles, as do international cultural tourists visiting the Hunza valley on the Karakoram Highway. Cultural destinations, such as the Baltit Fort in Hunza and other projects completed by the Aga Khan Trust for Culture, have received numerous international awards and offer attractive destinations for high-value international tourists. But tourists cannot reach these destinations—access is too difficult. Over 40 percent of all PIA flights to Gilgit and Skardu are canceled every year; the Karakoram Highway, once touted as the eighth wonder of the world, is in such bad repair that the journey from Islamabad now takes twenty-four hours in the best of circumstances; and access from China via the Khunjerab Pass is now blocked by the landslide dam and lake at Attabad north of Hunza (World Bank, Asian Development Bank, and Government of Pakistan 2010, 58). Upgrading the Gilgit and Skardu airports to allow instrument landings would address access issues and promote both international and domestic tourism, but so far the Civil Aviation Agency has not implemented this recommendation.

Tourism and Terrorism

Gilgit-Baltistan itself remains a relatively peaceful area, with occasional, mostly low-level sectarian violence. Civilian deaths from terrorism are rare in Gilgit-Baltistan, and even rarer are attacks against foreign tourists.[11] In the rest of Pakistan, however, civilian deaths from terrorism have risen dramatically, with 1,335 in 2007 almost doubling to 2,670 in 2009 (National Counter Terrorism Center 2008, 26; 2010,18). Above all else, the volatile political and security situation in Pakistan is the main obstacle to attracting high-value international tourists.

The Ministry of Tourism's *National Tourism Policy 2010* recognizes security as the top constraint on tourism, an observation echoed by Javed Burki, who notes that "domestic terrorism [has] increased to the point that almost all foreign travel has stopped" (Burki 2010, 1) and by the World Bank, which dryly notes that "actual progress in the tourism sector largely depends on the stability in the country" (World Bank, Asian Development Bank, and Government of Pakistan 2010, 183). Although government statistics seemingly show that foreign tourist arrivals have increased, this is misleading. What has slowed dramatically is high-value leisure and adventure tourism, despite Pakistan's unique mountain attractions and rich cultural heritage.

What Pakistan's tourism statistics show is that overseas Pakistanis returning to visit family and friends form a stable core, resistant to shocks, that contributes a steady 0.3–0.5 percent annually to the GDP. These overseas

Pakistanis also provide a shock-resistant flow of remittances that contributes 4 percent annually to the GDP. This core is, perhaps paradoxically, linked to the United States and the European Union, from which 54 percent of remittances and 63 percent of international tourist arrivals originate.

Pakistan's tourism policy must be understood in light of these statistics; policymakers cannot be unaware of these linkages. Pakistan, despite the optimistic statements in Ministry of Tourism documents, does not have in place an effective program to promote any part of Pakistan as a safe destination for international leisure and adventure tourists. Nor has the government resolved regulatory issues, such as making thirty-day landing permits available on arrival, a policy that is on the books but is not implemented. Pakistan does, however, have a full-fledged Ministry of Overseas Pakistanis and an Overseas Pakistanis Foundation to support overseas Pakistanis and maintain separate counters for their special handling at arrival and departure lounges at international airports.[12] The importance of overseas Pakistanis is highlighted by a statement of the Secretary of the Election Commission of Pakistan, reported in the October 17, 2011, *Express Tribune*, that they be allowed to vote in Pakistan's elections. And, apparently, Overseas Pakistanis also serve the useful role of allowing Pakistan to claim that tourists are coming.

Tourism and the Eighteenth Amendment

Given Pakistan's consistent inability to promote tourism at a national level, it would seem that the devolution of tourism to the provinces under the Eighteenth Amendment of the constitution would be a positive step.[13] A 2010 study in the *Lahore Journal of Economics* comments that "basic services are better provided by governments that are closer to their intended beneficiaries. The decentralization of the government's authority should help in addressing the problem the country faces as the number of people living in absolute poverty increases" (Burki 2010, 14). Putting the provincial administrations and tourism stakeholders in charge of tourism in their province would seem to do exactly that. But will it?

Under the Eighteenth Amendment to the constitution, the National Finance Commission distributes a major share of government revenue to the provinces. This revenue is to support the devolved ministries, one of which is the Ministry of Tourism. The two key issues for success of devolution of tourism are autonomy and resources. Will provincial administrations have sufficient autonomy to be able to manage, promote, and grow tourism effectively? For Gilgit-Baltistan, this is a crucial issue. More important for this financially impoverished area, will the Gilgit-Baltistan administration have sufficient resources and the capacity to carry out these tasks? For example, Pakistan's international environmental treaty obligations, such as the Convention on Trade in Endangered Species and UNESCO World Heritage, which are directly relevant to tourism, mandate federal coordination. These responsibilities cannot be fulfilled on a provincial level.

So far, the signs are mixed. Resources were already being withdrawn from tourism prior to devolution (*Express Tribune*, June 1, 2011), and tourism officials felt the government had little interest in promoting and developing tourism (*Dawn*, October 10, 2011). As devolution drew near, Senator Pervaiz Rashid, a member of the Senate Standing Committee on Culture and Tourism, commented that tourism "is just not government's priority," and that "stronger, clearer support from the government . . . does not seem [to be] coming" (*Dawn*, February 28, 2011).

Whether the necessary resources will be provided remains to be seen. If they are not, as Burki has noted, "the autonomy promised by the [Eighteenth] Amendment will remain illusory" (Burki 2010, 8). Given the shortage of resources on the national and provincial levels, the impact of the devolution of tourism is not certain. Moreover, as of June 2011, the federal government had reportedly made no allocation to the provinces for tourism funding as required under the Eighteenth Amendment (*Express Tribune*, June 4, 2011).

For Gilgit-Baltistan the situation is even more dire. Gilgit-Baltistan lacks authority to raise revenue of its own and is totally dependent on grants from the federal government to meet all its expenses (World Bank, Asian Development Bank, and Government of Pakistan 2010, iv). Resolving the constitutional status of Gilgit-Baltistan by declaring it a province of Pakistan would resolve this challenge. However, it would also define borders for what is still a disputed territory between Pakistan and India, making this unlikely. The federal government recently denied Gilgit-Baltistan's request for a share of the annual National Financial Commission award on this basis (*Express Tribune*, December 1, 2011). For Gilgit-Baltistan there has been no fiscal devolution.

For Pakistan's international treaty obligations relating to tourism, the Economic Affairs Division (EAD) of the Government of Pakistan recently announced that it will assume responsibility for UNESCO and other treaty obligations (*The Business Recorder*, July 8, 2011). Yet the mechanism for coordination with the provinces is not clear, and the means and level of EAD support of Pakistan's efforts under these treaties remain to be seen.

Can the provincial governments, particularly Gilgit-Baltistan, mount an effective campaign to promote Pakistan as a safe and positive destination for international tourism? Structurally, it seems doubtful. The existing government capacity held in the Pakistan Tourism Development Corporation (PTDC) will likely be lost as PTDC employees are not being transferred to the provinces, and PTDC itself is being disbanded (*The News*, June 16, 2011). For Gigit-Baltistan, the lack of resources and local autonomy is especially challenging. The 2011–12 Gilgit-Baltistan Annual Development Plan allocates a mere 0.9 percent of the federally provided budget to tourism (Planning and Development Department 2011). Overall, the decentralization approach is fragmented in concept and seemingly precludes a coordinated effort to promote the country as a whole. Such an effort seems essential in Pakistan, and models could be taken from experiences in Malaysia, Thailand, India, and elsewhere. Such countries have national tourism promotion boards that present a positive county image and highlight destination desirability. International donor support for the tourism sector could boost those regions of Pakistan that remain relatively free of terrorism and provide an investment opportunity that has a reasonable chance of successful return. The steps toward autonomy offer an opportunity, but that opportunity will be lost without a coordinated campaign to capitalize on Pakistan's tourist resources and restore the image of peace and recreation for the mountains of Pakistan. Such a campaign would serve as an antidote to pervasive stereotypes of Pakistan, Afghanistan, and their inhabitants as dangerous and inhospitable.

Notes

1. Raymond Davis, a CIA operative working in Pakistan under diplomatic cover, was arrested in Lahore on January 27, 2011, after shooting and killing two Pakistani men following him on a motorcycle. Davis maintained they were trying to rob him. News reports indicated that the two men may have been Pakistan intelligence agents assigned to follow Davis. The Wikipedia article on the incident, available online, has links to all major media reports.

2. For more on the Pakistan public's attitudes toward militant attacks inside Pakistan, see Fair 2009. For a discussion of the trust deficit and policy divergences between the Pakistan and U.S. governments and their effects on the war on terror, see Siddiqa 2009.

3. The 2010 national tourism policy appeared in draft form but was not officially adopted due to the ratification of the Eighteenth Amendment to the constitution.

4. Saudi Arabia limits Hajj pilgrims from any given country to 1 percent of the Muslim population of that country ("Holy Cities Vital for Saudi Drive to Boost Tourist Numbers," *Gulf News*, May 6, 2011, 29).

5. Highest Pakistan GDP growth was 2005 (7.7 percent) and 2004 (7.4 percent), and lowest growth 2008 (1.6 percent) and 2001 (2.0 percent) (World Bank 2011).

6. The crucial role of kinship in Pakistani society and politics has recently been highlighted by Anatol Lieven (Lieven 2011, 12–19, 211–24).

7. The Chinese visitors include trade delegations, those working in trans-border trade, and possibly some engaged with the expansion of the Karakoram Highway (KKH). Few, if any, are adventure or leisure tourists.

8. Actual figures are 7,728 total international tourists, with 3,755 from China, 722 from Japan, 338 from the United States, 328 from Germany, 324 from U.K., 292 from Korea, and 214 from Spain.

9. In 2012, mountaineers returned to Pakistan in force, with 51 expeditions and 329 climbers, underscoring the unique attraction and comparative advantage of Pakistan's Karakoram peaks (Alpine Club of Pakistan 2012).

10. The Ministry of Tourism sets porter rates. For 2011, porter wages were Rs. 455 per day plus a Rs. 650 allowance for clothing and food. Additional allowances are paid when crossing passes over 4,000 meters.

11. However, in 2012 sectarian violence spiked as Sunni militants dressed in Pakistan army uniforms stopped a bus, checked the passengers' identification cards, and singled out and executed the Shi'ite passengers on the spot. Gilgit-Baltistan residents are now afraid to travel the Karakoram Highway, further impacting their access to employment, education, and health care (Gregory 2012).

12. For more information, see the opf.org.pk website.

13. The Eighteenth Amendment was signed April 19, 2010, by the president of Pakistan. The Ministry of Tourism was transferred to the provinces at the end of March 2011 (*The News*, April 1, 2011).

Reference List

Ahmed, Junaid, et al. "An Empirical Analysis of Remittances-Growth Nexus in Pakistan Using Bands Testing Approach." *Journal of Economics and International Finance* 3/3 (March 2011): 176–86.

Alpine Club of Pakistan. "Report of Mountaineering Expeditions Visiting Pakistan in 2006." Islamabad: August 25, 2006.

———. "List of Expeditions Which Visited Pakistan, Summer 2012." Available on the alpineclub.org.pk website.

Burki, Shahid Javed. "Provincial Rights and Responsibilities." *The Lahore Journal of Economics* (September 15, 2010): 1–14.

Business Recorder. "Worker Remittances Increases by 25pc." July 8, 2011. Available on the brecorder.com website.

CPPG (Centre for Public Policy and Governance). "The State of Migration in Pakistan: Patterns and Challenges of Internal Migration." Lecture given December 14, 2011, at Forman Christian College, Lahore.

Dawn. "Tourism Promotion in GB Not Govt. Priority." February 28, 2011. Available on the dawn.com website.

———. "Boosting Tourism in Pakistan." October 10, 2011. Available on the dawn.com website.

Express Tribune. "Devolution: Over Thirty Projects on Chopping Block." June 1, 2011. Available on the tribune.com.pk website.

———. "Government Increases Development Spending by 9% to Rs. 730b." June 4, 2011. Available on the tribune.com.pk website.

———. "Elections 2013: Overseas Pakistanis May Be Given Voting Rights." October 17, 2011. Available on the tribune.com.pk website.

———. "G-B to Be Declared Tax-Free Zone—Decision Taken after Talks of Taxing the Region Failed." December 1, 2011. Available on the tribune.com.pk website.

Fair, Christine. "Pakistan's Own War on Terror: What the Pakistani Public Thinks." *Journal of International Affairs* 63/1 (2009): 39–55.

Gregory, Michael. "Pakistan's Threat Within: The Sunni-Shia Divide." Reuters, October 24, 2012. Available on the reuters.com website.

Kreutzmann, Hermann. "Tourism in the Hindukush Karakoram: A Case Study on the Valley of Hunza (Northern Areas of Pakistan)." In *Proceedings of the Second International Hindukush Cultural Conference*, edited by E. Bashir and I. ud-din, 427–37. Karachi: Oxford University Press, 1996.

Lama, Wendy Brewer, and Nikhat Sattar. "Mountain Tourism, and the Conservation of Biological and Cultural Diversity." In *Key Issues for Mountain Areas*, edited by M. Price, L. Jansky, and A. Iastenia, 111–48. New York: United Nations University Press, 2004.

Lieven, Anatol. *Pakistan: A Hard Country*. New York: Public Affairs, 2011.

Migration Policy Institute. "Remittances Profile: Pakistan." Washington DC: Migration Policy Institute, 2010. Available on the migrationpolicy.org website.

Ministry of Tourism. *Tourism in Pakistan–2009*. Islamabad: Government of Pakistan, 2009.
————. *National Tourism Policy 2010*. Islamabad: Government of Pakistan, 2010.

Mock, John. "Ecotourism Potential in Pakistan's Northern Areas." Paper presented at the Convention on Sustainable Tourism in Pakistan's Northern Areas. Gilgit Hunza, Northern Areas, Pakistan. June 12–14, 1999.

Mock, John, and Kimberley O'Neil. "Survey on Ecotourism Potential in the Biodiversity Project Area." In *Consultancy Report for IUCN–The World Conservation Union*. Islamabad: IUCN–The World Conservation Union, 1996.
————. *Trekking in the Karakoram and Hindukush*. 2nd edition. Footscray, Australia: Lonely Planet Publications, 2002.

National Counterterrorism Center. *2007 Report on Terrorism*. Washington DC: NCTC, 2008. Available on the nctc.gov website.

National Counterterrorism Center. *2009 Report on Terrorism*. Washington DC: NCTC, 2010. Available on the nctc.gov website.

The News. "Five Federal Ministries Transferred to Provinces." April 1, 2011. Available on the thenews.com.pk website.
————. "Devolution of PTDC: Over 900 Employees to Go Home." June 16, 2011. Available on the thenews.com.pk website.

Planning and Development Department. *Annual Development Plan 2011–12*. Gilgit: Government of Gilgit-Baltistan, June 2011.

Salazar, Noel B. "Developmental Tourists vs. Development Tourism: A Case Study." In *Tourist Behavior: A Psychological Perspective*, edited by Aparna Raj, 85–107. New Delhi: Kanishka, 2004.

Siddiqa, Ayesha. "Jihadism in Pakistan: The Expanding Frontier." *Journal of International Affairs* 63/1 (2009): 57–71.

UNESCAP (United Nations Economic and Social Commission for Asia and the Pacific). "Statistical Yearbook for Asia and the Pacific 2009." Bangkok: UNESCAP, 2010. Available on the unescap.org website.

United States Department of State. *Country Reports on Terrorism for 2007*. Washington DC: U.S. Department of State, 2007. Available on the state.gov website.

United States Department of State. *Country Reports on Terrorism for 2009*. Washington DC: U.S. Department of State, 2009. Available on the state.gov website.

UNWTO (United Nations World Tourism Organization). *Tourism and the Millennium Development Goals*. Madrid: UNWTO, 2010a. Available on the unwto.org website.

————. *UNWTO Tourism Highlights*. Madrid: UNWTO, 2010b. Available on the unwto. org website.

World Bank. "World Bank Open Data for Pakistan." Washington DC: World Bank, 2011. Available on the data.worldbank.org/country/pakistan website.

World Bank, Asian Development Bank, and Government of Pakistan. *Pakistan–Gilgit-Baltistan Economic Report: Broadening the Transformation*. Report no. 55998–PK. December 2, 2010. Available on the documents.worldbank.org/curated/en/home website.

10

The Importance of
Population Policy in Pakistan

ZEBA SATHAR AND PETER C. MILLER

Introduction

Making the connection between the well-being of Pakistan's population and the country's resources and size, General Ayub Khan was the first leader to announce emphatically and publicly in 1965 that Pakistan had a population issue that needed attention. He then assigned an important individual to the helm of the population program. This was a preemptive action, given that Pakistan's first census in 1961 yielded a total population size of only thirty million, and it preceded the rapid spurt in growth that occurred between 1972 and 1981. Civil society was even more advanced in its thinking, recognizing in 1958 that an active family planning program was needed. The Family Planning Association of Pakistan started its own voluntary nongovernmental program at that time and has had a huge impact on the government program, operating by its side for many years. This places Pakistan as one of the earliest countries to have a population policy. However, it also experienced one of the latest fertility declines in Asia, and its fertility levels appear to be settling at much higher levels than most of its neighbors. Fertility transition began just before 1990, about ten years later than in most of South Asia and at least twenty-five years after its clearly enunciated population policy.

Is a specific population policy, in the sense of setting demographic targets from time to time, enough to change families' reproductive behavior and diffuse ideas about family size and investments in children, or are other factors far more important? There has been an absence of a host of policies that support such changes, for example, investment in the social sector, especially in education and most especially in girls' schooling. Even in 2010,

Pakistan ranked 125 on the Human Development Index, despite some modest gains in per capita income that rank it as a middle-level-income country. Even though there have always been demographic targets on paper and in five-year plans, no serious attention beyond a handful of persons has been devoted to studying Pakistan's large population numbers or their distribution and the implications they hold for the country's development, politics, and ultimate stability. Population issues have not had an effective champion group that leads to those issues being given the attention they deserve in order to improve human lives, particularly health, women's status and well-being, and rights. In fact, the demography of Pakistan and population policy have largely been the responsibility of only a particular ministry, the rather minor Ministry of Population Welfare, along with a handful of professionals and organizations, and with virtual government denial of a population problem apart from occasional statements from state leaders on World Population Day or similar occasions.

Pakistan remains at the center of debate regarding population issues, with more attention coming from outside the country—from institutions such as Population Action International, the World Bank, the United Nations Population Division, and even the White House—calling for greater attention to be paid to population policy than from within the country (Hardee and Leahy 2008; Ohno et al. 2010; Lodhi 2010). This is because Pakistan remains an important and large contributor to world population. Its growth rate exceeds most countries in Asia, and it has been steadily rising into the ranks of the world's five largest populations, moving from #8 to #6 to #5 and possibly to #4 in a relatively short time. But international donor attention to the topic has been largely absent, especially in the last few decades.

The question posed in this chapter is whether there is any impact from Pakistan's population policy and programmatic framework on Pakistan's fertility trajectory (apart from earlier declines in mortality in the 1950s and 1960s). Conversely, can we conclude that the fertility transition in Pakistan has been disconnected from any policy framework? The development of population policy is described in the first section of the chapter. In the next section we compare Pakistan's efforts with those of neighboring countries, and in the third section we look at aspects of policy that appear to have been effective and those that remain disconnected with fertility behavior. This chapter then offers some suggestions for future change in Pakistan's looming population-related issues.

Population Policy—What's in It for Development?

We define population policy to include not only demographic goals and provision of contraceptives and family planning services, but also policies that deal with how those goals are to be met, as well as those factors that influence fertility, such as girls' education, employment alternatives for women, reduction in infant mortality, and overall development (Jain 1998). The following section is a synopsis of the course of population policy in Pakistan.

The First Push (1965–76)

The ten years after the first five-year plan (1955–60) saw the introduction of family planning activities through the Family Planning Association of Pakistan and other voluntary organizations. In 1965 the government introduced an independent family planning setup. Visible funds and directions were introduced into the population program through mass information, education, and communication activities, and a service delivery network was also established. In 1970 the government introduced the Continuous Motivation Scheme by employing male-female teams of workers at the union council level. This was considered a more vigorous approach to the distribution of contraceptives. The underlying assumption was that improved "supply" would take care of demand for family planning. In 1975 the Pakistan Fertility Survey showed a flat curve in the contraceptive prevalence rate (CPR), which remained under 5 percent, similar to the levels in 1968. In all likelihood the Continuous Motivation Scheme with its total focus on supply of contraceptives without any visible demand for such services was a misplaced strategy (Robinson et al. 1981). Unmet need for family planning services was negligible, and this early period may have been better used to create a demand for smaller families, for child spacing, and for gathering consensus for this policy. The strategy chosen and its misplaced priorities very much reflected a top-down decision to curb the rapid population growth rate. The infant mortality rate (IMR) declined in this period, but girls' education did not rise greatly.

The Lost Decade (1977–88)

While these problems could have been rectified and a course correction could have been made, the coup in 1977 that brought General Zia ul Haq to power led to a reversal of any possible ground that policy may have achieved. Over the next decade the program was only marginally operational due to reorganization, political unrest, and suspension of information, education, and communication activities. The Zia regime more or less put a moratorium on family planning activities. Right-wing religious parties became increasingly popular, and Zia's own conservative views gave rise to the perception of conflict between family planning and religion.

Furthermore, negative attitudes toward women combined with low investment in the social sector created a huge swamp of factors dragging down any changes in attitudes and behaviors leading to fertility change. The Pakistan Contraceptive Prevalence Survey of 1984 reflected this stagnation, finding that only 9 percent of women were using family planning services. This decade set back Pakistan most visibly, and having to restart a movement for change after this reversal was more difficult than starting anew. Further, any efforts at promoting fertility change were faced with the stigma of religious disapproval. IMR and female literacy continued their gradual improvement.

The Decade of Success (1989–98)

The Zia period was followed by a new beginning. With the election of Benazir Bhutto in 1988, the population program saw strong political support from the highest levels. Major achievements during this time included the devolution to the provinces of field activities, institutionalization of the role of NGOs through the NGO Coordination Council and the establishment of the National Institute of Population Studies. Social marketing was also introduced.

In 1993, the government announced a policy to provide special attention and funding for the social sector through its Social Action Program. This was a policy response, largely donor induced, to correct the course of Pakistan's lagging social indicators. Meanwhile, the International Conference on Population and Development (ICPD) in 1994 created a stir within the population policy arena. At that conference Bhutto stated, "I dream of a Pakistan, of an Asia, of a World, where every pregnancy is planned and every child is nurtured, loved, educated, and supported." This proclamation led to the initiative of the Lady Health Workers program. This was a huge public-sector program mandated to provide family planning and primary health-care outreach to 40,000 (later 100,000) communities in remote rural areas and urban slums. The National Trust for Volunteer Organizations, a successor to the similar NGO Coordination Council, was set up. The ICPD with its "beyond family planning" agenda began to attract two significant groups into the gamut of actors concerned with population policy: the health sector and women's organizations.

These ingredients, which included broadening efforts to incorporate women's issues in population policy, increasing efforts to invest in human development, addressing maternal and child health in rural areas, and diffusing responsibility of policy beyond the Ministry of Population Welfare, augured well for a successful policy environment. Initial results were encouraging. The

1997–98 Pakistan Fertility and Family Planning Survey showed a doubling of the contraceptive prevalence rate from 12 percent in 1991. Changes in reproductive behavior were visible in rural areas with prevalence rising to 19 percent in these areas and to 36.5 percent in urban areas. Fertility decline was on a fast track, with the total fertility rate (TFR) moving from 6.1 births per woman in 1991 to 4.8 in seven years. Feeney and Alam called this quick catch up the "fastest decline in Asia" (Feeney and Alam 2003). This was a period when services, institutional responsiveness to family planning needs, and a democratic government with fair commitment from both major parties came together to produce results for the population sector. Clearly, the demand for family planning had been created, and the improvement of services, especially in the rural areas, led to a surge in contraceptive prevalence. However, there was little change in mortality or female literacy.

Post–ICPD Policy (1999–2007)

Things appeared to be well placed for rapid improvement when the formulation of a new Population Policy was initiated in 1998. The process that led to a formulation of the Population Policy, which was finally passed by the cabinet in 2002, set a long-term vision for the population sector. There was every expectation that this rate of contraceptive uptake would continue, and it was plausibly predicted that Pakistan would reach replacement fertility by 2020. While reducing population growth rates remained the primary concern of the Government of Pakistan and was part of Population Policy 2002, there was greater emphasis on rights and providing accessible and better quality services to meet the needs of individuals. Furthermore, the need to collaborate with other public institutions on the part of the Ministry of Population Welfare and with the private sector and NGOs now appeared in all government documents and plans. The Population Policy appeared to broaden scope and partnerships to achieve its goals. After the restricted statements of earlier plans, Pakistan finally had a policy that followed ICPD principles and that extended beyond family planning.

There were, however, limitations. A policy announced in 2001 to transfer all responsibility for family planning services to the Ministry of Health was successfully resisted by Ministry of Population Welfare with the support of most of the stakeholders who had an interest in population issues. Also, once again, broader development issues, including girls' education and the status of women, were not included in population policy beyond general encouragement that such things should be attended to.

By 2006–7, the Pakistan Demographic and Health Survey and other sources provided some results. There had been significant if not dramatic improvements in health and education indicators, along with other development data. However, for fertility, especially family planning, the news was disappointing. At 4.1 births per woman, the TFR was continuing to decline, but at a reduced pace, and contraceptive prevalence, having reached a peak in 2003 at 32 percent, had leveled off at 30 percent. Unmet need remained high, and desired family size showed little change.

Why was there so little progress? In part, there was a failure of implementation. The issue of how services would be extended to meet the rise in demand and the gap in provision as seen in the high unmet need was not closely followed through in any plan. Very little attention was given to the details of coordination between the two mainline ministries of health and population welfare; or with their respective provincial departments, which are mandated to deliver services; or with the health system and the Lady Health Worker program. The Population Policy emphasized intersectoral coordination, but hardly any was visible within the education, youth, social welfare, or women's development sectors. The Lady Health Worker program (currently employing close to 100,000 women with basic education) was found to be very effective in delivering family planning services in 2001, but in a 2009 third-party evaluation was seen to be faltering in providing these services because of other demands especially polio vaccines (OPM 2009).

Amid the disappointment of lagging contraceptive prevalence and slower fertility decline, there was some surge of interest in population issues with the discovery of the possibility of the demographic dividend coming to Pakistan. The potential for this was laid out in the Vision 2030 document of the Planning Commission, which led to the Pakistan Development Forum 2007 declaring its theme to be "reaping the demographic dividend." While signaling declining dependency ratios as an opportunity to reap economic benefits, demographers clearly pointed out the need to invest in a more rapid fertility decline and in education and employment opportunities, especially for youth (Sathar 2007). Unfortunately, the good news was accepted in most circles without the accompanying provisos, so there was little understanding of what was required to reap the dividend. Nevertheless, the opportunity provided an occasion to focus on population issues more broadly as they related to the economy and across sectors, especially education, youth, and employment, providing some renewed focus to population policy. Political and economic events since 2007 have prevented continuation of this discussion of population as a development issue, which began to stir interest in the Planning Commission and the Ministry of Finance.

The Time of Reckoning (2008)

As policymakers began to consider adjustments to these sobering realities, Pakistan was beset by a series of severe shocks. The effects of the world economic crisis of 2008–9, the disastrous floods of 2010, and the security situation related to resurgent terrorism severely restricted attention and budgets. Meanwhile, in March 2010, the government passed the Eighteenth Amendment to the constitution, giving provinces full responsibility for many issues, including population, health, education, and women's issues, and abolishing the relevant federal ministries outright. The implementation of this measure is currently being worked out, but it clearly will require new approaches, concentrated at the provincial level, to providing social services of all types. National policies for population, health, and education, among other issues, will have greatly reduced salience beyond broad statements of intent.

Present Status of Major Population and Related Indicators

Before going on to more detailed analysis, it is worth summing up what has happened. Since 1965, except for a hiatus between 1977 and 1988, Pakistan has had a clearly stated policy of intent to reduce population growth through voluntary family planning. Initially, that policy was narrowly focused on direct efforts to increase contraceptive prevalence and reduce fertility. Over time, especially after the 1994 ICPD, population policy became more focused on meeting the rights and needs of individuals. Throughout, primary responsibility for both implementation and the adjustment of the policy itself were vested in the Ministry of Population Welfare, which had modest implementation capability and little influence beyond family planning issues. Implementation was largely left in the hands of that ministry and a relatively small group of supporting partners in the NGO and scholarly communities.

Some summary results are shown in Table 10–1. Most indicators have shown a slow but fairly consistent improvement over time, with improvements gaining pace over the last two decades (except for the plateau in CPR in recent years). Fertility is somewhat different; it remained consistently high until around 1990, when it began a rapid decline that has continued, although recently at a somewhat reduced pace, to the present. But even that more impressive trend may have less significance in relation to population policy than it may appear. Casterline (2010) estimates the relative influence of changes in wanted fertility, unwanted fertility, and marriage composition. The conclusion of his analysis is that changes in marriage composition had the greatest influence on fertility in Pakistan in the period 1975–2006, followed by changes in unwanted fertility, and last of all by changes in wanted fertility. Whatever factors were responsible for the change of age at marriage had little to do with population policy.

Table 10–1. Selected Population-Related Indicators for Pakistan, 1975–2007

Year / Survey		TFR	CPR	IMR	Literacy (MWRA)	GDP Per Capita (Current US$)[b]
1975	Pakistan Fertility Survey	6.3	55	–	11*	160 (1975)
1984	Contraceptive Prevalence Survey	6.0	9	106	14	338 (1984)
1990–91	Pakistan Demographic and Health Survey	5.8	12	91	21[a]	410 (1991)
1996–97	PFFPS	5.4	24	92	24	486 (1997)
2000–01	PRHFPS	4.8	28	–	–	551 (2001)
2003	SWRHFPS	4.4	32	–	28	561 (2003)
2006–7	Pakistan Demographic and Health Survey	4.1	30	78	35	881 (2007)

* *Married women of reproductive age*
[a] *Women with no schooling*
[b] *Source: The World Bank*

These questions then remain: What effect has population policy had on these rather modest results, and what alternatives may have produced better results?

Pakistan and Its Neighbors—A Different Scorecard?

It is interesting at this point to step out and assess the role of policy in Pakistan in relation to the experience of neighboring countries. Instructive contrasts can be found in the histories of policy and change particularly in Bangladesh, Iran, and India. Pakistan was the last among all its neighbors to experience fertility decline and continues to have the highest fertility rates. At the time of its inception, Pakistan's TFR of 6.6 births per woman fell between India's TFR of 5.9 and Iran's TFR of 7 births per woman, and was the same as Bangladesh's TFR (Figure 10–1).

Currently, Pakistan's TFR remains more than one birth higher than India's and Bangladesh's TFRs and around two births higher than Iran's, which has reached replacement level despite starting just as late as Pakistan. All countries in the region experienced high fertility rates until the late 1960s at which point India's fertility levels started a gradual but consistent decline. Bangladesh, with heavy investments in family planning programs, was the next to follow with the fertility rate beginning to decline rapidly by the early 1980s. Even Iran stepped up its family planning efforts by the late 1980s and started experiencing a very rapid decline in its fertility rate, reaching replacement in a remarkable period of barely fifteen years.

Figure 10–1. Total Fertility Rate by Country Over Time

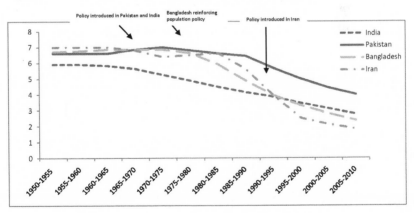

Bangladesh offers a particularly tantalizing comparison since it was a part of Pakistan and therefore had the same policies until 1971. In fact, much has been written about the comparative experience of the two countries

(Cleland and Lush 1997; Caldwell et al. 1999; Kabeer 2009). In essence, while politically joined but geographically separated, the two countries had many differences in terms of ethnic mix, population densities, marriage patterns, and landholding patterns. To reduce their different fates to merely different implementations of the same development policy is to view major shifts in human behavior through a narrow lens. An important difference between the two countries was that the newly formed Bangladesh had a chance to view its resources in line with population size and recognized much more clearly and categorically that it had an issue of unsustainable population growth. It went about dealing with this problem as a national priority. Pakistan in 1971 was in a different position; having lost half the country, it did have at that point more resources and other concerns such as a population fragmented across four provinces and multiple ethnicities.

It is important to point out that Bangladesh supported several other policies that strongly propped up population policy. Among the most important were the stronger economic role created for women and young girls and the priority given to providing education, both primary and beyond. Other important factors were the vigorous family planning program delivered through the Ministry of Health and Family Welfare to the doorsteps of families (announced as a priority by the president), the neutralization of the religious groups, and the involvement of the women's groups. All these were important ingredients for policy impact and success. A rapid fertility decline was under way in Bangladesh by 1980, a decade before Pakistan's decline.

Perhaps even more intriguing is Iran, a seemingly conservative country where Ayatollah Khomeini announced a population policy quite late, in 1992. Yet Iran has found routes to achieve fertility reduction much more rapidly than Pakistan. Population policy in all practical terms followed a fertility decline in the case of Iran; perhaps the policy was a mere means to endorse behavior that had already started to take root. In fact, the story of Iran's family planning program (UNFPA 2010) is an ideal one, showing how various groups converged. Planners, economists, and health specialists, among others, joined to create consensus on the issue, taking the powerful clergy on board slowly and surely. Iran illustrates that the success of policy lies in its wider endorsement. In any case, in Iran as in Bangladesh, a policy supporting family planning was accompanied by supportive policies such as education of women, an excellent rural health system with neighborhood health houses, and religious orientation counseling before marriage. This constellation of policies led to the very rapid decline shown in Figure 10–1.

Another interesting comparison is neighboring India, where the family planning program was instituted about the same time as in Pakistan. The demographic response in separate Indian states to supposedly the same program that was only implemented differently was quite a stark contrast. States in the south, such as Kerala, Tamil Nadu, and Karnataka, have reached replacement fertility levels, while states in the north, such as Uttar Pradesh, Bihar, Madhya Pradesh, and Rajastan, have levels of fertility resembling those of Pakistan.

India is in some ways similar to Pakistan—with multiple ethnic groupings, geographical expanse, and heterogeneity in caste—in economic and social terms. But the northern states with slow fertility declines are also states with poor records in terms of educational attainment, weak status of women, and poor health outcomes, among other factors. The lack of attention and progress in the accompanying factors may be a major factor for the weak policy impact, a mere symptom of weak commitment to social progress, and thereby reduced impetus for changes in family reproductive behavior. It is the southern states, also economically poor but egalitarian and committed to social-sector progress, that are reflected in the onset of India's fertility decline in the 1980s (Jain 2008). Politics and policy are just not enough. Development and literacy are important factors, and yet cultural differences between south and north India and resemblances of the latter with Pakistan argue for factors beyond population policies driving the process of transformation from a high fertility to a low fertility regime.

In the regional comparison certain issues emerge as very important. The key elements of success in achieving fertility change according to this brief comparison appear to be the following:

- a large base of support for promoting the policy and seeking broad popular and religious endorsement;
- good quality, extensive health infrastructure for delivery of family planning services and outreach; and
- improvements in women's status, such as promotion of female education and employment opportunities.

Unraveling the Disconnect— Where Has Policy Worked and Where Has It Not?

Based on the three criteria that appear to have supported the success of its neighbors, we can now look at Pakistan's population policy to see whether and how population policy might have contributed to Pakistan's long delay in bringing about a sustained fertility decline.

Broad Base of Support for the Policy

With the exception of the period of Zia ul Haq's rule from 1977 to 1988, Pakistan has articulated a policy of reducing population growth through voluntary family planning, generally accompanied by forceful statements of the dire consequences to be visited upon Pakistan in the event of continued rapid population growth. The first question is whether that policy is widely accepted.

For the most part, concern with population policy was and remains limited to a few population ministry officials, researchers, academics, and a handful of voices in civil society. Responsibility for periodic review of the policy was delegated to the Ministry of Population Welfare, which generally spoke for itself and this relatively small group. In the resulting policies the other two main criteria for success—a strong health infrastructure and enhanced women's status—were given little more than lip service. Hence, population policies prepared by the Ministry of Population Welfare that focused on the activities of that ministry were periodically forwarded to the cabinet and duly approved without troubling economic planners or requiring major changes in health or education—and things continued largely as before, with minor adjustments to suit the fashions of the day.

There have been no real champions who have gone about creating consensus on population issues. Politicians may understandably find population issues contentious and sensitive for religious reasons or for reasons to do with national distribution of resources. More surprising, economists and planners have been guilty of neglecting this important parameter, a neglect that is here to haunt them now and certainly will haunt them even more a few decades down the line. While there was mention of population growth impinging on resources from the third five-year plan (1965–70) onward, the implications for economic and social-sector policy were largely ignored.

Historically, NGOs have played a pioneering role in establishing family planning in Pakistan and in setting the reproductive health agenda. NGOs provided important clinical services, behavior change communication and community mobilization, research, and other inputs. Moreover, they have become increasingly vocal advocates for linking family planning and health and for improved education and status for women. However, the NGO sector has had little direct influence on policy at high levels, so its influence has been largely through the limited channel of the Ministry of Population Welfare.

An important requirement for a successful population policy is the support, or at least lack of active opposition, of religious establishments. As we have seen, Bangladesh has effectively neutralized religious concerns, and Iran has strikingly gained the support of the religious establishment at the highest level. (In India, religious opposition has never been a major concern.) In Pakistan, despite many attempts, there remains substantial hostility to family planning from Islamic leaders, partly for the reasons discussed below.

Donors have usually applied pressure in Pakistan to institute change in many areas. However, their support for family planning programs has fluctuated. International population movements and politics have definitely affected the twists and turns of Pakistan's policies. The real landmark was ICPD 1994, when the best possible balance was sought between population and development, laying out all possible dimensions. Ironically, this took its biggest toll on family planning programs. Instead of having the impact of penetrating and permeating all aspects of development, ranging from education and women's development to environment and health, to mention a few, the main message of the ICPD was the evolution of the term *reproductive health*, a holistic concept encompassing many aspects of family planning and safe motherhood, gender-based violence, and other factors. Responsibility for implementation cut across many ministries, NGOs, and partners. In Pakistan, the large and diffuse set of programs to be implemented led to a substantial dilution of attention and resources away from population and family planning without effectively creating a health basis for family planning or significantly improving women's status. In particular, the AIDS epidemic captured attention, and international funding for HIV/AIDS increased several fold at the expense of family planning. At the same time, the outreach structure of the Ministry of Health became heavily preoccupied with polio eradication to the detriment of family planning and other community-level health services. All this may change with very recent turnaround in international rethinking about the priority for family planning. But until now, while donors have been broadly part of the support for population policy, their support has not been consistently focused on creating and supporting the policies that have been effective elsewhere.

To gain the support of the population, advocacy and communication strategies have long been part of the Ministry of Population Welfare's agenda. Those strategies have been based largely on the idea of limiting family size. To elites, the benefits to the nation of lower population growth were stressed, and to ordinary people the message was boiled down to a "small family, happy family" message. This was successful to the extent that for decades more than 90 percent of Pakistanis have known about family planning. At the same time, it has caused a religious backlash because of the perception of family planning as a means of population control (which is perceived as against Islam) instead of as a means to improve maternal and child health (which Islam unequivocally supports). It has missed an opportunity to convince health officials and providers that family planning is an essential part of health care. And for elites, themselves often raised in successful large families, it has sometimes fueled the perception that family planning is related to an outside agenda that has little to do with Pakistan.

Thus, universal awareness of family planning has not translated into high levels of use. However, whether directly a result of official advocacy and mobilization or an indirect effect of ideational change, the concept of limiting childbearing has permeated widely and is now apparent even in rural Pakistan, among the uneducated, and across income groups. Figure 10–2 shows that the demand for family planning, as represented by the percentage of women wanting no more children, has risen more dramatically for women from the poorest quintile. In fact, the figure that shows the proportion wanting to limit childbearing has almost converged at a level of around 50 percent or more for all wealth quintiles, unlike the earlier period when it bore a sharp positive association with wealth.

Figure 10–2. Desire to Limit Childbearing by Background Characteristics Over Time

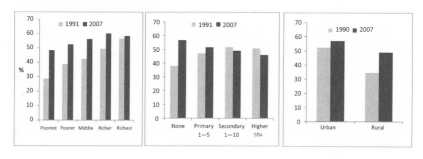

Nevertheless, levels of use of family planning have remained disappointing. In part, this is because the strategy has targeted women but has not effectively convinced any of the groups influential in making decisions; nor has it been able to garner support for the policy publicly. While women are the main beneficiaries, they certainly do not make decisions and were probably already prepared to be convinced of the benefits of family planning. Their main problem has been the absence of support for their desires within their families—notably from their husbands—and also in society. The most powerless were targeted while the most powerful remain unconvinced.

An alternative strategy that might have had more success in obtaining broad support for the program could have been to present family planning essentially as a health issue for mothers and children. A rephrasing of family planning as birth spacing is a convincing strategy both from the point of view of health benefits for the child and the survival of the mother and from the standpoint of greater compatibility with and acceptability to religious values. Such a repositioning is under way, and initial results seem to be strongly positive both within the public health community and in terms of the reception within families and communities. However, whether it will be effective in gaining high-level political and budgetary support remains to be seen.

A Strong Health Base for Family Planning Services

Unlike its more successful neighbors, Pakistan has not effectively placed family planning into the service structures of the Ministry of Health. The primary exception has been the Lady Health Worker program, but as we have seen, this has had limited success in supporting family planning. In part, this is because the Lady Health Worker program is at the periphery of a ministry that is otherwise largely uninvolved in family planning.

Why is this so? For many years, the Ministry of Health, on paper, has included family planning in its mandate, but that policy has not been translated into service delivery. To a considerable extent this has been because of a long-running turf battle with the Ministry of Population Welfare. The Ministry of Population Welfare consistently has resisted giving major family planning service responsibility to the Ministry of Health on the grounds that the Ministry of Health could not be trusted to take its responsibility seriously. Conversely, as long as responsibility lay with the Ministry of Population Welfare, the Ministry of Health was unwilling to become involved. The result was that the Ministry of Health, which has a far stronger service structure than the Ministry of Population Welfare, was not available to the public as a source of family planning information and services. Moreover, getting across the point that family planning is good for health has remained difficult as long as the body responsible for public health was not supporting the concept within its primary health-care system.

To understand why this failure is so important, it is necessary to look in more detail at the structure of demand in Pakistan. What is striking about the recent few years is the recognition and realization that family planning services have not kept pace with the increased demand. The high unmet need for family planning services, the high levels of unwanted fertility, and the large number of induced abortions (see below) to avoid having and rearing an unwanted child are reflections of this reality. These outcomes are largely a result of women, couples, and families not having easy, accessible, and affordable means to prevent unwanted pregnancies, such as good quality information and services. The stagnation of the contraceptive prevalence rate at 30 percent is testimony to this fact and to the fact that there is a disconnect between demand and the utilization of family planning services.

More than one out of three women want to space or limit their children but are not using contraception. Furthermore, out of a fertility rate of 4, one child on average is unwanted.

Unmet need—the percentage of currently married women who are fecund and do not want to be pregnant yet are not using contraception—increased from 33 percent of the population in the Pakistan Reproductive Health and Family Planning Survey 2000–2001 to 37 percent in the Pakistan Demographic and Health Survey 2006–7. Unmet need in rural areas, which was initially lower, is now more than urban unmet need, suggesting that the availability and affordability of family planning services is an obstacle to fertility change, especially in rural Pakistan. In line with these findings is the trend in unplanned childbearing (the combination of unwanted births and mistimed births). The proportion of recent births that are unplanned rose from 21 percent in 1990–91 to 24 percent in 2006–7. In the case of Pakistan, one of the major failures is the inability to deliver quality services, especially in the rural areas, beyond those provided by the Lady Health Worker program. The Ministry of Health, which has the larger public service delivery network with around fourteen thousand outlets, has not prioritized family planning. This is likely to change as a result of a recent commitment by the Ministry of Health to make family planning a priority in primary health care. Until now, however, the Ministry of Health clinics were not fully delivering family planning services. This, in brief, has been due to the refusal of the health sector to take responsibility for family planning, prioritizing other services such as immunization, HIV/AIDS, and maternal health, the last without seeing its strong connection with family planning. The Ministry of Population Welfare had the main responsibility for family planning, including controlling contraceptive supply chains.

The relationship of unmet need with other background characteristics has also changed over time. In 1991, women from the poorest households had the lowest unmet need. Over time, unmet need among these women rose substantially, and they now have the highest unmet need (Population Council 2009). The change in the relationship between unmet need and wealth can be understood by looking at the changes in the relationship between preferences and contraception and wealth in Figures 10–3 and 10–4.

This is in contrast to differentials in contraceptive use that appear to be almost as sharp across rich and poor women as they were in the earlier period. Current use differentials (in absolute terms) between the poorest and richest women were 34 percent in the earlier period and 32 percent in 2007, indicating a negligible leveling of contraceptive use, unlike the dramatic leveling seen in fertility preferences.

Figure 10–3. Unmet Need by Background Characteristics Over Time

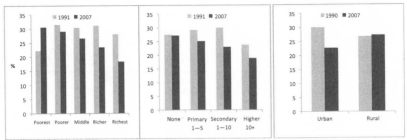

Figure 10–4. Contraceptive Use by Background Characteristics Over Time

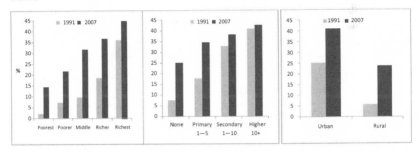

Ultimately, this explains the sharp increase in unmet need, a combined outcome of preferences and use, experienced by poor women who increased their demand to limit childbearing without much change in contraceptive use. By contrast, there was a sharp fall in unmet need on the part of rich women, who increased their contraceptive use in conjunction with their demand for it (Population Council 2009).

Unmet need for contraception and the proportion of births that are unplanned, along with the high rate of abortion, suggest that a large fraction of currently married women in Pakistan are at risk of an unwanted pregnancy and potentially an unsafe abortion. Despite the fact that induced abortions are illegal in Pakistan except when performed to save women's lives, a study carried out by Population Council and published in October 2004) estimated that there were 890,000 induced abortions in 2002 and an abortion rate of 29 per 1,000 women aged 15–49. The abortion rate is most likely an underestimate of the true abortion rate despite being moderately high by world standards. A majority of such abortions are taking place among poor, married women with more than three children. Results yielded a high unwanted pregnancy rate—one out of every seven pregnancies was unwanted; one out of three of these unwanted pregnancies ends in an abortion. Abortions are a clear response to the desire to limit and space births but are clearly operating outside of the population policy framework. (While post-abortion care has been considered a priority since 1994, as an essential part of reproductive health, the provision of abortions is clearly outside publicly supported services.)

Thus, by all measures there is substantial demand for family planning throughout the population. In addition to the public sector, the private sector through social marketing increasingly is taking on the responsibility for dispensing, advertising, and training in reproductive health, and is playing a very vital role in providing family planning/reproductive health services in the country. The Population Policy and the interim Population Sector Perspective Plan 2012 envisage an expanded role for social marketing in the pursuit of attaining the population stabilization goal by increasing contraceptive use prevalence. Social marketing was expected to intensify its efforts to extend beyond the urban areas, extending its outreach to rural areas. It was to broaden the scope of services through new interventions in order to enhance the contribution of social marketing to the national population goal. However, social marketing too has yet to fulfill its full role in expanding service delivery coverage, especially into the rural areas.

In sum, Pakistan's policy of vesting primary responsibility for family planning services in the Ministry of Population Welfare has led to a failure to establish a strong base for those services in the public health system. Partly as a result, for about two decades Pakistan has had one of the highest levels of unmet need for family planning in the world. A golden opportunity both to meet the needs of the nation's people and to bring down its population growth rate has been squandered.

Improved Women's Status

While it is essential that Pakistan do a better job of meeting existing demand for family planning, it is evident from the data that desired family size is inconsistent with completing the demographic transition in Pakistan. The ideal family size in Pakistan has hardly changed. Meeting unmet need can bring the TFR down to somewhat below 4, but further progress will be more difficult because Pakistanis, on average, prefer more than three children. This is unlikely to change unless there is a real transformation of society.

Clearly, many factors affect desired family size. Some are basically ideational, a self-reinforcing change in societal taste as the vision of a good life evolves. Perhaps more fundamentally, desired family size is a broad function of development in many areas, including income, education, health, and other factors. Even within the broad topic of development, however, there is much evidence that a central place in determining desired fertility is reserved for enhancing women's education and status. In studies in Pakistan, as throughout the world, the primary social determinant of a variety of variables involving fertility and fertility preference is women's education. At the societal level, status of women—notably, but by no means exclusively, participation in the labor force—is powerfully related to fertility. We have seen that for Pakistan's neighbors, improvements in women's education and status have been key factors in their success in reducing fertility. Bangladesh and Iran, especially, have an excellent record in making gains in female education. Iran, which has reached close to replacement fertility, has much greater proportions than Pakistan in higher secondary education and in high levels of female employment despite its conservative society in terms of hijab. The comparison between north and south India also reinforces the stark differences in investments in female education and the much lower status of women in the former (Jain 2008).

It was pointed out in the early 1980s by the economist Lawrence Summers, in an address at the Pakistan Institute of Development Economics, that Pakistan had to invest in *all* of its people, not just some people. Summers particularly singled out the draw-down effects of under-investing in female education (Summers 1992). Pakistan recognized in the 1990s that female education was lagging behind, and some efforts were made to escalate enrollment through the Social Action Program. Education levels have improved in Pakistan, notably in the early years of the past decade, and improvements have been somewhat more rapid for girls than for boys. For example, net primary enrollment for boys has risen from 49 percent in 1990–99 to 55 percent in 2000–2009, and for girls it has risen from 38 to 47 percent. The proportion of literate married women of reproductive age (a lagging indicator of education, since it reflects schooling levels in previous decades) has gone from 21 percent in 1990–91 to 35 percent in 2006–7. However, in comparison with Pakistan's neighbors, those changes are modest (see Table 10–2).

Similarly, the participation of Pakistan's women in public space has made only modest progress, a fact somewhat obscured by the prominence of a small number of upper-class women. Female labor-force participation rates slowly inched up to 20 percent in 2009, a meager rise from 11 percent in

Table 10–2. Literacy Rates of Adult Women in Pakistan, India, Bangladesh, and Iran

Country	Age Group (in years)	Female Literacy Rate (%)
Pakistan	15–49	45.9
India	15–49	55
Bangladesh	15–49	55
Iran	15+*	77.2*

*Adult female literacy

1991. Furthermore, labor-force participation remains limited largely to uneducated or highly educated women. By comparison, the effect of the large volume of female employment in Bangladesh's garment workers has been well studied.

These results are clearly functions of policy, especially on the education side. As with population generally, a broadly articulated policy of education for all is important but not adequate. It must be supplemented with more specific implementation policies and reified through budget allocations. Instead, Pakistan's education authorities have plodded on, building a certain number of schools and training a certain number of teachers each year with the budgets they are given. Plans are not in place to ensure, for example, universal primary education for all by a targeted date. Budget allocations for education as a proportion of the budget have hardly changed, ranging from 1 to 2 percent, not changes conducive to major achievement. Granted, increasing education for girls is not a population policy per se, but we would argue that a policy of reducing population growth is incomplete without an accompanying policy of universal education for girls.

Female participation in public space is perhaps less obviously a function of policy in a free-market economy and a traditional social structure. In particular, female mobility remains limited in Pakistan in comparison with many countries and resticts women and girls from activities outside the home. Nevertheless, policies can help prepare women for labor-force participation; they can encourage gender equity in public-sector hiring; they can support economic sectors that require female participation; and they can protect women who dare to venture into the labor market. Pakistan, while a signatory to various conventions on the status of women, has been limited in taking policy steps to make those commitments a reality.

Conclusions

Pakistan's population policy may have been misplaced in its priorities though not altogether deficient in design. Creating demand for smaller family size, extending the supply of services, and emphasizing demographic targets for development may have been the ingredients of a successful approach if concomitant efforts had been made in the past four decades to harness support for these measures and if the policy had been broadened to address some other issues. First, it is clear that the responsibility for and therefore support for the policy was restricted to the Ministry of Population Welfare, which did not succeed either in forging productive partnerships or in doing the job itself. The most glaring disconnect even today is that most educated Pakistanis, including economists, planners, and politicians, remain unaware of how important the achievement of fertility transition is for Pakistan's development and how important family planning services are for achieving improvement in women's and children's health. The base of support for the policy of supporting fertility transition remained too narrow and did not include women's groups, economists, and even donors, and consequently led to a limited impact.

Second, the health sector, perhaps as a consequence, did not accept its responsibility in including family planning as one of its priorities in the same vein as it did maternal-mortality reduction and child-mortality reduction. The link between contraceptive use and improved maternal-health and child-health indicators was not capitalized on. The only exception is the Lady Health Worker program, whose extensive outreach in the rural areas has contributed to raising prevalence levels in those areas. Even today, the outlets of the Health Department are probably insufficient to extend services to most Pakistani women, and the private sector will have to supplement the public sector, but the active contribution of the Health Departments would increase services in the public-sector manifold.

Third, and perhaps most important, there were few effective efforts or policies for improving the status of women. If there had been dramatic improvements in female education or in their economic participation, then the first two weaknesses of policy may have been mitigated as women themselves would have wanted fewer births and found ways to achieve their reproductive intentions. While Pakistan may have lost time in terms of the speed of its fertility transition, efforts in improving the gender indicators alongside the expansion of family planning services by the health sector can make a significant difference in making up for lost time.

Reference List

Caldwell, J., et al. "The Bangladesh Fertility Decline: An Interpretation." *Population Development Review* 25/1 (1999).

Casterline, J. B. "Demographic Transition and Unwanted Fertility: A Fresh Assessment." Paper for presentation at the annual conference of the Pakistan Society of Development Economists, Islamabad, March 16–18, 2010.

Cleland, J., and L. Lush. "Population and Policies in Bangladesh, Pakistan." *Forum for Applied Research and Public Policy* 12/2 (Summer 1997): 46–50.

Feeney G., and I. Alam. "New Estimates and Projections of Population Growth in Pakistan." *Population and Development Review* 29/3 (2003): 483–92.

Hardee, K., and E. Leahy. "Population, Fertility, and Family Planning in Pakistan: A Program in Stagnation." *Population Action International* 3/3 (2008).

Jain, A. *Do Population Policies Matter? Fertility and Politics in Egypt, India, Kenya, and Mexico.* New York: Population Council, 1998.

———. "A Tryst with Destiny: Demography Can Help Realize the Dream." Fourth Sat Paul Mittal Memorial Lecture, New Delhi, 2008.

Kabeer, N. "Snakes, Ladders, and Traps: Changing Lives and Livelihoods in Rural Bangladesh 1994–2001." *The Bangladesh Development Studies* 32/2 (June 2009).

Lodhi, M. "Boom or Doom." *The News International*, June 15, 2010.

Ohno, N., S. Chowdry, I. Haq, and S. M. Karim. "Fertility Decline in Pakistan: 1980–2006. A Case Study." World Bank, 2010.

OPM (Oxford Policy Management). *External Evaluation on National Program for Family Planning and Primary Health Care (Lady Health Worker Program).* Quantitative Survey Report. 2010.

Population Council. "Unwanted Pregnancy Post-abortion Complications in Pakistan: Findings from a National Study." Islamabad: World Bank, 2004.

———. "Examining Fertility Change and Its Impact on Household Poverty and Welfare." Background paper for the *World Bank Pakistan Poverty Assessment Report.* Islamabad: World Bank, 2009.

Robinson W. A., M. A. Shah, and N. M. Shah. "The Family Planning Program in Pakistan: What Went Wrong?" *International Family Planning Perspective* 7 (1981): 85–92.

Sathar, Z. "Stagnation in Fertility Levels in Pakistan." *Asia-Pacific Population Journal* 22/4 (2007).

Sathar, Z., and F. Fikree. "Estimating Induced Abortions in Pakistan." *Studies in Family Planning* 38/1 (2007):11–22.

Summers, L. "Investing in All the People." *The Pakistan Development Review* 34/4 (1992).

UNFPA (United Nations Population Fund). *Family Planning Programme, Primary Health Care, and Safe Motherhood Programme.* Tehran: UNFPA, 2010.

11

Religion and Development
Challenges in Pakistan

MUHAMMAD KHALID MASUD

Religion generally has been considered a formidable challenge to political, economic, and social development in Pakistan. However, the recent growth of mosque and *madrasa* networks has led some development studies to see possible interactions between the Ulama[1] and civil society. It has given currency to phrases like "Ulama, Agents for Social Change"[2] and "Ulama as Custodians of Change"[3] but has also incited labels like "Donor-Driven Islam."[4] In this chapter I explore how the Ulama's participation has been affecting development challenges in Pakistan.

This chapter, in three sections, traces the genealogies of the concepts of development and religion, overviews and assesses the Ulama's participation in community-development projects, and analyzes the possible reasons for the Ulama's reluctance to promote and support development and modernity. I suggest that religion and development challenges are integral to the politics of development in Pakistan.

Definitions of *Development* and *Religion*

Growing interactions between religion and development in recent years have prompted several studies to revisit their conception as dichotomous terms, almost as an ideological assumption. To start with, the etymology of the English word *development* suggests an ideological trajectory. Beginning with the simple meanings of "unfolding" and "growing," it became associated as early as 1756 with "advancement," and in 1836 with the theory of evolution to the extent that in 1862 *developmentalist* meant "follower of the theory of evolution."[5] The term also drew upon ideas of enlightenment, scientism, constitutionalism, reformation, liberalism, autonomy of the self, human rights, and democracy, which modernity indicated as signposts during its recent journey.

During its encounters with non-Western societies, the West objectified development in terms of advancements in science, technology, and the economy. Development came to mean achievement and progress in terms of modernization, and the world was divided into developed and backward or underdeveloped countries. The concept was thus limited to community development and came to focus on restricted targets like community education, public health, alleviation of poverty, and help for the underdeveloped (now called developing) countries, defined in terms of needs.

In this narrative tradition and modernity were both projected as static concepts. A number of scholars now disagree with the dichotomous and essentialist construction of the terms *tradition* and *modernity*.[6] Development in this narrative was a function of modernization, and religions functioned as part of tradition, resisting modernity. The narrative suggested a deterministic course of history ending with (Western) modernity. Ideological perceptions not only placed development in dichotomy with religion but also often posed it as a replacement for religion.[7]

Muslim societies are religiously quite complex, and scholars find it difficult to suggest a simple typology of Muslim social formations, especially in response to development and modernization.[8] Available typologies usually objectified the Ulama as the embodiment of religion. The Ulama, on the other hand, saw modernity as a new religion aiming to replace Islam.

Louis Cantori identifies two types of Muslim responses to modernization: (1) defensive responses that "literally intended to safeguard and maintain the social and political positions of the Ulama" and (2) apologetic responses, retorting that "Islam had anticipated modernity and development."[9] Cantori does not provide any details about these two groups. He argues that Islamic revivalists such as Sayyid Qutb,[10] Hasan Turabi, and Sayyid Mawdudi reformulated the traditional Islamic concept of development, responding to the nineteenth-century Western polemics against Islam from the perspectives of human control of nature, materialism, commitment to economic progress, individualism, and secularism. At a convention of the Association of Muslim Social Scientists in 1977, Muhammad Qutb and Isma'il Ragi al-Faruqi (d. 1986) defined *development* from an Islamic perspective.[11] Khurshid Ahmad, explained that Islamic development was based on Islamic theological concepts like *tawhid* (unity), *tazkiya* (purification), and *taghayyur* (change); socioeconomic concepts such as *al-'adala al-ijtima'iyya* (social and economic justice), *takafuliyya* (corporatism), and *masalih/maqasid* (five basic needs);

and political concepts such as *umma* (Islamic community), *shura* (mutual consultation), and *bay'a* (mass allegiance).[12]

Contrary to Cantori, Fazlur Rahman prefers to call the above formulation "neo-revivalist" or "neo-fundamentalist," both postmodernist trends. Revivalism or fundamentalism had existed in Muslim societies since the eighteenth century, before classical modernism. Those reform movements wanted to reconstruct Islamic spirituality and morality on the basis of a return to the pristine "purity" of Islam.[13] The postmodernist revivalist (neo-revivalist) is essentially anti-Western, and his or her "pet" issues are the "ban on bank interest, the ban on family planning, the status of women (contra the modernist), collection of zakat and so forth—things that will most distinguish Muslims from the West."[14] Neo-revivalism rectified several excesses in classical modernism and secularism and reoriented the modern-educated lay Muslims emotionally toward Islam, but it has done a great disservice to Islam because it totally lacked positive Islamic scholarship. The traditional Ulama had an imposing tradition of learning but suffered from disorientation toward the purposes of the Qur'an.[15]

The Ulama and Development in Pakistan

In *Faithlines*, a study published in 2000 based on interviews conducted in 1996–98 with forty-five hundred Muslims from Indonesia, Pakistan, Kazakhstan, and Egypt, Riaz Hassan observed a religious renaissance in Pakistan.[16] This was contrary to the frequent statements by the Ulama and Islamists that Muslim society had been drifting away from religion. More significantly, he also found that the number of people in Pakistan who trusted the Ulama was less than in other countries. Even though the people trusted the Ulama more than Pirs, political parties, and Parliament, the ratio of trust in intellectual, educational, and judicial institutions was higher (see Appendix, Table A–6). The disconnect between religion and the Ulama in this renaissance often goes unnoticed. Hassan found a shared self-image of Islam in Pakistan grounded in scripturalism, but the people constructed piety as being socially influenced by current global and local conditions.[17]

Development studies often overlook these factors and credit the Ulama for the success of development programs in Pakistan.[18] "Ulama and Development," a National Research and Development Foundation (NRDF), Peshawar report on some projects in Pakistan, for instance, argues that the Ulama's participation in development programs ensured their success because they were highly trusted and could effectively motivate people toward development behavior and practices. NRDF undertook this project to sensitize the Ulama to the productive and reproductive rights of women and to utilize their influence in dealing with these issues. It also organized a series of participatory orientation workshops to sensitize the Ulama to these issues.[19]

The report, however, does not provide any information about the actual impact of the project. It notes some modest success in introducing changes in the syllabi and curricula in thirty key *madrasas*, and the Ulama's approval of 160 Friday sermons prepared by NRDF. The report focuses on potential benefits as it concludes that the services of the Ulama can be utilized effectively in realizing the development goals, provided they are approached properly, carefully, and sincerely, because the Ulama are highly sensitive as a group. The report also argues that low levels of achievement in community participation, ineffective mobilization of local resources, gender discrimination, opposition to the work of NGOs, and little success in government-run family planning and other development programs were all due to the exclusion of the Ulama from such development projects. The report's recommendations, however, suggest that the Ulama's participation is still problematic. In dealing with the Ulama, it advises,

- avoid confrontations and try to understand their responses in a positive manner;
- learn from their experiences;
- respect them and do not ridicule, even if they are millennial in their approach;
- avoid discussion of controversial issues until trust is built;
- cooperate with them wherever they show a desire for change.

A similar stance is reflected in the report "Ulama, Agents of Social Change," which is based on a six-year (2004–10) project designed to reduce maternal, newborn, and child mortality through promoting positive behaviors, providing skilled health-care services, and improving the health-care infrastructure in a total of twenty-four districts in all regions of Pakistan. Since it is the men who are the sole decision makers in such matters, the project identified the Ulama as a crucial link to reach them effectively in the mosques.[20]

The project prepared a booklet, *The Role of Ulama in Promoting Maternal, Newborn, and Child Health*, explaining its objectives in light of the Qur'an and the Sunna. It networked over eight hundred Ulama and encouraged them to speak on these issues in their Friday sermons. About twelve hundred persons who attended these sermons were later interviewed to assess their perception of the sermons. These interviews revealed that the sermons contained general appeals. For example, appeals to women to be examined by a health professional during their pregnancies were clearly understood by all the attendees. The perception of the message was highest among those who regularly came to these sermons (91.6 percent); it was 80.5 percent among those who did not attend regularly, and 66.1 percent among those who did not attend these specific sermons. Sermons on more specific behavior changes, such as that a woman should be examined by a health professional at least four times during her pregnancy, were less successful in being understood: 49.4 percent among the regular attendees, 39.5 percent among the irregular attendees, and 34.8 percent among those not attending the sermon. Two observations in the above analysis are notable. First, it interprets "understanding" the sermon in the meaning of "agreeing" to the advice in the sermon. The report finds that the sermons giving general advice (for example, a pregnant woman should see a health professional, meaning a midwife or lady health worker, not necessary a medical doctor) were understood better than those which gave specific advice, such as visiting the health professional for a specific number of days. Second, the data include a category of persons who did not attend these sermons at all and yet understood the problem. This analysis reveals that the sermons with general advice were clearer than the one with specific advice. It raises the question, Are the Ulama reluctant to give specific advice? If so, why?

Apparently, the Ulama did not want to speak clearly on issues that they considered contrary to religious teachings. For instance, speaking on the importance of breastfeeding was not a problem, because it is prescribed in the Qur'an. But speaking on specific actions, such as early initiation or exclusive breastfeeding, was not acceptable because it may be perceived as promoting family planning that the Ulama regard as contrary to Islamic teachings. The report develops a complex and detailed argument to explain this reluctance on the part of the Ulama. According to the report, either the Ulama feared that their statements would be misunderstood because of high levels of illiteracy among their audience, or the Ulama were reluctant to speak on such issues because they themselves lacked the necessary technical knowledge. Nevertheless, the Ulama clearly showed reluctance in participating in these projects. Several imams agreed to speak on breastfeeding but refrained from delivering messages specified by the project and asked questions about the motives, funding, and partners of the project. According to the reports, diversity, heterogeneity, and adherence to different sects, the hierarchical nature of the religious organizations, and the requirement of blessings of the senior Ulama inhibited the junior Ulama from participating effectively.

The report observes that Ulamas in Pakistan are widely respected and often perceived as among the few reliable channels of communication, especially among the rural population and in areas where literacy is low and access to mass media is limited. Through a wide network of mosques and seminaries, the Ulama are endowed with a powerful platform for shedding misperceptions and promoting positive behaviors, especially among men who congregate regularly in sizable numbers at events like Friday prayers.

The report does not provide any data to show if the Ulama's interventions were successful in improving public health issues, reducing the rate of population growth, or lowering maternal and infant mortality. World Bank data, on the other hand, show no significant improvement in population growth and literacy from 2006 to 2010 (see Appendix, Table A–1and Table A–4). Pakistan did slightly better in public health (Table A–2 and Table A–3) and female primary education (Table A–5), but it is arguable whether these results were due mainly or exclusively to the Ulama's participation. The report also confines evaluation of the project's success to the Ulama's willingness to participate and to people's grasp of Friday sermons. Repeated stress on the significance of the Ulama as an agent of social change in this situation suggests the contrary—that the Ulama demonstrated reluctance toward development. The report concludes that successful integration of the Ulama into the development process can greatly help in achieving development goals. The position of the Ulama, as a potential agent of change, has attracted a number of academicians and development scholars to explore this possibility. In 2007, Carol Rakody noted with surprise the neglect of religion and influential faith-based activities in development theory and practices.[21] She launched an international research project to study how religious values and beliefs drive individuals and faith organizations, how they influence relationships between state and society, and how faith communities interact with development actors. The project undertook research on these topics in four countries, including Pakistan. Mohammed Waseem and Mariam Mufti, the coordinators of the project in Pakistan, noticed the influence of the Ulama, but more as a political pressure than as a harbinger of social change and development.[22] They found that politics and governance were heavily influenced by the nature and direction of pressure of an Ulama's group, which they call the Islamic establishment, especially because they are well organized both in the government and in the opposition. The state has frequently used Islam as a source of legitimacy in the absence of a mass mandate. In this effort the state has been relying on the Ulama to manage religious affairs, Islamic taxes, shrines, and *madrasas* and to play a role in sectarian conflict, peace efforts, and interfaith harmony.

In the authors' words, "It is necessary to go beyond a purely instrumentalist explanation of how religion is used by the state to understand the structural dynamics of Islam as a constant, pervasive and intense force that includes, but at the same time transcends, the manipulations of the ruling elite."[23] Parallel to the state's struggle to define religion as part of its political discourse, the Ulama have always held the state to its promise to establish *sharia*. The Ulama organized themselves as a group of religious political parties whose alliance, the Muttahida Majlis-e-Amal (MMA), came to power in 2002–7. Waseem and Mufti's study, conducted in 2008, found that the MMA was quite pragmatic in its political interests. It adjusted to the prevailing legal-institutional framework of authority in order to survive in office and established working relationships with the central government and donors on whom it depended for resources and with provincial government bureaucrats on whom it depended to implement its policies. It compromised on several issues on which it had a hard-line position before coming to power, for example, the presence of U.S. bases. It tried to improve health care while restricting women's roles, especially in the public sphere. The Ulama seem to have used their influence to enhance their political power, but they have been ambivalent about development issues.

The Ulama's Resistance to Modernity and Development

In order to understand the Ulama's resistance to modernity, one needs to look at the development of the institution of the Ulama in South Asia in the colonial context. The Ulama of Deoband emerged as one of the prominent religious groups in India during the nineteenth century, and it held a politically anti-imperialist stance.[24] That was also the time when modernity and modernization issues began challenging religious thought and practices. Deoband was a revivalist reformist school founded in 1867, but its anti-Western attitude shaped its concept of reform differently from that of the nineteenth-century modernists like Sayyid Ahmad Khan (1817–98), who supported British rule and modernization. This disagreement with modernists became more pronounced when Sayyid Ahmad Khan began urging Muslims to learn modern sciences and embrace new ideas of reform and development. He called for New Theology to find Islamic answers to modern challenges.[25] He expounded new principles of Qur'anic exegesis and reviewed critically the principles of Islamic jurisprudence. He suggested laws of nature to be rational criterion for understanding the Qur'an and explained miracles as natural phenomena in the light of scientific discoveries. The Ulama of Deoband were foremost in opposition to Sayyid Ahmad's views.

In 1890 Mawlana Qasim Nanawtawi (1832–80) refuted Sayyid Ahmad Khan's exegesis, and Mawlana Ashraf Ali Thanawi issued a detailed *fatwa* (religious pronouncement) in 1886 against what the Ulama of Deoband regarded as Khan's heretical views. The Deobandi Ulama's conceptions of modernization and development evolved to essentially defending its position against Khan's views on modernization. As the limited space of this chapter precludes even a brief overview of the vast literature that exists on this subject, I will simply say that I find Mawlana Ihtishamul Hasan Kandhlawi's critique of modernity and development typical of the Deobandi Ulama. He was the foremost ideologue of the Tablighi Jama'at, a mass reform movement that began in India in the 1930s and is now a global movement with a large following all over the world.

Mawlana Kandhlawi argued that confusing concepts of development (*taraqqi*) were keeping Muslims backward. The Islamic concept of development requires going back to the Prophet, not going forward and disregarding the past. He explained, "Other religions have lost their original teachings but we have them safe and secure. Other religions can make progress by staying away from religion, but if we deviate from it we go farther away from human values and perfection."[26]

In this situation Muslims had one of two choices: to safeguard and preserve Islamic education and culture or to acquire new knowledge and sciences so as not to lag behind other nations. Consequently, Muslims were divided into three groups: (1) the religiously educated who abided by the religion but had lost its spirit; (2) the modern educated who were fascinated with modern ideas and were disinterested in Islam; and (3) the masses who were illiterate and ignorant. The modern educated criticized religion openly, but since they had no true knowledge of religion their criticism was irrelevant. As a rule, if you were sick you should go to a physician, not to a philosopher or a scientist.[27] The modern educated pretended to be their own physician.

Kandhlawi elaborates that ever since the European nations colonized Muslim countries their concern for their own security and stability had been compelling them to keep confusing Muslim hearts and minds so that they could no longer distinguish bad from good.[28]

The Ulama in this period particularly felt threatened by modernity. It was particularly fearful about the impact of modernization on women. More than modernists, the Ulama took female education seriously.[29] Mawlana Muzaffar Husayn Kandhlawi warned the women in his family and advised them to abide strictly to the teachings and works of the Deobandi Ulama.[30]

This continuing concern for safeguarding and preserving has restricted the Ulama's perspective to a very local view of its community tradition, which is more convenient than constructing a comprehensive response to new challenges. The Ulama's *fatwas* still invoke two juristic tools—*bid'a* (novelties) and *tashabbuh* (resemblance)—to examine social and scientific developments they suspect of being threats to Islam. The criterion of *bid'a* is applied to ascertain if the matter in question is in accordance with tradition, that is, if it has precedent in the days of the Prophet or in Islamic history.[31] The criterion of *tashabbuh* (similarity) is applied to examine whether the matter in question has any resemblance to infidel cultural and religious practices.[32] Although in principle the Ulama distinguish between the religious and nonreligious nature of ideas and practices and reject only what is religious in intent, the selection of these criteria is itself very restrictive. The Ulama define development and modernization from the perspective of the community of religious scholars.

It is significant to mention that the Ulama show flexibility and allow exceptions only in individual cases but not as a policy. For instance, the Council of Islamic Ideology's Report on Family Planning allowed birth control in individual cases under certain conditions, but its adoption as a policy was contrary to the nature and spirit of Islam. The council, therefore, recommended that the government campaign for birth control must stop immediately and be excluded from economic planning strategies. Contraceptive medicines and devices must be available only to married couples upon the production of a marriage certificate or written medical advice.[33]

In addition to the epistemological restriction and anti-imperialist stance, the growth of the Ulama since 1950 as organized political groups also solidified their opposition to modernization. In the absence of a critical history of the Ulama and their institutions in Pakistan, it is not possible to comment on the growth and transformation of religious organizations and institutions. However, two recent studies suggest nationwide religious, political, and educational networks.[34] The Ulama's groups are also well-connected to the masses through *madrasas*, mosques, the press, and TV. Combined with their political affiliations, these groups make up a formidable community. They have real potential to be leaders of change at the grassroots level, but as they are restricted by the tradition of their respective sects, they depend on neo-traditionalist groups for idelogical and intellectual leadership, especially in responding to development challenges.

Conclusion

I have argued in this essay that religion and development challenges are integral to the politics of development in Pakistan. The threat of socialism during 1950–60 particularly brought the Ulama together. It necessitated reformulation of the concept of development. Jama'at Islami's Islamic formulations of political, economic, and social developments as alternatives to the Western theories brought the Jama'at closer to the Ulama. Political, educational, and media networks enhanced the Ulama's influence as an authority in religious matters, and the continuous resort to religion by the

Government of Pakistan to avert political crises has in turn reinforced the Ulama's confidence in its religious tradition.

The global politics of development has also fortified religious fundamentalism in Pakistan. The emphasis in the 1960s on building liberal middle classes in underdeveloped countries shifted in the 1970s to advocating dependency on the developed world and aid for lower-income groups. In the 1990s emphasis shifted again from dependency on the state to empowering civil society and NGOs for development work. The significance of non-state actors in political and economic development softened resistance to religion and religious organizations. Western countries as well as the Government of Pakistan began seeking the Ulama's cooperation in their development policies, particularly relating to public health and female education. Since the Ulama still maintains reservations toward development policies, attempts to enlist the Ulama's cooperation have strengthened their authority at the cost of development targets. Such recognition of the Ulama's influence has further politicized both religion and development in Pakistan.

Notes

1. *Ulama* is the plural of the Arabic word *Alim,* meaning "knowledgeable person." Usually it is used for Muslim religious scholars in general. In English usage it is spelled *Ulema* and refers to the general body of Muslim religious scholars. Since, in this chapter, the term does not refer necessarily to a specific body, the general term *Ulama* has been used to refer to religious scholars who are engaged in teaching, leading prayers, and delivering Friday sermons.

2. Atif Ikram Butt, Surushi Sood, Shailaja Maru, Margaret Edwards, and Fayyaz Ahmad Khan, "Ulama, Agents for Social Change: Muslim Scholars Speak for Mothers Rights" (Baltimore, MD: Johns Hopkins Bloomberg School for Public Health, 2010). Also available on the paiman.jsi.com website. References in this chapter are to the web edition at JHU/CCP, 2010.

3. Muhammad Qasim Zaman, *The Ulama in Contemporary Islam, Custodians of Change* (Princeton, NJ: Princeton University Press, 2002).

4. Afiya Shehrbano Zia, "Open Democracy," AWID 50.50 (January 21, 2011), available on the opendemocracy.net website.

5. Douglas Harper, "Online Etymology Dictionary," *Etymonline* (2001–10), available on the etymonline.com website.

6. For an overview of the debate, see Armando Salvatore, "Tradition and Modernity Within Islamic Civilization and the West," in *Islam and Modernity: An Introduction to Key Issues and Debates*, ed. Muhammad Khalid Masud, 3–35 (Edinburgh: Edinburgh University Press, 2009).

7. See, for instance, Oscar Salemink, Ananta Kumar Giri, and Anton van Haarskamp, *The Development of Religion/the Religion of Development* (Delft: Eburon Publishers, 2005).

8. See, for instance, William E. Shepard, "Islam and Ideology: Towards a Typology," *International Journal of Middle Eastern Studies* 19 (1987): 307–36. Riaz Hassan refers to Montgomery Watt, Ernest Gellner, Fatima Mernissi, and Fazlur Rahman on this subject; see

Riaz Hassan, *Faithlines: Muslim Conceptions of Islam and Society* (Karachi: Oxford University Press, 2003), 116–22.

9. Louis J. Cantori, *Modernization and Development* 3, in *The Oxford Encyclopedia of the Modern Islamic World*, 123–26 (New York: Oxford University Press, 1995), 124. Cantori is the major source for the brief account of the changing ideas of development in Western and Muslim societies. His discussion is limited to the Arab world, however, and therefore misses the peculiar South Asian perspectives. Wherever needed, I have added remarks to highlight this missing perspective.

10. Sayyid Qutb's *Al-'adalata al-ijtima'iyya*, originally published in 1949, came to prominence in 1960–70 and was translated into English by John B. Hardie (New York: Octagon Books, 1970 [1953]).

11. Sayyid Muhammad Qutb, "The Islamic Stages of Development," in *Islam and Development: Proceedings of the Fifth Annual Convention of the Association of Muslim Social Scientists* (Plainfield, IN: Association of Muslim Social Scientists, 1977), 1–11; and Isma'il Ragi al-Faruqi, "Foreword," in ibid.

12. Khurshid Ahmad, "Economic Development in Islamic Framework," in *Islamic Perspectives: Studies in Honour of Mawlana Sayyid Abul A'la Mawdudi*, 223–40 (Leicester: the Islamic Foundation, 1979)

13. Fazlur Rahman, *Islam and Modernity: Transformation of an Intellectual Tradition* (Chicago: University of Chicago Press, 1982), 136.

14. Ibid.

15. Ibid., 136–37.

16. Hassan, *Faithlines.*

17. Ibid., 74.

18. See Husnul Amin, "Re-imagining the Role of Ulama Poverty Alleviation and Development in Pakistan," in *Religion and Development: Ways of Transforming the World,* ed. Gerrie ter Harr, 273–94 (New York: Columbia University Press, 2011).

19. Butt et al., "Ulama, Agents for Social Change."

20. Ibid.

21. Carol Rakody, "Understanding the Roles of Religions in Development: The Approach of the RaD Programme," working paper 9, International Development Department (Birmingham, UK: University of Birmingham, 2007), available on the religionsanddevelopment.org website.

22. Mohammed Waseem and Mariam Mufti, "Religion, Politics, and Governance in Pakistan," working paper 27, Religions and Development Research Programme (Lahore: Lahore University of Management Sciences, 2009), available on the religionsanddevelopment.org website.

23. Ibid., 1.

24. I am referring here to the Ulama of the Deoband School founded in 1867. For details, see Barbara D. Metcalf, *Islamic Revival in British India: Deoband, 1860–1900* (Princeton, NJ: Princeton University Press, 1982).

25. I have discussed this point in detail in "Islamic Modernism," in Masud, *Islam and Modernity*, 237–60, and "Iqbal's Approach to Islamic Theology of Modernity," *Al-Hikmat* (research journal of the Department of Philosophy, University of the Punjab) (2007): 1–36.

26. Ihtishamul Hasan Kandhlawi, *Islah-i-Inqilab* (Delhi: Idara Isha'at Diniyat, 1956), 7.

27. Ibid., 26.

28. Ibid., 22.

29. Ibid., 25.

30. Ihtishamul Hasan Kandhlawi, *Din Khalis, Tabligh Kiya Hay* (New Delhi: Idara Ishaat Diniyat, 1956), 58.

31. For a detailed analysis, see Muhammad Khalid Masud, "The Definition of Bid'a in the South Asian Fatawa Literature," *Annales Islamologique* 27 (1993): 55–75.

32. Muhammad Khalid Masud, "Imitating the Infidel: The Doctrine of Tashabbuh in Modern South Asian Fatawa about Cosmopolitanism and Cultural Authenticity," forthcoming.

33. Council of Islamic Ideology, *Report Khandani Mansuba Bandi* (Islamabad: Council of Islamic Ideology, 1992 [1984]), 20.

34. Muhammad Amir Rana, *A to Z of Jihadi Organizations in Pakistan* (Lahore: Mashal, 2011); and Saqib Akbar, *Pakistan ke Dini Masalik* (Islamabad: Al-Basira, 2010).

Appendix

Table A–1. Population Growth (Annual %)

Countries	2006	2007	2008	2009	2010
Pakistan	2.1	2.1	2.1	2.1	2.1
Afghanistan	2.7	2.7	2.7	2.7	2.7
Bangladesh	1.5	1.5	1.4	1.4	1.3
India	1.4	1.3	1.3	1.3	1.3

Source: http://data.worldbank.org/indicator/SP.POP.GROW

Table A–2. Maternal Mortality Ratio per 100,000 Live Births, 2008

Country	Ratio
Pakistan	260
Afghanistan	1,400
Bangladesh	340
India	230

Source: http://data.worldbank
.org/indicator/SH.STA.MMRT

Table A–3. Contraceptive Prevalence (% of Women Ages 15–49)

Countries	2006	2007	2008	2009
Pakistan	–	30	–	–
Afghanistan	15	–	15	–
Bangladesh	–	56	53	–
India	56	–	54	–

Source: http://data.worldbank.org/indicator/SP.DYN .CONU.ZS

Table A–4. Literacy Rate: (% of Females Ages 15–24)

Countries	2006	2007	2008	2009
Pakistan	58	–	61	–
Afghanistan	–	–	–	–
Bangladesh	–	–	–	77
India	74	–	–	–

Source: http://data.worldbank.org/indicator/SE.PRM.GINT .MA.ZS

Table A–5. Gross intake Rate in Grade 1, Female and Male (% of Relevant Age Group)

Countries	2006		2007		2008		2009	
	Female	Male	Female	Male	Female	Male	Female	Male
Pakistan	91	114	96	112	98	114	96	111
Afghanistan	–	–	82	119	–	–	93	129
Bangladesh	116	113	99	97	100	99	105	101
India	126	134	124	132	–	–	–	–

Source: http://data.worldbank.org/indicator

Table A–6. Trust in Key Institutions (%): 1996–98

Institution	Pakistan	Indonesia	Egypt	Kazakhstan
Ulama	48	96	90	24
Imam Masjid	44	94	83	22
Pirs/Kiyai	21	91	52	21
Parliament	22	53	34	19
Courts	55	55	76	16
Civil service	26	58	44	11
Political Parties	12	35	28	12
Armed Forces	82	68	78	33
Press	38	84	54	33
Television	31	80	49	37
Universities	60	88	70	33
Schools	71	92	68	48
Intellectuals	66	92	81	37

Riaz Hassan, Faithlines: Muslim Conceptions of Islam and Society *(Karachi: Oxford University Press, 2003), 153.*

12

Faith-Based Versus Rights-Based Development for Pakistani Women

AFIYA SHEHRBANO ZIA

The instrumentalization of religion as an entry point for development initiatives has been under-discussed among feminists in Pakistan. During the 1980s, several women's research and activist groups embraced the idea of the strategic worth of using the religious (Islamic) framework as a tool for negotiating and advancing women's rights. This, in turn, saw the introduction and growth of Islamic feminist consciousness—both funded and political—in Pakistan, Malaysia, Algeria, and several other countries. Some of these groups were knitted together under networks such as Women Living Under Muslim Laws and other such transnational Muslim women's rights groups. Many of these had critical strategic value, despite their limited measurable success, particularly in innovative interpretation of Islamic texts, especially with reference to Islamic jurisprudence. Still, this approach has diluted and ultimately weakened secular feminism and created considerable space for the recent right-wing Islamist political backlash witnessed in Pakistan in general. It has had more serious implications for the women's movement specifically.

Simultaneously, although more interrogative of cultural rather than religious identities, the nature of subaltern studies in Western academia opened new avenues of critical inquiry regarding the Western gaze over "third-world women."[1]

This scholarship has gradually been supplanted in the wake of 9/11, especially since Operation Enduring Freedom sought to rationalize the U.S. occupation of Afghanistan under the guise of Afghan women's emancipation from the Taliban. This political charade provoked a new impetus for some feminist scholarship that sought to challenge the moral hypocrisy of the purported feminist altruism of the Bush regime.[2] It also sought to unpack self-referential positions of power within Western feminist theory regarding Muslim women.

The pragmatic challenge for secular feminists in Pakistan today comes from the momentum gained by anthropological and ethnographic revivalist scholarship on Islam as a liberation theology, which has emerged largely from Western academia over the last decade. Much of this has translated and crept into tangible development policies and projects across the country, as a celebrated confirmation of the pragmatic possibilities of development subsumed and framed by religion/Islam. Some Pakistani feminists, meanwhile, have become complicit in such exercises, unwilling to concede the contradictions in portraying a secular political identity while engaging in funded development projects that reinforce the communitarian logic of religion.

Most often, the policy-directed research I refer to does not focus on engagement at domestic levels. Instead, it takes an interesting route whereby Pakistani consultants or development experts are contracted to carry out semi-academic research in collaboration with foreign universities. Sometimes, the consultant hired is an academic embedded in the foreign university as a doctoral student or under a fellowship. In other words, the process of policy is often shaped and directed by factors and actors completely outside the collective developmental or indeed the political or activist paradigm of the country itself. Pakistani development activists and feminists then tend simply to contract themselves out to the received wisdom of such developmental policy as a career path.

The content of the very well-funded research emerging from such collaborative efforts from Western academia focuses on the *sharia, madaris,* the veil, and faith-based politics and their institutional links with Muslim women.[3] Such efforts have produced a body of literature that attempts to reinscribe these very sites where gender roles and identities have been constructed. It suggests that Muslim women now have opportunities to convert such patriarchal symbols and structures into potentially liberating possibilities for themselves.[4] This is due to the much celebrated discovery of the "agency of Muslim women," which, the revivalist scholars argue, could be docile and non-feminist, and may seek resistance by way of symbols, such as dress and domesticity, rather than political change and challenging patriarchy[5]—or, as I have argued elsewhere, what may be termed a "political nunnery."[6] What such research selectively ignores is that where the form of (Muslim women's conscious) resistance does engage with the political, it has tended to uphold conservative, anti-feminist, and often, nonmaterialist agendas.[7]

Theocratization of Development

This essay is based on observations that have emerged from a broader study of women and religious identities in Pakistan, recognizing the thrust of a simultaneous and linked process that can only be termed the theocratization of development. The main argument here is that during the 1990s the "progressive" women's movement in Pakistan broadly defined its objectives within a universalist human rights approach, but over the last decade or so, this has redirected itself such that the rights-based discourse has been enmeshed in and forced into a religious framework.

As a feminist scholar, I am always reluctant to date anything to 9/11 because social scientists in Pakistan, those who are intellectually honest anyway, know that the direction and depth of the development debate was already being affected by faith-based identities before that event. While these identities may have been exacerbated after the occupation of Iraq and Afghanistan, they were certainly not simplistic, post-9/11 new developments.

The fact that many within Pakistani civil society started tagging "Islam" onto all their project proposals is simply reflective of the kind of opportunistic politics that have historically been played out by sections of civil society.[8] Incidentally, what can be dated is the birth of this imagined collective now called civil society. The date is 2007, when at the height of the Laywers' movement in Pakistan, many NGO careerists realized that a force larger and more political than them was taking on the state in a far more effective, direct, old-school activist manner. This afforded an opportunity to many development activists to discard their "NGO-ized" reputation—one could argue, a reputation that was increasingly perceived as a compromised one. This rechristening also allowed the NGO community to wash away memories of collaborative politics when many NGOs had supported or collaborated with the military-led but purportedly "enlightened and moderate" regime of General Musharraf (1999–2008). The term *civil society* allowed a reinvention of their more apolitical and accommodationist earlier lives as Musharraf's image-enhancing NGOs.

The most obvious example of this change is when, practically overnight, the Aga Khan–funded NGO Resource Centre in Karachi changed its sign at the gate to "Civil Society Resource Centre." In any case, that is an aside from the main argument of this essay, which is that many identity issues within the development discourse perhaps were catalyzed by compelling external factors but were by no means surprising or new. The one discussed here has to do with the specific role of development practitioners, advisers, and consultants, and some diasporic scholars, and the kind of development research they have been invited to produce (I use this term deliberately) in the last decade.[9] This essay notes that many of them started prioritizing the religion question over all other identities and categories, including and especially class differences. If, as many people argue, class was already dead, then in this case it was exhumed, revived, and repackaged as Muslim militant poverty.

This new brand of development research has been systematically informing Western think tanks and offering policy advice to them. Journalists, novelists, activists, retired military officers, fresh ivy-league graduates, technocrats more than government representatives, or as their representatives, are the new policy elite that sit at the roundtable sessions held in London and Washington. It's democracy interrupted and represents a very Musharrafian legacy.

The influence of this new generation of local consultants and researchers, who are hired for joint projects with Western academia/think tanks, according to my readings, enables them to argue often for negotiating a place for religion, particularly this thing called "moderate Islam," into the development discourse. Essentially, the justification for such a recommendation stems from a criticism of Western, liberal, secular-rights-based approaches in/for Pakistan and the need, therefore, to consider alternatives, such as "indigenous," "culturally appropriate," "Islamically sanctioned" modes of relations and development.

However, if now, a post-9/11 new school of those who advocate for an indigenous, religious-revivalist approach to development is agreed upon the need to reject Western liberalism, humanist theories, Western feminism, modernity, and the hegemony of Western development paradigms, surely there should be an overall consensus about the rejection of foreign-sourced development funds too? Not so fast. Humanitarian and development assistance apparently can stay (although also a product of Western liberal humanism), and, of course, USAID must stay, since it funds so many of these think tanks, universities, and their studies, which come up with these ideas of accommodating religion within development in the first place.

Somehow, between left-leaning and right-leaning developmentalists, there has emerged an unspoken consensus that suggests that funds are somehow a neutral category. Left-leaning developmentalists insist that governments should accept funds only for progressive social development, whereas the conservatives suggest that if development funds can be unlinked from the concept of liberal human rights and can be used for conservative purposes, they are kosher. Only the more radical on both sides of the ideological divide insist that the political economy of funds needs more careful scrutiny and redirection and should be decided on the basis of an economic vision at the very least.

Where Are These Ideas Emerging From?

The Lahore University of Management Sciences (LUMS), also referred to in tongue-in-cheek fashion in Pakistan's feminist circles as the Lahore University of Madrasa Sciences in reference to its conservative reputation, has produced a few studies that are exemplary in highlighting the "theocratization of development" trend discussed above.[10] These are quoted below but it should be noted that, if reputed civil society organizations and the donor community in Pakistan were not so secretive about more of their "research," those studies would perhaps be equally revelatory.

LUMS engages in this interesting approach to research through visiting fellowships and collaborative studies with overseas academia, whereby its own faculty often serve as consultants for both the private and government sectors and/or sometimes work with Pakistani diasporic scholars. Jointly, they represent native Pakistanis for the purpose of recommending development policy. So, for example, a given British public-sector university and government development agency collaborate with Pakistan's private-sector university and free-lance consultants to charter policy recommendations for the U.K. development program for the average Pakistani citizen.

Over the past decade a series of such efforts have attempted to look for alternatives to radical, political Islam; out of their many recommendations, they have come up with ideas such as "support for madrasas," "culturally appropriate justice systems," harnessing the potential of faith-based development, and even investment in the promotion of a softer or "Sufi Islam"—as if Sufi Islam will not be patriarchal or worse in its implemented, institutional form. Neither is this restricted to Western academic interest; now politicians globally have, in an Obama-esque manner, embraced this moderate, Sufi Islam option as a viable alternative to radical Islam.

All the attempts to redefine and rebrand what is essentially a complex political identity that is in itself a dynamic and intangible mixture of the ideological, material, and social is incredibly ambitious. Certainly, some of these studies outline what may be academically interesting. However, the explicit relevance of these findings—how religious violence or social development or, indeed, political identities are actually articulated in the Pakistani context—seems to be a far cry from the, frankly, nonrigorous and questionable conclusions of some of these studies. However, Pakistani audiences never get to question these conclusions. The idea that if only there could be a method to neutralize some of the radical groups; or reinterpret religious texts (many of which are not even in written form) in a progressive way; or, according to a LUMS/DFID study,[11] "'support' rather than 'reform' the *madrasas*"[12]; or convince the jihadis to struggle for the personal but not the political is reminiscent of the NGO approach to sociopolitical development. That method is to circumvent the state and apply "band-aid" fixes for structural failures by methods such as "raising awareness," "empowering the communities," putting up more private schools/shelters, and promoting income-generation programs. These may be commendable projects, but they are certainly not political solutions.

The value of research is not in question here. However, when this research begins to morph into projects at institutional levels or as developmental or educational joint ventures between Western governments and home institutions, there is a danger.

Research that indicates results from projects such as Respecting the Veil, Afghanistan-Pakistan peace jirgas to resolve tribal violence, pro-state *lashkars* (armed militia reminiscent of warriors from Islamist history), women's empowerment in the Muslim (not Asian) context, support of *madrasa*-taught *sharia*-compliant progressive justice, faith-based organizations, Islamic Relief rather than Red Cross, and so on . . . raises some flags that alert us to a risk-laden development path for the future. More important are the processes that inform the actors, production, and politics of this research.

Main Concerns of Theocracy-Development Scholarship

This essay discusses three main concerns regarding analysis that invests and links development output through theocratic lenses. The first is that such analysis is found to be overwhelmingly and consistently nonmaterial-ist. There is little or no discussion of class identities to be found in such studies, or if there is, it is always in sweeping references to "the poor." One such study suggests that research on faith-based organizations will help us understand the needs of "the poor."[13] Thereby, all class differences become subsumed under a presumed communitarian logic using religion as a unit of analysis. The temptation then is to categorize people according to sectarian affiliation rather than social classes.

The second concern is that such scholarship tends to be defeatist and therefore makes a pragmatic call for negotiating rather than demanding rights. The language of such research will suggest that activists should "make space for more rights" rather than "ensure equal rights." It posits the need for *madrasas* for girls as a practical demand-driven necessity or recommends some mosque space for women in the absence of secular public alternatives. This research accepts that access to health care for women should come through the approval and involvement of and mediation by local clergymen, what I call Rent-a-Maulvi projects. It avoids the contradiction that such a strategy negates other potential social empowerment for women, as if paying the price for overall women's rights can be justified because any tactic is acceptable if it allows entry into the community in order to meet those Millennium Development Goal (MDG) targets. In the process, sexuality is ignored and women's health is reduced to the MDG enumerable maternal health while land rights/inheritance rights remain within the framework of *sharia* compliance. In the realm of such research there is no recognition of a demand for equality; therefore, religious minorities should be treated with tolerance not equality.

Thus, the entire rights-based discourse for marginalized groups has been relinquished and rationalized into a pragmatic proposal. This proposal may continue to depend on funds as long as it qualifies and is cognizant of faith-defined identity politics.

On the concept of women's empowerment I have argued that such research draws an imaginary line between personal empowerment of the Muslim female subject through pietist practices and rituals, on the one hand, and the political expression of the Muslim woman, on the other. So when sometimes the faith-based, personal agency of this celebrated Muslim woman morphs into a political expression of her faith-based agency, as in the case of Jamia Hafsa women,[14] supporters of the faith-based empowerment path back down and completely disown that this is even possible—that the personal can be directly linked to the political. This should raise important ethical alarm bells for the said researchers.

The last concern discussed here has to do with this new theocratic development path and what it has revealed about the identity crisis among donor or aid agencies in Pakistan. Specifically, the turn in the rights-based discourse, as it now attempts to include faith-based approaches, has resulted in highlighting some contradictory pursuits of donor organizations in the field of development assistance.

Many such funding organizations in the new millennium had already begun to redefine themselves as "partners" rather than donors. Even at the time, women development activists were wary of this change in vocabulary, arguing that when calling for a paradigm shift in developmental relations they didn't mean simply that labels should be changed. However, as neo-colonial as this proposal struck many people, several new "partnerships" were launched, and the activities of donors started creeping directly into Pakistan's social delivery process. Ironically, the conservative sectors were not as worked up about the cessation of national sovereignty at that time as they have been more recently.

At the risk of singling out one agency, this chapter quotes an anecdotal example of donor relations; it should be pointed out, however, that such contradictory and troubling relations between donor agencies and activists is not only uniform but, sadly, quite regularly experienced.

About two years ago, while undertaking some personal-interest research on honor crimes, I called the Oxfam office in Islamabad because it had been running a supposedly successful campaign called We Can (eliminate honor-based violence against women). When I called to inquire about this project, Oxfam said that actually it had run out of funds in Islamabad, so it had to subcontract the project to South Asia Partnership (after all, what are partners for?). My immediate response was one of anger over the now quite regular and questionable practice of donors who willfully engage directly in service delivery rather than simply providing funds to local organizations and then disengage whenever they please. However, rather than getting into a political argument, I chose instead to laugh it off and jokingly asked if the new title for the project was going to be, "No We Can't and So Maybe *You* Should Instead." The Oxfam employee did not find it funny.

The point here is that if donor agencies can be so directly engaged in social development—with a physical presence within bureaucracies and government departments and also (disputedly) micro-managing the Government of Pakistan's budgets, while their local officials demand and bully their "partners" for due paperwork and line-item details—how can the same agencies possibly complain about the presence of militant, faith-based groups that, despite their bigotry and bullying, also dispense social assistance and aid to communities? How have donors decided upon the strategy of co-opting the more tractable among the faith-based actors into the field of social development? Further, who decides on the question of legitimacy as far as social delivery is concerned? Who accepted the hierarchy or discretion, so that some faith-based organizations qualify for funds and others do not?

The underlying argument of this essay is just this—that if we begin to abandon the moral imperative of a universalist human rights approach and relinquish increasing space to faith-based social development, then anything is possible on this slippery slope. I am suggesting that in recent years too many donors and too much Western government assistance are showing just how greasy or oily this development assistance path can really become. This, and the issues outlined above regarding development research, are issues that women's rights activists need to be extremely wary of. This chapter suggests that if these issues are not addressed, these unresolved debates will arrest democratic social and political developmental possibilities rather than advance and expand them for marginalized groups in Pakistan.

Notes

1. Examples of post-colonial feminist theory are found in Gayatri Spivak, "Can the Subaltern Speak?" in *Colonial Discourse and Post-Colonial Theory*, ed. P. Williams and L. Chrisman, 66–111 (New York: Columbia University Press, 1994); and Chandra Mohanty, "Under Western Eyes: Feminist Scholarship and Colonial Discourses," in *Feminism Without Borders: Decolonizing Theory, Practicing Solidarity*, ed. Chandra Mohanty, 17–42 (Durham, NC: Duke University Press, 2003).

2. The historical connections between contemporary domination and colonial conquest in the context of the War on Terrorism are made by Leila Abu-Lughod in "Do Muslim Women Really Need Saving? Anthropological Reflections on Cultural Relativism and Its Others," *American Anthropologist* 104/3 (2002): 783–90; see also Judith Butler, *Precarious Life: The Powers of Mourning and Violence* (London: Verso, 2003).

3. For a detailed critique of such scholarship, see A. S. Zia, "Donor-Driven Islam?" in *Opendemocracy 50.50* (January 2011), available on the opendemocracy.net website.

4. Membership and the body of work presented at the regularly held Islamic Feminist Conferences are indicative of this approach. For more info, see the feminismeislamic.org website.

5. Saba Mahmood, *Politics of Piety: The Islamic Revival and the Feminist Subject* (Princeton, NJ: Princeton University Press, 2005); and Humeira Iqtidar, "Secularizing Islamists? Jamaat-i-Islami and Jamàat-ud-Dàwa in Urban Pakistan" (Chicago: Chicago University Press, 2011).

6. Afiya S. Zia, "The Reinvention of Feminism in Pakistan," *Feminist Review* 91, and also in *South Asian Feminisms: Negotiating New Terrains*, ed. Firdous Azim, Nivedita Menon, and Dina M. Siddiqi, 29–46 (London: Palgrave Macmillan, 2009).

7. For a detailed review of the debates and policy decisions by Jamaat-i-Islami women in Pakistan's Parliament, 2002–7, see Afiya S. Zia, "Faith-Based Politics, Enlightened Moderation, and the Pakistani Women's Movement," *Journal of International Women's Studies* 11/1 (November 2009): 225–44, available online.

8. For a more detailed critique of opportunistic politics with reference to civil society, see S. Akbar Zaidi, "State, Military, and Social Transition: Improbable Future of Democracy in Pakistan," *Economic and Political Weekly: Special Articles, India* 40/49 (December 3–9, 2005).

9. For an idea of the broad range of donor efforts toward research focusing on religion, see all of DFID's Religions and Development Research Programme (RaD) policy briefs and working papers, in particular "Islam and Pakistani Politics: Partners or Adversaries in Social Development?" Policy Brief 5 (2010), based on M. Waseem and M. Mufti, "Religion, Politics, and Governance," in *Pakistan*, working paper 27 (2009); and "Rethinking Madrasa Reform in Pakistan," Policy Brief 1 (2009). All RaD publications are available on the relgionsand-development.org website.

10. One example of the revivalist scholarship and debate on religion that is emerging from LUMS can be found on the baytunur.blogspot.com website. For specific studies please refer to the previous three notes.

11. "Rethinking Madrasa Reform in Pakistan," an information leaflet based on Masooda Bano, *Contesting Ideologies and Struggle for Authority: State-Madrasa Engagement in Pakistan* (Birmingham: Religions and Development Research Programme, 2007).

12. Ibid., 3.

13. Information leaflet on the project Religions and Development Research Programme that summarizes what is stated to be "output from a project funded by the UK Department

for International Development (DFID) for the benefit of developing countries." The document also carries a disclaimer by the funding agency: "The views expressed are not necessarily those of DFID." The back page identifies the "Audiences for the research" and claims that "the ultimate purpose of the research is to benefit poor people in developing countries." More details may be found at on the www.rad.bham.ac.uk.

14. For more details on Jamia Hafsa and the debate of Islamic and secular feminisms, see Zia, "The Reinvention of Feminism in Pakistan" and "Faith-Based Politics, Enlightened Moderation, and the Pakistani Women's Movement."

Part Four

ONGOING CHALLENGES OF MILITANCY, INSECURITY, AND POLITICAL PATHS

13

Gendered Peripheries

Structuring the Nation, the State, and Consensus in Pakistan

Nazish Brohi

In the Nara desert in southern Sindh province, a woman told me about her son working as a driver with an oil and gas exploration company in its Islamabad office. What she said was, "Woh mulk mein nokri karta hai. Saal mein aik dafa watan waapis aata hai. Mein yahaan apni qaum ke saath rehti hoon." Islamabad was the *mulk*—the country where her son worked. Sindh was the *watan*, the homeland to which he returned on his holidays. Her tribe and family made up the nation, the *qaum* with whom she lived while he was away.

When I repeated her words to others in her community, they immediately understood what she meant and did not find her phrasing particularly remarkable. For her, the country, the homeland, and her nation were separate enclaves within the geographical boundaries of Pakistan. Where did that leave the nation state?

The distance between the multiple self-identified nations and the state is a result of the absence of internal conceptual consensus around the state of Pakistan. Given that foundational ideas have been sites of contestation since the inception of the country, this chapter excavates grounds on which solidarity has been possible across subnational groups and between citizens and the state. It suggests that a gendered social contract ensures domestic political consensus as well as confers governance legitimacy on ruling regimes. The social contract allows for impunity to violence within delineated enclaves where the state reserves the right to violence in the public sphere while allowing men impunity in the private sphere, creating a "community of interest" around the use of force that promotes masculinist accord across subnational cleavages. The state is bound to maintain it because it lacks the legitimacy to assert itself without resort to violence, and men accept the otherwise alien state because it allows for private patriarchies and its concomitant political economy.

This essay attempts to unearth why development prescriptions for women's equality produce only marginal results in Pakistan. The National Plans of Action, Millennium Development Goals (MDGs), CEDAW Points of Action, countless reports on the status of women, and efficient recommendations from conferences pile up into an archive of dreams, and yet even minimum benchmark indicators remain unmet. It finds that current inequities are based on foundational precepts that intrinsically tie together the "woman question" with that of the state, the nation state, and society through a social contract that consigns women to peripheries of citizenship. It suggests that if diffusion of state power leads to broader ownership and consensus over the state, it would lessen the need for the state to rely on violence, hence giving it the legitimacy to intervene on violence within the private sphere. In conclusion, it proposes reconfiguration of state-citizen relations to create possibilities of a new social contract.

Theoretically, states merge the status of the citizen and the identity of the nation to make the political boundary correspond with the psychosocial boundary. In conventional theories of nation-building, the process is portrayed as a gradual unification of disparate territories under the control of nation-building elites. This process is typically carried out in stages: territorial consolidation, rise of participatory decision making, administrative apparatus for development of a welfare state with capacities of redistribution, and cultural standardization.

A summary review shows that the nation-building project of Pakistan has been contested since the country's independence and, at best, remains incomplete. Territorial consolidation remains illusory. Examples are replete, for instance, with the Federally Administered Tribal Areas in conflict with links and identity ties with Afghanistan; Khyber Pukhtunkhwa's questioning of the Durand Line; a secessionist movement in Balochistan; and until recently, the indeterminate status of Gilgit-Baltistan and India's and Pakistan's strident claims over territories of Kashmir.[1] Another listed indicator, the rise of participatory decision making, is low on the list of priorities of political parties, with a track record of local governments being instituted by dictatorships and conversely dispensed with by elected governments. There are competing diagnoses of the health of Pakistan's democracy, which remains sporadic between military interregnums. Similarly, it is also evident that while the country was envisioned as a welfare state with redistributive functions, it is now characterized more as a garrison state with traditional security concerns eclipsing human security. Provision of basic services and safety nets is the most commonly cited failing of the state across a plethora of development-sector literature.

This leaves the nation-building toolkit with the indicator of cultural standardization, where I suggest the state has been able to make more headway in Pakistan. There are many tools a state has at its disposal to do so, such as linguistic uniformity, perspectives on history, what is taught in textbooks, religion, and reinventing culture and traditions. These cultural characteristics shape a shared narrative, creating and communicating the foundational ideas that arguably contour the state itself. This formulation suggests that three core elements constitute the state: the physical base of the state, the idea of the state, and the institutional expression of the state. The strength of a state correlates not only to the use of force but is also characterized by shared narratives and the level of internal political consensus centered on the idea of the state. This aspect is vital to the coherence and purpose of the state because it provides a mechanism for persuading citizens to subordinate themselves to the state's authority.

Mapping the divergence between the nation and the state in Pakistan, this chapter suggests that a lack of internal political consensus leaves the state reliant on the use of force in the domestic arena. In domestic discourse, the referent for the state in Pakistan is "the establishment," an amorphous yet recognizable matrix that protects and promotes a particular discourse and interpretive trajectory as fundamental ideas of the state. Anyone can identify and belong to the establishment by becoming an agent of this discourse, though it is usually indicative of a core elite spanning the army, bureaucracy, political actors, security agencies, and intelligentsia. Attributed to the establishment is the attempted crafting of a singular Pakistani identity based on religion, a centrist view of history that filters out people's lived realities, investiture of power at the center, security concerns overriding democratic considerations and triumphing development, the convenience of religious ties in determining foreign relations, and the preoccupation with threat perception from India and its construction as the constant Other. The common denominator is the calculus of interest-protection of the security establishment and the political economy of the army's preeminence. What is of particular interest is that this perceptual matrix has been packaged in terms of the nation and not in terms of either the state or the establishment. Decisions in Pakistan are gauged against national interest, national security, and national sovereignty. The establishment viewpoint of the ideas of the state remains contested, and it has been unsuccessful in establishing hegemony.

The other attempt at crafting consensus around the idea of the state is the positioning of religion as the glue that would bring disparate territories into the identity parameters of Pakistan. The inception of the country was grounded in the two-nation theory that posited that Muslims living in united India constituted a distinct nation. Islam was positioned at the crux of the Pakistani identity, even though alternative commentaries suggest that the doctrine was buried at sea in the Bay of Bengal.[2] Increasingly, Islam has become a bitterly and violently contested terrain, with divides between Shias and Sunnis, Deobandis and Barelvis, Wahhabism and Sufiism; the declaration of Ahmedis as non-Muslim; and varying interpretations of religious-pacifist groups, religious-militant groups, revivalist social movements, and those who invoke religion in service of foreign-policy objectives. Whether this proposition of Islam cementing together Pakistan as a nation has worked or not remains debatable.

The above summation shows ideas that have not worked, or have worked only partially. This chapter now attempts to draw attention to a domestic political consensus that has, in fact, worked: a covert gendered social contract. I suggest that centrifugal and centripetal forces in contestation over ideas of the state do not exist as binaries and that impunity toward violence against women in the private sphere has created a "community of interest" that promotes masculinist solidarity across subnational cleavages.

The Gendered Social Contract

The state has not managed to create a domestic political and societal consensus that eliminates the need for force and "domestic" violence to contain recurring challenges to the nation state. This has left the state preoccupied with domestically generated security threats, and it has responded with a perpetual invocation of national interest and national security, while directing force at the nation itself. The state then uses violence and the threat of violence to interpellate people as subject citizens. However, justification of this power is still necessary because it involves negative features, including exclusion, restriction, and compulsion in addition to physical violence. Legitimization is important if the power-wielder is to enjoy moral authority in addition to bare power. This legitimacy is created by the distribution of power to the subordinate, creating a "community of interest." The power that is distributed mirrors the power of the state, including physical violence, exclusion, restriction, and compulsion, as the domestic violence the state retains as its right in the public sphere it then contracts out to men in the private sphere. The terms of engagement are between men and the state, and they function by carving out spheres of influence where men can retain the capacity for domestic violence within the home. This heuristic social contract creates consensus over impunity for the use of force, by sharing entitlement to it and allowing participation in a shared moral order.

Classic contractarian philosophers have theorized how society moved from the state of nature to modern political life and how people consented to being governed. Envisioned differently by various writers, the common thread is the idea that people gave up some independent action that the state of nature allowed them in exchange for the security of greater benefits that could be accrued to them, and that the need for an entity to moderate this interface led to the formation of government. Carole Pateman revisited the social contract to point out that it was predicated on a sexual contract based on exploitation of women, with an agreement between men to diffuse the rule of the father to modern patriarchy. She examines the implication of the marriage contract, the prostitution contract, and the contract of surrogate motherhood. Continuing with Pateman's supposition that it was a contract between men, I attempt a somewhat different reading of the Enlightenment-proposed contract that posits it as the historic moment of consent to government. Instead, I argue it as the moment of taming, a domestication of violence, and a delineation of spheres for its use. The primitive condition that Thomas Hobbes described as "war of all against all" gave way to defined circumferences within which violence was permissible, and government emerged as the arbitration authority that mediated the use of force, while withholding for itself the right to use force in the interactive space of the public. The process and structure are consensual in that men agree to limit their use of force in order to be protected from the violence of the other, and agree to a central regulatory body.

Therefore, I argue that the idea of the state includes the public-private divide where the state regulates the public and men regulate the private in a power-sharing arrangement. Sovereignty at the state level extrapolates into autonomy/authority at the household level—to make decisions about individual (male) self-interest without external interference. The compact is the legitimization of violence, hence the creation of a "discourse community," and by tentatively using the binaries of sanctioned violence and deviant violence, it allows me to place state-sponsored violence, internationally mandated violence, and violence against women in the same category—that of sanctioned violence—sanctioned by either states or societies, or by both.

In Pakistan, the state intervenes whenever the use of violence by men over women moves from the private enclave into the public sphere—whether it occurs spatially in a community site, such as the public gang rape of Mukhtara Mai; incidents of stripping and parading women naked, such as the Tando Bhawal case or the woman councilor in Noshera; the public flogging of Chand Bibi in Swat recorded and broadcast on television; the four women buried alive in Balochistan; or when women bodily carry the spectacle of violence into the public space, such as particularly grotesque cases of domestic violence in which women die, or go to hospitals or to police with physical evidence of abuse—such as the case of Zainab Noor, one of the first high-profile cases of marital torture. Men have territorial jurisdiction over and therefore impunity for violence only within the private sphere, where extreme forms of violence breach the fourth wall, the boundary between the spectator and spectacle. The terms of the contract mirror the colonial strategy of allowing natives to settle "personal laws" governing marriage, divorce, and family matters that regulate the private sphere, whereas regulation of the public realm was the reserve of empire.

Even a cursory look at contemporary Pakistan shows that the state does not exercise a Weberian monopoly over violence and that the authority to discipline, punish, and even kill has been distributed and subcontracted. There is no dearth of empirical evidence of the honor killings and forced confinements, the forced marriages and the forced prevention of marriages, and domestic marital violence that form the everyday narrative of violence, and the state not only does not intervene, but often does not see it as its "place" to intervene. Women's bodies are a critical site for mapping and maintaining the circulation of violence, which generates legitimacy of violence as a mediator of conflict. The circular referencing among different levels of violence in society allows a norming that permits the state to have moral authority as opposed to mere de facto power, and facilitates interpellation by acts of routine violence to the logic that violence can settle conflicts. This "logic" is most widely communicated through domestic violence.

The appeal of masculinist solidarity based on impunity in apportioned zones of violence converges into a systematized code of violence that interpellates people into being subjects of the order. Julieta Kirkwood, a Chilean feminist, argues that in order to impose authoritarianism, the military not only calls for the power of the armed forces, but also a brutal, underlying authoritarianism in civil society, like domestic violence, resulting in the total imposition of the patrimonial state. Seeing the domestic and the public as mutually constitutive realms, fighting an authoritarian state would require dismantling *all* authoritarian structures.[3] According to Kirkwood, "Authoritarianism . . . has its roots and causes in all of the social structures, and that one must question contents not previously considered 'political' because they were attributed to day to day life."[4]

The effectiveness can be gauged by the conflation of honor with protection of the zones in both the state's and men's stature. In the state's discourse, national honor is outraged when forces external to the state intervene without invitation. In recent times national honor has been brought into debate by perceived breaches such as questions over Pakistan's nuclear arsenal; the Kerry-Lugar bill that tied U.S. aid to continuity of democratic regimes and the crackdown on terrorism in specified locations; and the entry of U.S. Marines for the operation that killed Osama bin Laden. In individual men's value codes, their honor is violated when "outsider men" breach their bastions by sexual contact with women within their apportioned zone, resulting in honor killings, including that of the woman in question. The chastity of the woman at home and the purity of the motherland both must be protected against uninvited penetration. In this framework only men can accept other men to marry women within their realm, and only the state can decide who can intervene and realign its domestic terrain (such as the IMF). The *ghairat* (honor) code bridges state-citizen and other class and ethnicity fault lines.

Women are configured into this not as actors but as the site itself. Women have *izzat* (respect), *sharm* (shame), *haya* (modesty), but not *ghairat* (honor); they are the site where honor is asserted, and hence their actions can result in a loss of honor for men but not in gain of it for themselves. Women, however, are part of nations. Given the near-complete hegemony of the idea of the nation state as a global political construct and its intrinsic liberal conception of citizens' equality, this creates a conundrum: women were not party to the original (heuristic) social contract but were subject to it and the object of it, yet they are still consenting partners in secondary (material) contracts. While women inhabit the physical base of the state, they operate primarily in the private realm, which the state does not govern or protect directly, and they have little interface with institutional expressions of the state, because in the original position they are not consenting parties to the idea of the state and, in fact, constitute the site of consent itself.

How then do women engage as citizens of the nation state? What happens when they enter a political arena when they were in themselves an arena in earlier configurations? This essay finds explicatory strength in the sociological insights of Pierre Bourdieu,[5] whose framework understands power processes as operating from a basis of consensus, or rather, "acquiescence." It allows for breaking away from the structure-agency dichotomy by focusing more on the full process taking place at the agent level, explaining how the actor may simultaneously be discontent, uneasy, and compliant, as well as take strategic action.

Bourdieu terms *field* as the site of struggle for power between the dominant and the subordinate. In a variety of semi-autonomous fields, there is perpetual competition to amass maximum capital—material, symbolic, and cultural. Participation requires shared commitment to field-specific capital, and who inhabits it is a contest to establish legitimate domination within the field. The nation state in Pakistan can be understood as a competitive field because it was grafted on to different preexisting nations, ethnicities, languages, cultures, and identities. Therefore, the idea of a singular nation corresponding with representation through a singular state led to competition between nations and sub-national identities over who defines and represents the singular nation. Since there is no internal political consensus over the idea of the state, cohesion remains absent, and, in this conflictive terrain, citizenship is the symbolic capital to be accrued.

Habitus for Bourdieu is the internalized schema through which the world is perceived, understood, and evaluated.[6] It is also the mental structure that allows "society to be deposited in persons in the form of lasting dispositions or trained capacities and structured propensities to think, feel and act in determinant ways."[7] Habitus explains how certain behaviors or beliefs become part of a society's structure when the original purpose of those behaviors or beliefs can no longer be recalled and become socialized into individuals of that culture. The social contract that regulates use of force by creating spheres of violence and granting impunity within them forms part of the habitus. The historic marginality of women in power arrangements forms the consciousness of both men and women. Women enter this field disadvantaged because of their habitus as women, while men enter it relatively empowered by their habitus as men—even when compromised by their other identities. This creates within the field of the nation state a continuum of citizenship, with different actors situated in proximity and distance on it. Rather than in spatial terms, this essay suggests that it is here in this field that the center and periphery of the state are determined.

The Pakistani nation state is the field of contestation where different groups vie for claim over the nation state. Women as a group exist on the margins of the field, whether the indicators are women's use of tangible symbols such as identity cards, invocation of basic rights, access to the voting system and courts of law, or measured through elusive personal investments that create communities of belonging, such as nationalism, ownership of elected representatives, and consciousness of relational ties. Citizenship is not a level playing field but a continuum, where women are positioned in the peripheries by habitus and may either stay at the fringe or begin to move inward, toward the center. To do so, women must derive symbolic capital from other fields, such as class, ethnicity, profession, and livelihood to change their position within the field of the nation state and even begin to compete for the symbolic capital that denotes citizenship. Bourdieu's actors are not denied agency, counter to some critiques, but positions of innocence. In this framework it is not possible for women to compete in the field without accepting the rules of the field—resistance requires some degree of complicity in the power structures. Class privilege is a common criticism against the women's movement in Pakistan, which remains "state-centric" in its appeals for equality, just as having kinship ties to male politicians is the common criticism of women politicians. Writing of upper- and middle-class women in Pakistan, Shahnaz Rouse states, "They were clearly involved in a struggle over their position and location in the public and private realms; but the articulation of their struggles within and as a response to, existent social and sexual norms often led to a confrontation with and reproduction of the very structures women were challenging. . . . While they were not excluded from public or state apparati, the emphasis was on women's differential insertion into them."[8]

Alternately, women have the choice of exiting the field entirely. Those who cannot draw on symbolic capital of other fields—the abjectly poor women, the rural, marginalized women across Pakistan—circumvent the state and state institutions. They prefer arranged *watta satta/badal* marriages (in which a woman's brother is married to her husband's sister) to preempt domestic violence; if her husband inflicts suffering on her, his sister suffers the same fate as revenge by the woman's brother, ensuring a balance of power. They agree to marriages within the family and turn to heads of their family/tribe/caste rather than approach the police or judiciary unless their lives are threatened. Marriages become a tool of governance in absence of state institutions, in which marital choices configure social mobility, residence, access to water, joint family manual labor for economies of scale, and political voting blocs. Withdrawing from claims of citizenship, however, still leaves these women vulnerable as combative actors in the fields of family, culture, and tradition, because they can leverage little symbolic capital there either.

The common invocation of the lack of "political will" to bring about substantive change is therefore not a reference to a monolithic, rational, conscious, organic state, nor to a de-centered, fragmented one, but to the instinctive recognition of field and habitus. Through interactions with the poorest of women across rural areas of Pakistan, it seems that they have an intuitive understanding of this field. They do not attribute structural issues to the *riyaasat* (state) but speak instead of the asymmetrical *nizaam* (order). So when the once all-important ex–Federal Information Minister Sherry Rehman of the Pakistan Peoples Party (PPP) vowed to take concrete steps for women's empowerment, it was less indicative of development trajectories than a statement by the head of a marginal portfolio, Federal Minister for Postal Services, Israrullah Zehri, who defended honor killing as essential to tribal culture and tradition. Similarly, General Musharraf's mantra under his presidency—"moderate enlightenment"—was suspect, with his one (aberrational and even then retracted) statement about women wanting to get raped for foreign passports believed by most to be the "true face" of the regime.

While social actions do reconstitute structures of domination, this happens within and through the process of social change. Habitus "is not fixed or permanent, and can be changed under unexpected situations or over a long historical period,"[9] in part due to the dialectic between common-sense perceptions and actual experiences and the resistance within these interstices. It is these sudden or unexpected situations that allow the center-periphery paradigm to be challenged.

Introduction of alternate governance models that change the premise of state-society relations could be such unfactored determinants. If consensus emerges on alternative configurations, it could replace the need for "domestic" intrastate violence, and the state could withdraw the impunity men retain for domestic violence in the private sphere. It is only once congruence is assumed between the people and the state that the state develops the social legitimacy to intervene in order to offer protection in the space of the people—the private sphere—changing the terms of its social contract. With powers of ideation and consent, the state's reliance on domestic force declines as does its need to permit spheres of violence, because the impunity it derives from the community of interest legitimizing and endorsing the moral code becomes irrelevant.

This chapter reflects on one such possible entry point in Pakistan today: devolution. While the procedural changes via the Eighteenth Amendment relate to bureaucratic rearrangements, the basic purpose is to diffuse power so decision making can take place at points physically closer to the level of implementation instead of administrative concentration in the country's capital. This has been a longstanding demand of nationalist political parties and leaders in Sindh, Balochistan, and Khyber-Pukhtunkhwa. Opposition to concentric federal powers has highlighted the distance between political authorities and subjects. Dispensing with arguments that all decision making is under federal control and that provincial government are "puppets," empowered provincial governments could increase ownership by the people. In the long term this could contribute toward viability of alternative political models, such as the multi-nation state.

The modern state's monopoly of violence is premised on a fundamental shift to the nation state because, via representation, it allowed the state/central authority simultaneously to straddle both spheres: the governors and the governed. Pakistan, as pointed out earlier, is a state with many nations, and religious identity has not succeeded in erasing other sub-national identities. The proximate political structure that can allow congruence between the governors and the governed is devolving state power to structures most contiguous (though not entirely) to parameters of sub-nations—the provinces. They are better positioned locations for ideation and internal consent around it. A more representative political authority structure can then delegitimize other spheres of violence because it does not need violence to interpellate citizens as subjects. Citizens are in ideational sync, whether ideological, identity-based, or through shared vision.

Diffusion of state power to representative and inclusive political authority structures can bridge the difference between the governor and the governed; between the nation and the state; among the *mulk*, the *watan,* and the *qaum.* This would change the substance of legitimacy of the state from its current legalistic form to one that has social resonance and acceptance—taking on attributes of the nation state, and challenging private loci of violence that allow for the existence of the anti-women positions of the male community councils like the *jirga*, community-sanctioned honor killings, familial constraints on mobility, and domestic violence. As institutional expressions of the state, decentralized representative and participatory political structures can inhabit both, the state itself and the interior, inner space of the private sphere, the society. Their creation also potentially changes the center-periphery continuum by altering the field of the nation state itself. The state may be better positioned to bring the margins into the fold of citizenship by bridging the distance, creating new forms of symbolic capital to be gained. It may also be among the "unexpected situations" that change habitus, though the change would not be structural without changing the social contract itself. While the causal pathway is indirect, and possibly even an overreach, it may offer a way of approaching the insidious, deeply gendered structures that the plethora of development interventions do not even begin to scratch the surface of. I tentatively argue that the current debate in Pakistan over devolution, cast in the center-periphery paradigm, suggests that the tectonic plates of the country's power structures are shifting and may offer new possibilities to address violence against women. Whether the state then goes on actually to revoke such impunity or not is a deferred debate—the contention here is that as things stand currently, the state cannot do so because it simply lacks the social legitimacy to do so. The acceptability of the state is built on a gendered social contract, and till it finds another set of terms for engagement, it cannot isolate and change one of the pillars of the compact: violence against women in the private sphere. Simply put, the state cannot act against domestic violence till it stops using domestic violence itself.[10]

This chapter builds a case for a gendered theory of politics that situates domestic violence as a core political issue and gender as an organizing principle of the state. It proposes as an analytic lens a continuum of citizenship; in addition, it proposes that gender relations form part of the structural and ideological grid upon which state power is based. That grid has class, ethnic, and gendered content, and it is not fixed but constantly in flux, reflecting the struggles that take place both within and outside the state. The social contract recounted in this chapter indicates that the issue is not as much about state presence versus lack of writ of state as it is about what state penetration means—direct enforcement in centers, versus state's powers subcontracted out to other masculinist hierarchies in the peripheries, as positioned on the continuum of citizenship.

Violence and the peace deficit are among the main challenges to development in Pakistan—ranging from gender-based violence to ethnic and faith-based militancy and use of force by state institutions. In exploring the spectrum of violence within the country, this essay analytically separates acts of violence from the legitimacy of violence, concentrating on the latter, and finds it undergirded by impunity. Violence is legitimized by a warped democratization that distributes entitlement to violence between state and men, operationalized through a social contract that benefits both the dominant and the subordinate by creating terms of consent. In keeping with the feminist contention that violence is central to the maintenance of patriarchal order, this chapter shows that the configuration of state-society relations rests on authorizing enclaves of violence to create a shared moral order. As long as that configuration of state-society relations remains intact, impunity to violence will continue. The essential prerequisite to overcoming development challenges is changing the compact by bridging the gaps among the state, the nation, and society.

Notes

1. David Beetham, *The Legitimation of Power*, Issues in Political Theory Series, series ed. Peter Jones and Albert Weale (London: MacMillan, 1991).

2. This refers to the separation of East Pakistan and the statehood of Bangladesh after much violence and war, showing religion was not enough to cement together a nation, even in Pakistan.

3. Julieta Kirkwood, discussed in Lessie Jo Frazier, "Medicalizing Human Rights and Domesticating Violence in Postdictatorship Market-States," in *Violence and the Body: Race, Gender and the State*, ed. Arturo J. Aldama, 388–403 (Bloomington: Indiana University Press, 2003), 397.

4. Julieta Kirkwood, *Feminarios* (Santiago: Ediciones Documentas, 1987), translated and quoted by Sonia E. Alvarez, *Engendering Democracy in Brazil: Women's Movements in Transition Politics* (Princeton, NJ: Princeton University Press, 1990), 7.

5. See Pierre Bourdieu, *Outline of a Theory of Practice*, Cambridge Studies in Social and Cultural Anthropology (Cambridge: Cambridge University Press, 1977).

6. Habitus is created by the interplay of structure and agency; it consists of dispositions shaped by past events but is also conditioned by our perception of these (ibid., 170). Acquired as the result of occupation of a position in the social world, different positions would have a different habitus. It is a way of analyzing how social relations become constituted within the self, but also how the self is constitutive of social relations. As Bourdieu defines it, "The habitus—embodied history, internalized as second nature and so forgotten as history—is the active presence of the whole past of which it is the product" (ibid.). As habitus is also generative, dominant groups constitute new forms of patriarchies, even when ostensibly challenging them.

7. Loic Wacquant, "Habitus," in *International Encyclopedia of Economic Sociology*, ed. J. Becket and Z. Milan (London: Routledge, 2005).

8. Shahnaz Rouse, *Shifting Body Politics: Gender, Nation and State in Pakistan* (New Delhi: Women Unlimited, 2004).

9. Zander Navarro, "In Search of a Cultural Interpetation of Power: The Contribution of Pierre Bourdieu," *IDS Bulletin* 37/6 (November 2006): 17.

10. While this chapter focuses on Pakistan, preliminary thoughts about other countries also bear out this logic. Most countries introduced and implemented laws against domestic violence only after rebellious uprisings against the state were quashed or curbed and mainstreamed. Only once states stopped using violence to regulate their own citizens did they intervene to offer protection within the private sphere.

14

Pakistan's Political Development

Will the Future Be Like the Past?

ASHLEY J. TELLIS

Pakistan's short history is littered with repeated failures of political development. The justification for this claim is self-evident: since achieving statehood in 1947, the country has had three constitutions, witnessed four military coups, and experienced a regular alternation of civilian and military governments wherein no representative dispensation has yet actually served out its full term in office. Missing from the beginning of Pakistan's crisis-filled past to today has been the key to political development—institutionalization, or the creation of norms, structures, and patterns of behavior that are conducive to the peaceful production of political order, economic growth, and social justice through representative instruments of rule. The result has been a trail of corrosive consequences that plague Pakistan to this day.

The conventional wisdom about Pakistan's ills often attributes its stunted political development to the pernicious effects of the military's domination of its political life. This conventional wisdom is not wrong, but it is incomplete. The chief cause of Pakistan's problems is not military control per se, but rather bureaucratic domination—of which military rule is only one of many problematic species. The notion of bureaucratic rule, in this context, refers to "the form of rule in which the elite is composed of officials,"[1] and, by extension, it implies the oligarchic exercise of power by trained individuals-in-organization, either civilian or military, whose principal distinctiveness is their expertise rather than their selection through electoral procedures that designate the collective choice of the polity. As evidenced by the history of Pakistan's weak political institutionalization, the usurpation of political power by the bureaucrats began long before the first declaration of martial law in 1958, thereby suggesting that the repeated bouts of military authoritarianism—1958–71, 1977–88, and 1999–2008—represent only the apotheosis, rather than the font, of compromised authority in Pakistan.

Pakistan's stunted political development is rooted in the choices made by its founders, who, when confronted by a set of unfavorable political circumstances, made the fateful decision to attempt to resolve their conundrums by accepting bureaucratic rule as the way out of their troubles. As a result of those initial decisions, key bureaucratic actors—the military, the intelligence services, and their allies in the civil services—were able to slowly coalesce and progressively form a Pakistani "deep state" that controls decision making related to key aspects of the nation's life: the allocation of financial resources for state endeavors, including those available to the military; the character of the nuclear weapons program; the nature of foreign relations with a few critical countries; the "grand strategy" of the country at large; the sponsorship of civilian proxies in domestic politics; and the freedom of action permitted to civilian governments when in power and to other "public associations in civil life," in de Tocqueville's phrase.[2]

Control over these arenas of political activity has remained durably in the hands of the bureaucratic formations for two reasons: first, the unelected bureaucracies can leverage their control of state resources to extend their own silent rule; and second, they have been able to negotiate a tacit social compact that secures the support of the "establishment"—a small conservative elite in society, composed of mostly agrarian landowners but sometimes supplemented by other industrial and commercial interests.

Together, this social compact perched itself at the apex of the Pakistani state and has remained there since, occasionally in a military guise but always aided by allies in the civil services. The consequences for Pakistan have been ruinous. When rule by cabal becomes the norm and executive power is exercised by unelected bureaucracies whose decisions cannot be reviewed, contested, or countermanded through the normal instruments of competitive politics, that power increasingly comes to serve mainly the interests of a small privileged group that is not accountable to the country at large. The evidence accumulated over the last sixty years of Pakistan's history suggests that the country's multifaceted deficiencies—at the level of governance, social change, economic management, and foreign and strategic policy—are all deeply rooted in its core failure of political development.[3] The comprehensive domination by unrepresentative bureaucracies has proved unable to resolve the nation's constitutional dilemmas, to settle conclusively the ideological bases of Pakistan's legitimation, or to relieve the country's external challenges. In fact, the record suggests that bureaucratic domination probably exacerbated the hazards on all three counts. And by so doing, it not only created the preconditions for repeated usurpations of power subsequently but also, and more dangerously, strengthened the perception of oligarchic seizures as the "normal" exit from all failures of constitutional politics.

These shortcomings cannot be remedied overnight, given the consolidation of bureaucratic rule that has occurred over many decades, but the solution—if and when it comes—will not materialize until the development of an appropriate democratic order that is centered on genuine civilian rule governed by a constitutional framework with appropriate checks and balances. This "fix" has numerous entailments, ranging from the need for a liberal and modern political culture, to vibrant mass political parties that are programmatic in orientation and democratic in internal structure, to new civil society institutions that represent both hitherto marginalized groups and alternative economic interests. These requirements imply that Pakistan's political transformation cannot occur merely as a result of alterations in the "superstructure" of the political system, but rather will be part and parcel of the larger processes of social change and economic development, which must involve transmutations in class structure, the growth of a modernizing bourgeoisie and the expansion of the trading classes, and the rise of new interest groups in Pakistani politics.

In short, representative democracy is the key. What threatens to retard this remedy, however, is the tenacious endurance of the bureaucratic deep state. Its continued dominance is self-perpetuating, and whether in civilian or in military guise, bureaucratic power ensures that genuine representative institutions cannot either take root or grow deep roots in Pakistani soil. Even when civilian regimes occasionally appear in Pakistan, they are permitted to govern, but never to rule. Andrew Wilder summarized the nature of the problem succinctly when he noted:

> The fundamental electoral dilemma confronting Pakistan's ruling elites since Independence has been how to accommodate the legacy of rule by elected representatives without threatening the legacy of bureaucratic rule. The objective has always been to hold elections that would legitimate but not change the status quo.[4]

Because this dilemma has never been satisfactorily resolved, even representative governments—on the occasions they have appeared—have been unable to set Pakistan's political development on sturdy and lasting foundations. The magnitude of the constraints besetting them is emblematized by the fact that not once in Pakistan's history has a civilian government served out its complete term. In every instance, civilian dispensations have had their tenures in office truncated by authoritarian overlords because of various perceived failings. And, in every instance, civilian governments *have* indeed behaved in exactly the disappointing fashion that the apologists of bureaucratic rule have always accused them of. These pathologies, however, do not derive merely from the venality of civilian politicians as is often supposed—though that exists in plenty too—but rather from three constraining circumstances.

First, the ever-present threat of military intervention has compelled civilian regimes to focus, when in office, primarily on self-preservation, thus dulling their capacity to take any bold initiatives because of the fear that promoting consequential change—especially one that alters the internal balance of power within the state—might run afoul of key bureaucratic actors and thereby provoke the government's demise.

Second, the persistent presence of shadowy bureaucratic power has distorted the competition among civilian politicians themselves by creating opportunities for rivals to appeal not to the electorate to adjudicate political differences but to the army and its allies, which then manipulate such contentiousness in order to strengthen their own hold on power.

Third, the uncertainty surrounding the survival of civilian governments, when they do appear episodically in office, induces them to focus—quite rationally—on self-enrichment rather than on good governance, because a quick expropriation of state and societal resources is perceived as occult compensation for a truncated term in office while bequeathing transient gains that promise to advantage its possessors in the power struggles to come.

The cumulative consequence of such behaviors has been the maladministration witnessed every time civilian governments take office in Pakistan. These failures, in turn, have provoked repeated military intervention that, at least initially, is aimed at cleaning out the rot, often to the relief of the body politic. In time, however, these bureaucratic usurpations outlive their welcome as the military rulers of the day find themselves incapable of managing the enduring challenges of satisfying popular demands for political voice and economic development. Before long, these regimes too decay amid returning public resentment and are replaced by another iteration of civilian governance, surrounded by widespread aspirations for change, but the cycle continues once again, drearily, as before.

This continual alternation between nominal civilian rule and formal bureaucratic seizures of power exemplifies the enduring legacy produced by the initial undermining of civilian authority at the time of Pakistan's founding. At that time powerful political interests in the new country were determined not to surrender their power by becoming subject to genuine majoritarian rule, and their machinations resulted in the failure to consolidate early a constitutionalism that ensured that all political disputes would be addressed solely by reference to the people. This failure created a hard-to-reverse tradition that enshrined the bureaucratic "rescue" of democratic politics as a legitimate—and, in time, increasingly expected—means of managing political problems, even though the real challenges to national direction, far from being resolved, were only progressively aggravated by such solutions.

It might be tempting to think that the allure of such remedies has been laid to rest in Pakistan because of the stable presence of the current representative government led by President Asif Ali Zardari, which has been in office since 2008. This impression is misleading on two counts. First, for all the activism characterizing civilian politics in Pakistan, Zardari's government still does not control the nation's fundamental direction. Important decisions pertaining to policy, both in the external and the domestic arenas, are still made by the bureaucracies constituting the deep state, with representative institutions either compelled to accept the prevailing realities or at best to legitimize them by providing tacit or token "consent."

Furthermore, when the Zardari government appeared weak and incapable—as was the case in the months leading up to the U.S. military action in Abbottabad—not only did individual politicians (some within Zardari's party itself) encourage the army to consider autocratic replacements of leading government officials, but there was also a remarkable willingness on the part of the Army's chief of staff, General Ashfaq Parvez Kayani, to contemplate a constitutional coup d'état as a solution. Only the embarrassment inflicted on the Pakistan Army and its bureaucratic allies by the U.S. military mission against Osama bin Laden provided Zardari's regime with a reprieve—though whether Zardari is capable of utilizing his renewed freedom to maneuver to restore the credibility of democratic rule and set Pakistan's political development on a surer footing remains an open question.

Even contemporary events, therefore, suggest that authoritarian interventions still remain persistently attractive as solutions to Pakistan's maladies of political development. The analysis offered by one scholar early in the last decade, thus, remains both prescient and relevant:

> Ironically, sections of the "attentive public" [that] are still counting on the military to deliver the elusive desideratum of good governance . . . forget that Pakistan's crisis of governance stems in large part from the formidable political power and influence of an autonomous military establishment, with clear corporate interests, superimposed on civil society and the political scene. The military's entrenched hegemony over civilian affairs has dictated the "do's and don'ts" of government in Pakistan for more than 50 years. While it is true that civilian

governments in post-Zia Pakistan did make matters worse, they had little room to maneuver in the face of overwhelming policy constraints imposed by heavy debt and defense burdens, the demands of political survival, and an overbearing military establishment working at odds with its civilian bosses as it pursued its own political, security, and foreign policy agendas.

In the long run, Pakistan's political stability depends on the restoration of an uninterrupted democratic process, as does any chance of real institutional reform. No single group, be it the military officer corps, the politicians, or the bureaucratic elite, can or will reform Pakistan on its own. Sustained reforms will require public pressure exerted through representative public institutions. Only by embedding democracy in society can the capacity and incentives for reform be created. The long term governance gains from political democracy, though uncertain and reversible, will far outweigh any short-term gains in administrative efficiency that might accrue from military-style "surgical measures."[5]

This argument suggests that any reform effort that attempts to attack Pakistan's complex problems through reliance on bureaucratic devices will only produce temporary palliatives that actually retard larger national evolution, as demonstrated by the repeated, alternating episodes of weak civilian governments interspersed amid formal military rule.

The critical analytical question at this juncture, however, is whether Pakistan's future political development will be different from its troubled past. Many observers believe that there are two emergent grounds for qualified optimism: the rise of a vibrant and often rambunctious media and civil society, and the promising reassertion of prerogatives by a now-confident judiciary. Both developments are undoubtedly welcome, because they move toward the creation of alternative centers of influence in a state otherwise choked by unresponsive bureaucracies.

Both institutions have already made an important difference in Pakistan's political life. The media have been an indispensable forum for debate where all manner of opinions find expression and, to that degree, support the growth of civil society. Yet, the chaotic effervescence that characterizes the Pakistani media today disguises critical weaknesses from the viewpoint of advancing political development. The media in Pakistan still remain incredibly dependent on the state as a source of information and, where the printed press is concerned, as a source of revenue as well. The capacity for analysis and critical assessment is unacceptably low in general, with the Urdu press in particular often being little other than an echo chamber for nationalist propaganda.

Even the elite press, however, remains more often than not highly susceptible to pressure from state organs, such as the military and the intelligence agencies; lacking alternative sources of information, it becomes a de facto conduit for the party line fostered by the establishment. Above all else, the media and civil society organizations more generally appear capable of transiently mobilizing social power when political conditions veer toward desperation, but they lack the endurance, consistency, organization, and, ultimately, the power to transform the deep structure of the Pakistani state. Whether they possess the appropriate *weltanschauung* that values liberal democracy is also unclear; the approbation offered by some elements of the Pakistani public to Mumtaz Qadri in the aftermath of his assassination of the Punjab governor, Salmaan Taseer, raises uncomfortable doubts about whether civil society can be an unambiguous vanguard of political transformation in Pakistan.

Similarly, the recent resurgence of the higher judiciary in Pakistani politics is a welcome development after many decades of abnegation. After numerous judicial decisions that legitimized the serial military usurpations of power—which the judiciary was admittedly powerless to prevent—the current apex court in Pakistan has attempted to retrieve the previously lost powers of judicial review and to enforce the fundamental rights of the citizenry in the face of executive abuses. In so doing, its actions at various moments have threatened the stability of the current civilian government because its "constructionist" approach to remedying both past mutilations of the Pakistani constitution and the previous political deals that brought the current crop of leaders back into the power were at odds with the necessities of stability.

The court's new and energetic self-insertion into a wide set of issues ranging from enforcing minimum-wage laws to modifying commodity price caps to revoking carbon taxes has raised understandable fears about the problems likely to ensue from such judicial activism. Such a crisis was narrowly averted early on when the court, in response to its *suo moto* review of the Eighteenth Amendment, finally accepted, despite its displeasure with certain individual articles, the proposition that the power to amend the constitution lies solely with the people of Pakistan as expressed through their elected representatives in Parliament.

While this decision certainly demonstrated the court's maturity and protected its credibility initially as an arbiter of the constitutional balance, it is still uncertain—given its later judgments in the reopening of the corruption cases against President Asif Ali Zardari—whether the current resurgence of judicial power will become a permanent—or a desirable—feature of Pakistani politics. More important, it is also unclear whether the higher judiciary's renewed assertiveness will transcend the personalities presently on the bench and mutate into a real constitutionalism that is capable of both slowly rolling back bureaucratic dominance and preventing military usurpations of power in the future—or whether it will evolve into merely another bureaucratic chokehold, albeit in different guise. Whether the court can lay the foundations for strengthened representative rule through strong protection of individual rights, effective checks and balances among different organs of government, and a robust system of prerogative writs, remains a fundamentally open question today. The claims made by the current leadership of the Supreme Court, which assert expansive judicial prerogatives in the name of constitutional supremacy, actually threaten to negate the power (and undermine the conduct) of representative government, thereby setting back the cause of resuscitating democratic rule in Pakistan—all in the name of protecting democracy. Even if the worst dangers on this score were to be avoided, the fact remains that the lower judiciary in Pakistan is still overburdened, ineffective, and unable to provide impartial justice in response to legitimate grievances for a whole host of institutional and procedural reasons, again leaving considerable doubt as to whether the most utilized elements of the judicial system can help reverse the disillusionment with secular state institutions in the country.

At the moment, therefore, it is too early to conclude that the media and the judiciary will be successful in the manner necessary for representative rule to thrive in Pakistan. Even if they are, they remain surrounded by numerous other factors that offer considerable grounds for pessimism about the larger success of democracy.

First, bureaucratic power in Pakistan has become deeply entrenched in wide swaths of public life in a manner hitherto unprecedented—in politics, in economics, and in society—and none of the traditional devices for weakening its chokehold—military defeat, political failure, or social revolution—either appears on the horizon or could be considered desirable even if it did. The Pakistan Army, as the historical record illustrates, has suffered repeated military defeats—in 1965, 1971, and 1999—leading to its political discredit on many occasions; while these outcomes have forced a transient lightening of praetorian pressure, they have never produced a permanent retrenchment that has allowed genuinely representative governance to take root.

Ironically, the episodic presence of representative government, even when ineffective and unable to wrest control of national policy comprehensively, has turned out to be one of the key elements deterring social uprisings of the kind now witnessed in the Arab world. The simulacrum of democracy has provided enough of an outlet for popular resentment to blow steam, while its effigy ensures that the underlying structures of power and privilege lie undamaged. The demise of labor as a social force in Pakistan, the overwhelming power of the agricultural elite in the rural areas, the presence of a relatively weak middle class, and a virtually nonexistent intelligentsia, have only made social revolutions even more distant.

As a result, whenever "mass" political mobilizations in Pakistan have occurred, they have been propelled by disgust with the government of the day, whether civilian or military, and have sought only its replacement within the existing framework rather than a thorough renovation of the entire regime, as usually occurs in a social revolution. Pakistan's weak democracy, paradoxically, has therefore been effective enough to prevent revolution, even if it has been otherwise incapable of producing good governance.

Second, Pakistan's continued enmeshment in external conflicts with India and Afghanistan, as well as in internal wars with various insurgents and jihadi groups previously sponsored by the state, only reinforces the durability of bureaucratic power, especially military institutions. The prospect that Islamabad will be able to negotiate successfully an end to its rivalries with New Delhi and Kabul appears highly unlikely in the near term; if anything, the continued crisis in Afghanistan ensures that the relations among these three states will remain highly unsettled. The prospective security transition in Afghanistan, occurring as a result of the drawdown in U.S. military forces, will likely intensify the competition involving Afghanistan, Pakistan, and India (not to mention Iran and the Central Asian republics) even further, making the role of the Pakistan Army and its intelligence services even more central in Pakistani politics as the struggle over "strategic depth" in the West continues unabated.

To complicate matters further, the decrease in American forces in southern Asia does not by any means presage a reduction in Washington's counterterrorism operations in the region. On the contrary, the U.S. military is likely to stay engaged in military operations in the borderlands between Afghanistan and Pakistan for the remainder of this decade, a task that will involve both "kinetic" missions on Pakistani territory and training and support for security forces in Afghanistan. The upshot of all these activities is that the Pakistani military will remain enthroned at the heart of decision making within the state as conflict and insecurity further cement its continued primacy to the detriment of the elected arms of state and other civilian institutions.

Third, despite the likelihood that the current civilian government will be the first in Pakistan's history to complete its term—an inadvertent consequence of the military's humiliation due to the Abbottabad raid—the human terrain supporting democratic renewal does not look inspiring. Although there are many political figures of admirable rectitude in Pakistan, they are for most part second- or third-tier leaders in their political parties. The exceptions to this rule are found in Islamic parties, such as the Jamaat-i-Islami, but the mainstream parties are distinguished by a conspicuous absence of charismatic *and* competent civilian leaders capable of building confidence in a democratic consolidation that permits slowly wresting power away from the bureaucracy.

Because all the major Pakistani political parties are still primarily patrimonial rather than agenda driven and internally democratic, competent auxiliary leaders are inevitably prevented from rising to the top to shape their political direction. As a result, even these nominally representative institutions end up highly ossified, focused more on rent-seeking behaviors than on transforming the vestigial "viceregal" system when in power.

Fourth, the liberal political culture pervasive in Pakistan at its founding, despite all the contemporary struggles over its ideological coloration, has now dangerously eroded as a whole. The rise of highly conservative strains of Islam imported from the Middle East, which are quite suspicious of both liberal politics and representative rule, has made it harder for the supporters of democracy to thrive. Although these elements are still contested by large numbers of Pakistanis, the latter's freedom of maneuver has gradually decreased over time.

The various state-supported efforts at Islamization over the years, which now find manifestation in blasphemy laws and the Hudood Ordinance, strengthen a culture that constrains human rights and raises questions about the quality of democracy that may finally triumph in Pakistan. Most dangerous of all, the still resilient affinity between some anti-democratic Islamist elements in Pakistani politics and the military bureaucracy for multiple internal and external reasons—despite the ongoing campaign against other Islamist threats along the western border—vitiates the hope that the dominant state institutions see value in supporting the comprehensive triumph of moderate social forces.

Fifth, and finally, Pakistan appears condemned to face substantial economic stress in the foreseeable future. For reasons that vary from injurious competition with India to the enervating domination of agrarian elites in Pakistan, the nation's economy has failed to either diversify or modernize, leaving it highly dependent on agricultural exports, external remittances, and foreign aid for state revenue. The thin tax base in Pakistan, which is owed entirely to its constrictive political economy, has prevented the country from making the kinds of public investments in power production and water management—not to mention public health and education—that would have been essential to sustain growth.

As a result, Pakistan is likely to face significant crises in the coming years at least in energy production and flood control, both of which threaten to undermine the agricultural system that underpins the domestic economy as well as foreign trade. The slower growth of the international economy in the aftermath of the financial crisis could also constrain the increase in external remittances—which will be essential by way of compensation, given the problems besetting other domestic revenue streams—while the intensifying political difficulties in U.S.-Pakistan relations because of terrorism and Afghanistan could result in a diminution of foreign assistance at a time when Pakistan might need it the most.

Although Pakistan's size, population, and nuclear weaponry make it a state "too important to fail"—and hence will likely assure continued international assistance at some level—the internal challenges of rapid population increases, inadequate economic growth, and restricted foreign investment all combine to suggest that the country's economic performance is not likely to improve dramatically in the coming decade. The prospect that Pakistan will therefore lurch from crisis to crisis—caused, if nothing else, by continued economic stress and enduring resource constraints—implies that the propensity for any further divestiture of powers from the unelected arms of the state to representative institutions is rather low.

Under conditions of crisis, the military bureaucracy will probably attempt to protect its already high share of national resources on the grounds that its defensive capabilities become even more important when Pakistan is vulnerable, but even if this were not the case, it is unlikely to contemplate surrendering its political powers to what will still be fragile civilian governments when the country is engulfed by substantial dangers.

On balance, therefore, it appears as if Pakistan is likely to be beset by crises for a long time to come. The roots of these dangers lie in structural problems that cannot be eradicated instantaneously, even if the political will to do so existed. However, precisely because these challenges are intimately connected to the balance of power within the state and because resolving them involves eliminating the prerogatives of the dominant organs of rule, it is to be expected that even the more hopeful developments witnessed recently—the rise of the media and civil society and the resurgence of the judiciary—will be insufficient to fundamentally transform the character and the direction of the Pakistani state. In circumstances where state collapse, social revolution, and climacteric military defeat all remain unlikely possibilities—for different and even welcome reasons in each case—continuing stasis appears to be the most plausible prospective future for Pakistan and that, in turn, promises only feeble improvements in its political development.

Is there an exit from this cul-de-sac? It is possible to envisage two alternative but complementary paths, even if neither is imminent or plausible right now. The first is the rise of genuinely charismatic leaders, in the Weberian sense, who possess strong and authentic democratic commitments. If such personalities come to the fore, they could lead agenda- and broad-based political parties in effective mass mobilization that progressively wrests power away from the currently dominant bureaucracies. For this process to succeed, however, charismatic leadership—once in office—must be both effective and successful in both governance and economic management, thereby denying the bureaucracies the excuse that they must always control the reins of power because failures of popular rule remain an abiding possibility.

The second outlet is offered by possibilities in the international arena. If Pakistan were to achieve reconciliation with Afghanistan and India with regard to its outstanding disputes, the sense of siege that justifies the continued bureaucratic domination of the state would dissolve substantially, thus creating greater space for democratic forces within the state to operate and thrive. Such a transformative reconciliation, however, would require Pakistan to alter its longstanding aims and strategies toward both Kabul and New Delhi: in regard to the former, Pakistan will have to learn to live with the reality of Afghan autonomy, ceding to the Afghan state the right to choose its own policies and friends; vis-à-vis the latter, Pakistan will have to accept the current territorial status quo and the reality that it cannot match India in power, capability, or standing, and hence ought not to pursue any forms of competition that threaten regional stability and undermine its own integrity.

Additionally, with regard to both states, Pakistan will have to recognize the benefits of deeper regional integration, which advances its own national economic and political development. Both Afghanistan and India, in turn, must adopt, singly and in collaboration, those policies that help Pakistan pursue geopolitical reconciliation, and Islamabad's international partners too must be willing to prioritize their long-term interests over short-term exigencies in their relations with Pakistan. All this is undoubtedly a tall order, but it constitutes at least in principle an exit from the current dead end that impedes Pakistan's political development.

Because the two conceivable avenues that aid Pakistan's transformation will be a long time coming, it is imperative that civilian regimes in Islamabad—despite all their real and serious imperfections—be permitted to survive undisturbed. The creation of a new tradition in which representative governments, irrespective of their efficacy, remain in office and are replaced only through constitutional processes by other representative dispensations exploits time to create a new tradition that slowly abrades the deleterious consequences of the original decision to permit bureaucratic capture of political decision making.

If a convention that bureaucratic rule is unacceptable under any circumstances slowly develops in Pakistan, the prospect of military usurpations, the traditional bête noire, or judicial arrogation, the newest deformity, will gradually diminish as the recognition of their intrinsic illegitimacy becomes universal; the extant temptation of civilian politicians to appeal to bureaucratic power to constrain their opponents will also progressively diminish if such interventions cannot deliver office as before; and the pernicious practice by civilian leaders of raiding state resources immediately upon taking the helm will also disappear once it is recognized that their terms cannot be cut short except by legitimate constitutional means and that there will always be opportunities for a lawful return to office so long as they deliver on their promises to the electorate. For all these reasons, persisting with representative governance, however inefficient and frustrating right now, is imperative, because it alone provides lasting hope for the slow recovery of the democratic power that was first lost immediately after Pakistan's formation as a new state.

The recognition that such an outcome is necessary for the permanent success of Pakistan's political development does not mean that it will materialize. To imagine so would be to fall victim to the fallacy of voluntarism. The structural factors conspiring against stable and genuine representative rule in Pakistan are indeed formidable. Although a slow improvement in the salience, quality, and worth of representative institutions is likely to obtain—if Pakistan's luck holds amid the corrosive countervailing trends—the nation, most likely, will still be unable to overturn or undermine the hitherto robust domination of unelected bureaucracies any time soon. The upshot of this reality, unfortunately, will be continued political, social, economic, and strategic challenges, outcomes that persist because all the agents involved will make individually rational decisions that nonetheless produce systemically suboptimal results. Consequently—and regrettably—the future of Pakistan's political development will likely resemble its troubled past.

Notes

1. Harold D. Lasswell and Abraham Kaplan, *Power and Society: A Framework for Political Inquiry* (New Haven, CT: Yale University Press, 1950), 209.

2. Alexis de Tocqueville, *Democracy in America*, vol. 2 (New York: Vintage Books, 1945), 114.

3. These deficiencies are summarized in Ashley J. Tellis, "U.S. Strategy: Assisting Pakistan's Transformation," *The Washington Quarterly* 28/1 (2004): 97–116.

4. Andrew R. Wilder, *The Pakistani Voter: Electoral Politics and Voting Behavior in the Punjab* (Karachi: Oxford University Press, 1999), 17.

5. Aqil Shah, "Democracy on Hold in Pakistan," *Journal of Democracy* 13/1 (January 2002): 74–75.

15

The Intersection of Development, Politics, and Security

Moeed Yusuf

When it comes to examining the Pakistani state's priorities in the development and security arenas, Pakistan can hardly be characterized as a normal country. One of the world's largest countries in terms of population, Pakistan presents a dismal picture across virtually all meaningful development indicators even as it boasts a strong military and a nuclear weapons capability. Volumes have been written by scholars attempting to explain this anomaly. Most have come out criticizing the military for its domination of politics and its tendency to stifle genuine debate on a vision for the state.[1] These analyses often bank on the military's vested organizational interests—broadly speaking—as the explanation for the relative negligence of the development needs and the failure of the political elite to reign supreme. The interaction among development, politics, and security then is seen as a military-dominated enterprise where this powerful institution safeguards its vested institutional interests above any other.

The argument in this chapter does not necessarily disagree with the fact that the military's behavior underpins the development-security anomaly in Pakistan's case. However, it goes beyond the purely organizational argument that portrays the military as deliberately manipulating the environment in a Machiavellian manner for its own gains. The chapter develops a constructivist explanation, rooted in a threat from an external actor—India—and its internalization by a military that exhibits a "guardian" mindset. The military is seen less as an institution deliberately seeking to maximize its own gains as its primary concern and more as an entity that is convinced of its own sincerity to Pakistan's cause but is not nearly as certain that other national institutions are equally sincere. As the argument is developed, the military is seen as exhibiting misplaced nationalism—defined as the need for Pakistan to hold its own against India above all other concerns of the state—but one that it truly believes serves the country's best interest. The outcome: an obsession with India, internalized benignly by the military as a necessity given Pakistan's regional environment, has forced the country to be overly focused on its physical security, to the detriment of its socioeconomic development and the well-being of its people. It is this dynamic that is responsible for much of the internal weaknesses for which Pakistan makes global headlines today. The domestic implications, interlinked as they are, discussed in this chapter include: (1) failure to consolidate democracy; (2) preference for "guns" over "butter"; (3) "security-centric" foreign policy and forgone regional integration; and (4) backlash in terms of anti-state militancy.

The chapter begins with a brief explanation of the "India factor" in Pakistan's thinking and a recounting of the roots of the obsession with its eastern neighbor. Next, it conducts a detailed discussion of the above-mentioned domestic distortions. I conclude by highlighting what these distortions mean for Pakistan's development-politics-security interplay and examining ways to break the deadlock, thereby opening up possibilities for transforming the present set of national priorities.

The Primacy of the "India Factor" for the Pakistani State

Since this chapter argues that it is the Pakistani military's belief, itself a function of the institution's guardian mindset, that its outlook vis-à-vis India is the only logical one, it is important to define the "India factor." Simply put, it amounts to an outright focus on ensuring that Pakistan remains independent of India's policy dictates. It is this security-centric desire to hold its own against India's overbearing presence in the region—not to fall in line with India's vision of South Asia—that is responsible for fixing attention on security as opposed to development and consolidation of democracy. To be noted, the India factor, as expounded here, is different from the more often discussed real or perceived Indian threat to Pakistan per se; the threat levels may fluctuate and their veracity can be debated at any point, but the drive to avoid falling within India's ambit of influence is both broader and more structural in nature.

In South Asia's case, India, with nearly 80 percent of the region's GDP, vast majority of the population, nearly three-fourths of the total regional exports, by far the strongest conventional military, and geographical and historical centrality in South Asia, is the natural pivot for this region. The overwhelming power differential has meant that peace and conflict in the region have largely been a function of how easily India is able to establish ties with its neighbors on terms preferential to itself. Whenever India and one of its neighbors are able to find an equilibrium that approximates the power realities of their bilateral equation, relative peace has ensued. And in every instance that one of the neighbors has tried to defy India on issues the latter considers central, tensions, crises, or worse yet, conflicts have resulted.

Ultimately, only one of India's neighbors has taken it upon itself to remain outside the sphere of India's influence. From the very outset, Pakistan has sought to affirm its presence as a state too strong to behave as "just another Nepal," as some Pakistani nationalists like to put it. Pakistan, on its own and courtesy of assistance from friends like China, has remained strong enough to avoid being forced into submission by India but not strong enough to claim equality on its own. This uneasy equation, coupled with outstanding bilateral disputes both sides consider to be much more critical and acute than those between India and its other neighbors, has led to perpetual hostility and intermittent conflict between the two sides. Indian and Pakistani attempts to redefine their relationship on terms preferable to themselves have affected domestic priorities in both countries. There is a case to be made that both New Delhi and Islamabad have had to absorb a net negative impact due to their troubled ties. This chapter, however, limits the analysis to Pakistan while noting the need for a comparative chapter on India.

Tracing the Roots of the India Factor

The primacy of the concern vis-à-vis India has been present in the Pakistani imagination since the partition of British India. The deep-seated tensions between Muslims and Hindus on the eve of partition, the role of the British in leaving key territorial issues between the two sides unresolved, the popular message of the Pakistan movement as seeking a state that relieved Muslims from the possible subjugation of the "Other"—the Hindu India—and the objective reality of segments of the Indian decision-making enclave being bitter about the creation of Pakistan all but ensured an initial preoccupation with India. The situation was not pleasant for India either, but for the weaker of the two states, which genuinely feared Indian aggression and hegemony at the beginning, an outright focus on New Delhi was all but natural.

Pakistani concerns were exacerbated by a number of threatening statements by the Indian leadership early on and subsequently, when the two sides got embroiled in a limited conflict over Kashmir less than a year after their birth. Trade ties suffered soon thereafter on grounds related to trade policies.[2] Meanwhile, as domestic political developments kept Pakistan internally weak and divided, the state became even more wary of its troubled neighborhood.

The nature of the concern regarding its eastern neighbor began to change once Pakistan had survived the first few years and there were clear signs that the Indian state had reconciled with Pakistan's independent presence next door. The discourse moved from one of survival to "otherness"—the "we were meant to have a destiny independent of India" message. This was now a Pakistani state willing to, and in its own mind capable of, staying outside India's orbit of influence, and more specifically of forcing a revision of the status quo on outstanding disputes. From here on in, periodic developments—ironically, these were often initiated by Pakistan's own policies—continued to provide reason to retain centrality of the India factor. India's intransigence on Kashmir during the 1950s and 1960s; Pakistan's botched efforts to force the issue, for example, by igniting trouble in Kashmir in 1965 and ending up in a bilateral conflict; and finally the loss of East Pakistan in 1971 only strengthened the state's view of India. The 1971 debacle was the turning point because for many it confirmed Pakistan's original concerns about India all over again. Pakistan's decision to start a nuclear weapons program shortly thereafter is perhaps the single most obvious example of the India factor playing out in decision making—it had the need to stand up to India at any cost written all over it.

Interestingly enough, in the early years the concern about India was not an outcome of any deliberate manipulation by the military per se; rather, it reflected a broad consensus among the decision-making elite. However, politico-military developments were soon to thrust the military, along with large parts of the civil bureaucracy and later some politicians, to the forefront and make them the custodians of the India factor as representing a fundamental national character of the state. This conglomerate (popularly dubbed the Establishment), led by the military, the strongest national institution and constituting a substantial portion of the decision-making elite, remains in the driver's seat on this issue even today.[3] Three factors allowed the conglomerate to take center stage. First, parts of the civilian bureaucracy and the Pakistani military were the only institutions in the newly born state that had some residual structure inherited from British India.[4] They were therefore able to organize themselves much quicker than the political leadership, most of which had migrated from what became India. Second, the first decade after 1947 saw political turmoil and a gradual ascendance of the bureaucracy in positions of political power. The bureaucracy, in turn, created openings for the military to become partners in rescuing Pakistan from what was already being seen as the ineptitude of the politicians. Finally, the military gained significant public support as General Ayub Khan's rule in the 1960s brought about an aura of stability and progress that was touted as the military's success. By the mid-1960s,

Pakistan had stabilized as a state, it had escaped initial fears of externally orchestrated collapse, and it had a military that was fairly well liked within the society for its respectable performance at the helm of affairs even as it undermined democratic institutions and co-opted a new breed of civilian politicians to serve the government of the time. The military would only continue gaining strength as time went by.

The "Guardian" Military Takes It Upon Itself

Merely pointing to Pakistan's obsession with the India factor does not necessarily explain why the Establishment has managed to perpetuate its outlook. It also does not suggest why an argument purely based on vested institutional interests does not hold in this case. To explain this, it is important to introduce the military's "guardian" mindset. Without this mindset it may not have been as easy to perpetuate the primacy of the India factor and absorb the extreme domestic costs (discussed later) for doing so.

Often, policies that lack will or conviction are the easiest to change. The Pakistani military's position on the India factor is anything but that; this explains the longevity of the state's stance vis-à-vis India.

One can find a clue into the military's thinking by examining the institution's perception of itself and how it justifies its actions and policies internally. Perhaps the most accurate depiction of the Pakistan military in this respect is one of a "guardian" institution (Staniland 2008). A prototype is a military that is professional and focused on national defense but extremely intolerant of political instability, which it sees as undermining the unity and, in turn, the security of the state. Guardian militaries also tend to be very image conscious because they see their ability to affect domestic change as a function of a degree of respect and acceptance from the people. Nonetheless, the primary focus of guardian militaries remains on war fighting; they do not alter their organizational form and ethos merely to become entrenched in political roles (Huntington 1968). Such institutions may well develop political and economic vested interests—in fact, they almost always do—or even have individuals interested in personal gains, but the institutional structures and norms do not allow such thinking to become a characteristic of institutional learning as such. Moreover, even when narrowly defined interests dictate specific actions, they are internalized and often truly believed to be in line with the guardian spirit. In other words, the internal narrative is strictly professional even when actions are not. To be sure, a guardian military's self-image does not necessarily conform to the objective reality; how it sees itself drives its actions, but it may well be seen as (and be) counterproductive by outsiders. The guardian spirit, then, need not be seen as a positive attribute per se, and as we discuss below, it has certainly not proved to be so in Pakistan's case.

The Pakistan military exhibits virtually all the characteristics associated with guardian outfits. It considers itself the ultimate arbitrator of national interest. The institution has a strategic culture that presents the military as the principal, in fact, the only institution genuinely capable of guaranteeing Pakistan's security.[5] It has often seen the political elite with a degree of apathy, and even suspicion, and it therefore demands institutional supremacy vis-à-vis the civilians when it comes to issues relating to national security, broadly defined. Since the understanding of this "security" flows directly out of the quest to keep out of India's domination, the military has chosen to embody the state's quest to address the India factor. It has not lost track of its chief objective of maintaining high standards of professionalism as a war-fighting machine—to fight against India, that is. Moreover, it considers a minimal level of stability, defined broadly in terms of the political, economic, and law-and-order situation within the country, to be a prerequisite for Pakistan to act upon the country's heightened threat perception from the east. This prompts the military to consider intervention in times of political instability or in case of a serious challenge to its institutional supremacy. Yet, the military as an institution sees the intervention as a temporary but necessary act aimed merely at correcting civilian fallacies. The fact that its actions do not always seem as benign to outsiders as they may to its own members is often rejected as a fault of the "Other"—this is consistent with what one would expect from such an institution.

The military's mindset has been most evident at times of political transitions in Pakistan. The military has interfered regularly and remains a key player in politics. Its preference has been to use its political leverage from behind the scenes; therefore, all coups in Pakistan's history have taken place only at times when a "constitutional" mechanism to force political change was unavailable to the military. Internal dynamics within the military top brass prior to each coup or when it has given blessings to a constitutional overthrow of an elected government point to little other than a conviction that the political leadership of the time had crossed the military's self-defined red lines, whether in terms of challenging the national security paradigm or misgovernance and growing internal instability. Moreover, once in power, each military ruler has sought to prolong his rule by manipulating domestic politics and leveraging external patrons to fill the legitimacy void. Yet, as an institution, the military has always remained concerned about its image as a war-fighting machine. Therefore, traditionally, its top brass only tolerates the whims of the military ruler, who over time operates more as a political actor and thus a liability than as an asset for the military, till the domestic political landscape is relatively stable and the military's image is not being tarnished by complying with the ruler's desires. Open and prolonged resentment against military rule is perceived as instability inducing, and if extended to its logical conclusion, as a potent mechanism for the society to challenge, potentially successfully, the military's supremacy and, in turn, the national security paradigm. Each act of military withdrawal from power has been a result of a decision among the military top brass to pull back; the top man is asked to step down, and the military quickly reverts to manipulating the political process from behind the scenes to ensure that the national security outlook remains unaltered.

It is the military's (more broadly, the Establishment's) predominant position among state institutions coupled with a benign image of itself and the conviction of being an entity truly engaged in upholding the country's national interest—read: satisfying the India factor—that is responsible for ensuring the permanence of the India factor in Pakistani thinking.

The India Factor: Affecting Pakistan's Core

The quest to retain Pakistan's outlook as "not India" has led to a number of domestic distortions. We discuss the ones most relevant to Pakistan's development-politics-security interplay; together, these have affected Pakistan and Pakistanis to the core. The national discourse on domestic priorities, the country's global outlook, the national vision, and even what it means to be Pakistani have been colored by the resolve to defy India's hegemonic presence in South Asia.

Failure of Democratic Consolidation

The civil-military tussle in the political sphere is a constant for Pakistan. Linked to the India factor, the Pakistan military, and more broadly the Establishment, it has persistently overreached into the political sphere.

The Establishment's interference, underpinned by the military's guardian mindset, has ensured Pakistan's failure to consolidate democracy. Its efforts to tailor the political situation to its outlook have led to a covert or overt disruption of the democratic process time and again. Political evolution has therefore been stunted, and this has prevented more efficient political and governance models from taking root.[6] Ironically, the net result of this overreach has been not only a weakening of the democratic process, but also greater internal vulnerability of the Pakistani Federation, which undercuts the very reason the interference is seen as necessary in the first place.

Apart from the first decade of Pakistan's existence, when the bureaucratic principles seemed more responsible for undermining political actors than the military, the military has constantly chosen favorites among political actors and often facilitated the rise of some while quashing others. Empirical evidence from the past five decades suggests that the overriding concern of the military was not to allow any single political actor or coalition to become strong enough to challenge the conventional wisdom on the India factor. While an outsider may rightly see this as a means to further the military's vested interests, the military's internal institutional narrative has always been one of genuine concern for the well-being of the Pakistani state—as the institution defines it, of course—were the India factor taken lightly. This explains why local government structures that undercut the efficacy of political parties (of all leanings) have been the preferred governance model for each of Pakistan's military dictators (this also has the added advantage of undermining organized political resistance to military rulers of the time, which itself is justified to correct fallacies of the previous government).[7] At times when civilian governments are in charge, the military's efforts to prop up political fronts against clear frontrunners who could potentially become too strong on their own—the Islami Jamhoori Ittehad's (IJI) rise against Benazir Bhutto's PPP in 1990 being the best example—is also explained by the same overall objective.[8]

Regardless, years of political manipulation have perpetuated weak political parties dependent on patronage-based politics.[9] Political actors themselves have exhibited extreme immaturity, both in terms of their failure to transform the landscape into one dominated by consociational politics and also in their own eagerness to rise at the behest of the Establishment. Yet, these actors have managed to retain a hold on national politics courtesy of their entrenched patronage networks. In addition, the Establishment's impatience with its governance failures and the resultant unconstitutional or forced "constitutional" changes has prevented the natural evolution of the democratic process whereby voters and non-veto-wielding institutions would be allowed to determine their fate through democratic means. A new crop of politicians more worthy of being called statesmen has thus never emerged.

In the final outcome, while there is little doubt that those, including the military, who criticize the political elite for their failure, have much to go by, it is equally true that they often shy away from identifying the Establishment's manipulation and periodic disruption of the political system as the principal underlying reason for the failure of democracy to throw up worthy leadership. As Chadda (2000) highlights, it is this structural anomaly that is responsible for a democracy that has resulted in uncertainty and lawlessness; the argument comes full circle as the Establishment points to these instability-inducing factors to intervene and reverse the democratic transitions periodically.

More "Guns" and Less "Butter": Trading Development for Security?

While it is too simplistic to argue for a causal relationship between high defense spending and poor development and social outcomes, an inverse relationship has often been noted. As Shuja Nawaz argues, "Apart from their strategic or political implications, defense expenditures have an obvious economic impact that can be particularly acute in the developing world, where resources are scarce and therefore the opportunity cost of such expenditures is high" (1983, 34).

Chari and Siddiqa-Agha (2000) state, "The proportion of national resources allocated to defense reflects the perceptions of national elite and decision-making circles, which is largely founded on the security milieu in which a country finds itself." In Pakistan's case, with a preoccupation with the eastern neighbor driving policy behavior, the fundamental prerequisite to satisfy the India factor was always going to be a strong defense capability against the larger Indian military might. Achieving this for an economically weak country was certain to be an uphill battle and was guaranteed to eat into other national priorities. Indeed, today the guns versus butter debate in Pakistan is an evocative one, where per capita income (in terms of current factor cost) still hovers around US$1,200 (see Government of Pakistan 2011), while the country maintains the seventh largest military in the world.[10] Indeed, Pakistan's situation is clearly one in which crowding out of resources has been a real problem. Even today, despite recent improvement in the development-defense spending imbalance in the former's favor, almost 45 percent of the total expenditure goes to defense and debt servicing; the number was around 70 percent just a decade ago.

Given the virtual consensus in Pakistan that the threat of Indian aggression was clear and present in the initial years, Pakistan's original allocation of 70 percent of the budget for defense was not altogether surprising. While the proportion of defense in the overall budget has declined to 18 percent, it is still higher than the South Asian average.[11] Overall, the distorted relationship of spending in the defense versus development sectors has remained intact. Since Independence, Pakistan's spending in the social sectors has been disproportionately lower than for defense. In fact, with health and education expenditures at 2.6 percent of GDP each, Pakistan's social-sector spending is low even by South Asian standards (UNDP 2011). The outcome is evident from the fact that Pakistan ranks an embarrassing 145 on the Human Development Index (ibid.)—especially embarrassing given that Pakistan boasts of a large conventional military and nuclear weapons capability.

Over the years, periods of high economic growth and direct foreign military assistance have been used to increase spending in the defense sectors. From the 1950s onward, and especially during military rule during the 1960s and 1980s, Pakistan successfully leveraged its ties with external allies—principally the United States—to gain direct foreign assistance, which, while contributing to economic growth, also laid the basis for a rather troubling political economy of defense (Jalal 1995). For instance, in the 1980s, a period characterized by the persistence of the Afghan-Soviet war on the western border, the average growth of expenditure on defense, in real terms, was a staggering 8.9 percent per annum. Development expenditure, in contrast, was growing at a paltry 2.7 percent per annum (Government of Pakistan 2007). At other times, such as the 1990s when Pakistan was under representative governments but when its international leverage dwindled and economic growth slowed down, both development and defense expenditures began to shrink, but the former took a greater hit (see Table 15–1).

Table 15–1. Growth in Real Expenditure

Year	Current	Development	Defense
1980s	10.5%	2.7%	8.9%
1990s	4.5%	−2.6%	0.4%
2000–2004	0.1%	9.4%	0.4%
2004–9	5.7%	13.5%	1.3%

Source: Government of Pakistan (2010).

The bulk of the growth in expenditure flows in this decade was for interest payments, as governments struggled to repay the international debt accumulated in the previous decade. The first five years of the last decade, from 2000 to 2004, were remarkable for the significant growth in development expenditures—a trend that seems to have persisted into the latter half of the decade. That said, one needs to be cautious when appreciating this improvement as some of it is attributable to statistical craftsmanship. For instance, since 2001–2, military pensions (amounting to over US$800 million in 2009–10) have been subsumed into the civilian head of "public administration." Salaries of personnel of defense-production establishments, and amounts allocated for the upkeep of cantonments, to name just another two heads of expenditure, are also routinely included in budget allocations for civil entities. In fact, historically, there has always been a differential between reported and actual budgets for the defense sector and between allocated and spent amounts; the defense sector, unlike development, is not prone to under-utilization of funds. In a press statement just after the federal budget for 2010–11 was announced, the principal adviser to the Ministry of Finance told reporters that the true size of the defense budget allocated for the coming year was closer to PKR 675 billion, as opposed to the PKR 442 billion reflected in budget documents.[12] The IMF's estimates highlight an even greater differential; its calculations would put the 2010–11 defense budget figures at 34 percent higher than the number reported in the federal budget under the head of defense (IMF 2010). This would represent a number about 32 percent higher than the allocated development budget.

Notwithstanding, the trend is pointing in the right direction, both in terms of demands for greater attention to development and for the military establishment to be more transparent in its budgeting. The fact that a military-led regime (which was in power in 2000–2001) had to resort to subterfuge to mask the defense expenditure is indicative of the changing mood and the growing tendency to question government allocation priorities. The questioning does not end at block allocations but was also manifested in growing calls for a breakdown of defense expenditure to be presented in Parliament—a practice that was discontinued after the India-Pakistan war of 1965. The year 2008 was the first time since the war that a broad categorization of defense expenditure was presented in the federal budget documents.

Beyond Numbers: The Political Economy of Defense

There have been a number of excellent commentaries on the Pakistani military's stake and role in the national economy. The most prominent explanations highlight the military's ability (especially under military rule) to leverage international support and monetary assistance to spike defense spending and build an incredibly large infrastructure while maintaining reasonable economic growth. This not only perpetuated a political economy of defense but also increased the military's direct role in the development sector. In her book *Military Inc: Inside Pakistan's Military Economy*, Ayesha Siddiqa-Agha argues that the military's stake in the political process manifests itself in the control of economic resources; the army's business networking is seen as its vehicle to power. Her concept of "Milbus" (military business) suggests that military capital "used for the personal benefit of the military fraternity" rests on the transfer of resources from the public to the (military-affiliated) private sector; that the growth of Milbus encourages the top echelons of the armed forces to support "policymaking environments" that will "multiply their economic opportunities"; and that such actions are "both the cause and effect of a feudal, authoritarian, non-democratic political system" (Siddiqa-Agha 2007, 3). In essence, the argument puts the military's manipulation of resources at the forefront of explaining the institution.

As critics of this argument have pointed out, a close look at the origins of the military's entities operating in the development sphere, its specific use of military and broader defense sector–related resources, and its political behavior and outlook do not seem to hold up any causal link between the military's behavior and Milbus. Short of this, the fact that the military's economic stakes have grown significantly is evident and worrisome. This, however, ought not to detract from the fact that the institution's fundamental defining characteristic remains its guardian mindset and not a hunger for greater economic stakes.

Next, the relatively large size of the defense budgets and any distorting effects of the military's economic interplay ought not to force a linear conclusion to the guns versus butter debate. Pakistan's development and social-sector woes can only partly be explained by a resource crunch. Failed economic models and misgovernance, both during military and civilian rule, have been as conspicuous. Pakistan's case presents an extremely complex relationship among economic growth, development and social outcomes, and budget allocations. Despite fairly impressive GDP growth rates on average, social-sector performance has remained abysmal. As Easterly argues, Pakistan represents a case of poor performance on most social and political indicators—education, health, sanitation, fertility, gender equality, corruption, political instability—for a country of its level of income. He contends, "While foreign aid and governmental programs may have contributed to overall economic growth, they were an egregious failure at promoting social and institutional development under the circumstances of elite domination and ethnic division" (Easterly 2001, 1).

To be sure, there is little evidence that the military favors weak economic and social performance as a matter of policy. In fact, the India factor is much better served by a well-performing macro-economy and relatively equitable distribution of wealth because these ensure availability of adequate resources for defense appropriations and promote greater societal stability, respectively. Not detracting from the massive defense spending over the years, most analyses of governance in Pakistan are categorical in suggesting that governments in charge could have performed far better on the development count with the available resource set than they did. In the development sector, high levels of pilferage; lack of capacity for efficient resource utilization, which regularly results in under-utilization of allocated funds; and skewed resource distribution driven by political expediency within the development sector have exacerbated Pakistan's governance woes throughout (Hasan 1998). In the final outcome, Pakistan's history is one of military overreach in claiming its share of the resources combined with abysmal governance failure in the development sector.

The Global Context:
India Factor Colors Pakistan's Global Outreach

The implications of the India factor are not limited to the domestic scene. Perhaps nowhere are they more obvious than in the foreign policy arena. There is ample evidence to suggest a direct causal link between Pakistan's view of the Indian presence next door and its decisions in terms of selecting global partners.

Since Independence, Pakistan's foreign policy toward South Asia and the great powers has been used to leverage support for Pakistan's position vis-à-vis India. The policy has been closely overseen by the Establishment. Flowing naturally from the civil-military disconnect discussed earlier and the reasons explained for the military's interference in politics, the Establishment has sought to dominate the direction of the country's ties with India, and by extension with other powers capable of helping Pakistan stand up against its rival. The characteristic is so strong that, often times, Pakistan's national security policy and foreign policy vision seem indistinguishable.

Pakistan has sought to deny India an overriding advantage by (1) ensuring that Pakistan's western borders remain calm and friendly so that it can focus energies on India—Pakistani strategists refer to this as avoiding a "two-front" situation; and (2) leveraging extra-regional relations that would help offset the Indian advantage and generate diplomatic backing for Pakistan on the international stage. Three relationships in particular are of note because these have been the most important ones for Pakistan and are ones without which Islamabad's ability to stand up to India would have been significantly compromised.

First, the Pakistan-U.S. relationship is a classic example of Pakistan's efforts to leverage an extra-regional player to strengthen its capabilities and diplomatic position vis-à-vis India. After some deliberation shortly after its independence, Pakistan chose to join the U.S.-led Western world against the Soviet Union and its allies. The rationale: to benefit from foreign economic assistance and to build up a defense capability to tackle the Indian threat. As mentioned earlier, during the 1950s and 1960s tremendous amounts of foreign assistance flowed into Pakistan as Islamabad boasted of being one of the key U.S. allies in a troubled neighborhood.[13] The angst between Pakistan and the Soviet Union (and later Russia) that has marked the entirety of their relationship is also a function of this choice. Pakistan's decision to support the United States to push back the Soviet invasion of Afghanistan in the 1980s was not prompted by the India factor per se, but Pakistan did use this and the following decade to overreach into Afghanistan to ensure a pliant, pro-Pakistan government that would not allow Indian clout to Pakistan's west.[14] The present-day tension between Pakistan and the United States over the future of Afghanistan and Pakistan's outlook toward its western neighbor is in no small part dictated by the fear of India's permanent ingress into Afghanistan (Ganguly and Howenstein 2009). In the final outcome, even though the Pakistani view criticizes the United States for not having supported it in crunch time over the years—Pakistanis remain bitter about lack of decisive U.S. support during the India-Pakistan wars, for instance—with over US$42 billion of aid and support to all three Pakistani coup makers, the United States has enabled the Pakistani state in its quest to build a strong defense capability (and Establishment) and thus helped it to satisfy the India factor.[15]

Next, Pakistan has relied on China over the years as the principal antidote to potential Indian hegemony in the region. If the United States is criticized for being a "fair-weather partner," China is praised for being the "all weather friend." China's own territorial disputes with India and its interest in keeping Indian power in check made Pakistan the perfect partner for it to ensure a balance of power in South Asia. China has been a major supporter of Pakistan's defense buildup since the 1970s; it has also supported Pakistan's nuclear program, allegedly including its weapons component (Garver 2001, 187–216). Equally relevant has been the Chinese diplomatic support in international and multilateral forums—principally the United Nations—on issues like Kashmir as well as during India-Pakistan wars and crises (the 1999 Kargil crisis being the only exception where China took a neutral posture, ultimately pushing Pakistan to back away from its position during the crisis).[16] It is fair to say that without China, Pakistan's international standing, its defense capabilities, and consequently its ability to stand up to India would have been substantially weaker.

The third relationship can be defined as the Muslim world connection, primarily focused on the Sunni block in the Middle East. Pakistan's self-image as a Muslim country well placed to play a role in the Umma meant that its outreach to the Middle East was ideologically underpinned to a large extent. In that sense, the India factor may not have been a necessary condition for cordial ties with Saudi Arabia, United Arab Emirates, Turkey, and so forth. Nonetheless, it did increase Pakistan's drive to leverage these relationships to ensure that forums such as the Organization of Islamic Countries (OIC) maintained an official position favorable to Pakistan's stance on Kashmir and barred India's entry into their midst,[17] and to gain economic concessions that would help Pakistan's growth and stability, much needed to remain a worthy challenger to India. Islamabad has also remained desperate to limit India's political and economic clout in Central Asia—this explains Pakistan's over-reach into Afghanistan—and to the Middle Eastern Muslim block, which it is geographically and ideologically well situated to do.

Forgone Regional Integration

In the foreign policy domain, the biggest casualty of the India-Pakistan rivalry has been the dream of South Asian regionalism. While this chapter is limited in focus to Pakistan, India has been equally guilty of its own emphasis on competing with Pakistan over the years. New Delhi has also been active in opposing Pakistan's positions in various forums and has leveraged its own relationships to strengthen its hand vis-à-vis its western neighbor. It is no exaggeration to say that both have been Machiavellian in their conduct toward the other and, as a direct corollary, exist in a region that is the least integrated in the world.

As the world has globalized and economies and policies have become increasingly integrated, regional associations and trading blocs are being seen as virtual necessities for swift progress. Short distances, natural geographical and economic complementarities, and often historical and cultural affinities are considered obvious reasons for neighbors to explore synergies. There is increasing evidence of a positive correlation between strong regional group-ings and individual member-state performances (Khan, Shaheen, and Yusuf 2009). Unfortunately, courtesy of the India-Pakistan rivalry, South Asia has been unable to cash in on this trend.

South Asia has a regional bloc—the South Asian Association for Re-gional Cooperation (SAARC)—and a free-trade agreement—the South Asian Regional Trade Agreement (SAFTA)—but both have proven largely ineffectual. While India and Pakistan have tended to point fingers at each other to deflect the blame for SAARC's failures, the truth is that together they have held SAARC hostage. For one, even though SAARC was set up in 1985 to create a vehicle for regional integration, bilateral political issues were left out of its purview. SAARC is therefore toothless in terms of being able to achieve integration in the true sense. This is especially so given that in South Asia's case, a high degree of conflict and political instability are responsible for dwarfed regional trade (Kahn, Shaheen, and Yusuf 2009).[18] Behera notes that SAARC has struggled to survive as "India perceived it as an attempt by the smaller neighbors to gang-up against it, while the latter especially Pakistan feared that India would use it as a vehicle to impose its hegemony in the region." Behera also makes the important point that other member countries view their engagement with SAARC "through the prism of their bilateral relations with India specifically" (Behera 2009). As a result, most countries are politically unable to make economic choices more conducive to their own growth and integration.

In terms of trade, India retains the highest non-tariff barriers (NTBs) in the region, while Pakistan has undermined economic progress by refusing to liberalize trade with India, instead traditionally taking a Kashmir-first approach: solve Kashmir before expecting a liberalization of economic ties (and other aspects of the relationship). Pakistan has only recently agreed to offer India MFN (Most Favored Nation) status, but it is yet to apply SAFTA provisions to its eastern neighbor.[19] It has thus passed on one of the largest sources of trade in the region, a loss for itself and the region as a whole. India has been keener to open up trade, both because its larger economy stands to gain more and also because it hopes that improved economic ties will deflect attention from the Kashmir issue. And yet, India's realist approach is evident by the high level of its NTBs, which are unlikely to be lowered for Pakistani exports until Islamabad agrees to liberalize ties.

For countries with a shared history, contiguous boundaries, and an initial trade relationship at independence whereby 70 percent of Pakistan's exports were directed to India and 63 percent of Indian exports went to Pakistan, Pakistan's and India's formal trade has been abysmal. Trade figures have risen remarkably over the past decade from around US$357 million in 2003 to over US$2 billion in 2011, but even the present number pales compared to the estimated potential trade (IMF 2011). A 1993 World Bank study concluded that Pakistan could have increased its flow of trade with India ninefold by entering into a truly operational free-trade arrangement (cited in USAID 2006).

Gravity-model predictions such as Baroncelli's (2007) estimated that in the absence of conflict from 1948 to 2000, the volume of trade between Pakistan and India would have been 405 percent higher than actual flows. In 2000, recorded trade flows between both countries (including informal trade) were at US$117 million, whereas the model suggests that in a state of peace, this figure would have been at US$591 million. Combined with the impact of a fully functional regional trade agreement, the peace dividend would have jumped to US$683 million in total trade in 2000.[20] Overall, Pakistan's trade with its neighboring countries is 79 percent lower than would be expected under the presence of a regional trade arrangement such as SAFTA (Baroncelli 2007). This is not in line with the classic gravity-model prediction that trade is directly related to the economic size of the partners and inversely related to the distance between them. And while these statistics tend to overstate the case in that they do not factor in short-term losses for the weaker economy and a need for individual countries to restructure production patterns to suit a South Asian economic liberalization (Yusuf 2007), the fact that overall trade ties will strengthen is undisputed.

To add to this, Pakistan's trade with SAARC countries is 17 percent less than that of the rest of the world, and mutual trade within the SAARC region as a share of total trade is the lowest in South Asia compared with other regions (Gul and Yasin 2011). India also possesses the smallest share of intra-regional trade in relation to its trade with the world. Given that India and Pakistan are the two largest economies in the region, intra-SAARC trade, at 0.8 percent of regional GDP, the lowest in the world (compared to the highest, East Asia and the Pacific at 27 percent), can be blamed squarely on the policies of these two sides—Pakistan's policies most obviously being a function of the India factor.

Another interesting trend, exhibiting behavior in line with our hub and spoke model, is the manner in which the two sides have gone about joining sub-regional and extra-regional groupings; they have actively tried to keep the other out of groupings in which they are involved. The most obvious example is that of the Bay of Bengal Initiative for Multi-Sectoral Technical and Economic Cooperation (BIMSTEC), a South Asian/South East Asian sub-regional grouping involving Bangladesh, India, Myanmar, Sri Lanka, Bhutan, Nepal, and Thailand, but not Pakistan.[21] The South Asia Growth Quadrangle involving Bangladesh, Bhutan, India, and Nepal is another economic grouping championed by India that has left out Pakistan. Till 2004, India was also instrumental in keeping Pakistan out of the Association of Southeast Asian Nations (ASEAN) despite strong support for its admission by a number of member states. India has also been actively cultivating ties with Iran and through it accessing Afghanistan over the past decade in what it sees as a strategy to bypass Pakistan's hold on this landlocked country. (Pakistan sees Indian moves to establish a formidable role in Afghanistan as an attempt to "encircle" it—the dreaded "two-front situation" that the Pakistani Establishment has so desperately tried to avoid.)

Pakistan, for its part, has always sought to look west. It joined the high-profile Economic Cooperation Organization (ECO)[22] along with Iran and Turkey. ECO later added a number of Central Asian republics and Afghanistan, but not India. Also, Pakistan refuses India overland transit rights through to Afghanistan and on to Central Asia, and also does not allow Kashmiri goods originating in Indian Kashmir to flow through Pakistan.

In the final outcome, the India factor and India's equally intransigent position have effectively undermined any hope for successful regionalism in South Asia. By all estimates, both sides have incurred losses amounting to billions of dollars by doing so. Their extra-regional efforts to undercut each other's economic alliances take these costs even further. And while it is true that the last decade has seen significant progress ranging from noticeable concessions on political and trade issues specific to Kashmir to growing formal bilateral trade to serious talks about trade liberalization just in the past year, the fact remains that there is a long way to go before South Asia will become truly integrated. Until then, all other South Asian states shall remain hostage to the whims of the India-Pakistan relationship.

Pakistan Burns From Within: The Militant Fallout

The India factor has not only shaped Pakistan's foreign policy choices, but some of these have even come back rapidly to haunt Pakistan. Militant violence within Pakistan is one example.

Post-9/11, the Pakistani intelligence agency, Inter-Services Intelligence (ISI), has been under severe criticism for its policies supporting militant actors over the past three decades. Most relevant to the India factor is the ISI's support of an originally indigenous armed insurgency in Indian Kashmir throughout the 1990s. After having played a critical role in supporting the anti-Soviet forces waging holy war in Afghanistan in the 1980s, the Pakistani state put its weight behind the insurgency in Kashmir, using trained irregular fighters to wage "jihad" against India's illegal—as Pakistan saw it—occupation of the territory.[23] Under the Taliban's Afghanistan, Afghan territory was used as one of the training outposts for the Pakistan-backed insurgents fighting in Kashmir. Many more camps were situated in Pakistani Kashmir and elsewhere in Pakistan. The rationale: the insurgents were a low-cost tactical option with plausible deniability aimed at reigniting the Kashmir issue, and ultimately, to alter the territorial status quo; Kashmir, after all, is one of the key reasons underlying Pakistan's obsession with India in the first place.

While support for militancy—or "freedom fight" as it was termed by Pakistan at the time—was a crucial element of Pakistan's security policy during this period, the country's military and intelligence agencies never wanted to radicalize Pakistan. The military was more than happy to employ radicalized elements willing to fight in the name of religion, but the official narrative notwithstanding, it never saw their use as more than a tactical tool. Therefore, the Establishment simultaneously took great pains to shield against the possibility of domestic repercussions resulting from its aggressive use of Islamists to satisfy regional security objectives. Even as they were supported, militants and the phenomena of extremism were constantly discredited internally, and the voice of the ultra-right remained on the margins of Pakistan's political arena. Key state institutions did not project an extremist character as a whole—they did, however, become increasingly conservative under General Zia ul Haq in the 1980s—and the state supported the line society drew to distinguish its conservative disposition from intolerable extremism.

In retrospect this policy was extremely shortsighted. Until the 9/11 attacks in the United States, the policy worked because the interests of the state and militant groups were relatively aligned. However, once 9/11 had forced the state to reverse its pro-Taliban policy in Afghanistan, which it had pursued since the mid-1990s, and Pakistan toned down its support for militancy in Indian Kashmir, the ability of the militant enclave to challenge the state became apparent. With the help of prolonged state patronage, militants were able to penetrate society and generate quite a following due to their wide social service networks. Militants were able to commonly recruit from within Pakistan, and they had become financially independent of the Pakistani state as a result of external funding—mainly alms from Muslims abroad and donations that foreign Muslim governments had contributed. Furthermore, the longstanding association of militant groups with the ISI gave them functional knowledge of the agency, which was extremely advantageous after they turned against their former patrons, the state.

Until 9/11, the Pakistani state rarely had to deal with internal militancy; in particular, militants felt no necessity to target the state due to its implicit support, which militants were guaranteed as long as they remained allied with the state's agenda (homegrown sectarian groups were somewhat of an exception). However, the state's tenuous grip over these groups became clear once Pakistan, under extreme international pressure, became compelled to reverse its stance on militancy. The result was that the state declared "terrorist organizations" the same militant outfits that for years it had nurtured. However, within the militant enclave, few were receptive to this shift. In fact, as the state was poised to pull back its support right after 9/11, the fervor for jihad against the "invading Americans" in Afghanistan was rising.[24] Subsequently, as General Pervez Musharraf ordered the Pakistan military to move, again under American pressure, to operate in the Federally Administered Tribal Areas (FATA) against pockets of newly declared terrorists, it instantly faced a massive backlash. However, while the situation would inevitably have been much different but for 9/11 and the U.S. invasion of Afghanistan—in that sense, it is erroneous to draw a direct link between the pro-insurgency policies of the 1990s and the post-9/11 scenario—a decade after 9/11 a number of factors have combined to strengthen the militants' hand in Pakistan.

The Pakistani state is now faced with a plethora of militant outfits fighting for varying yet overlapping causes; all of them are Islamist in their tenor, even if they have visible ideological differences among themselves. Virtually all of them have penetrated the social space and are active recruiters for jihad from among Pakistani society. In fact, some, like the Lashkar-e-Tayyaba (and its public face, the Jama'at-ud-Dawa), have mustered such a following in Punjab that the state's official plea for not targeting them is fear of an unmanageable backlash. To date, the state has had to expend tremendous human and capital resources only to fight back the most lethal of these, the FATA-based Tehrik-e-Taliban Pakistan. Even then, it still remains infested by it and a number of other radical outfits across various parts of the country.

The Pakistani nation has had to pay a heavy price due to the militant backlash. According to the Pakistan Institute for Peace Studies' security report for 2010, the proliferation of militant groups has overwhelmed law-enforcement agencies, providing small militant outfits the space to increase the number of terror attacks significantly, most notably in Punjab, Sindh, and Khyber Pukhtunkhwa provinces (PIPS 2011). From 2001 to 2011, over forty-three thousand Pakistani civilians and security personnel lost their lives, and many more were injured in terror attacks.[25] Militant aggression against sectarian targets has also intensified significantly, as has their propensity to target religious minorities. Indeed, it is no exaggeration to state that the once moderately peaceful Pakistan has seen a swift descent into chaos, with hardly any region of the country left immune to militant violence. To be sure, the state of Pakistan is fighting for its survival as a moderate, progressive entity; increasingly, though, growing intolerance and sympathy for radicalized elements are leaving the silent, moderate majority nervous about the country's future.

Breaking the Stronghold: Moving Beyond the India Factor

The primacy of the India factor in Pakistani policymaking has been fundamental to shaping Pakistan's direction as a state. Together, the above-discussed implications of the Pakistani state's preoccupation with the India factor define the interplay among the country's development, politics, and security. Simply put, it is one characterized by a security-centric vision; a national narrative that prioritizes all policy aspects believed to be necessary to uphold the India factor (read: a "securitized" narrative); a military-led Establishment that sees satisfying the India factor as key to Pakistan's identity and strength and acts on this premise; a military that finds political overreach to be justified; a political elite that has exhibited immaturity; a severe civil-military disconnect that has led these two pillars of the state to see each other as rivals rather than partners in ensuring Pakistan's prosperity; resource utilization patterns that are skewed in favor of defense at the expense of development; a development sector that has failed to translate macro-economic gains into social well-being; a global engagement colored by the need to stand up to India, one that has forgone the benefits of regional integration within South Asia; and a situation where past policy choices have even contributed to the militant violence and growing intolerance increasingly on display in Pakistani society today.

This is an anomalous situation, to say the least, one whose overall effect on the Pakistani nation has been squarely negative. To be sure, however, I do not wish this argument to be read as one passing a value judgment on the choices made by the Pakistani state. The idea is not to suggest that Pakistan is the sole responsible party for the troubled India-Pakistan relationship. Yet, there is a need to dwell upon ways to reduce the primacy of the Indian factor in Pakistani thinking. But this is primarily due to the fact that the current state of the development-politics-security interplay is undesirable and retarding the progress of the Pakistani state, and not due to any normative claims about how the Pakistani state conducts its business.

The discussion in this chapter points to three possible paths to effect change in the status quo: *convince* the military that its view of the India factor is misplaced; *make it impossible* for the Establishment to pursue the traditional policy; *make the traditional mindset redundant* by altering the Pakistan-India relationship positively.

Literature on institutional change readily highlights the difficulty in using normative arguments to influence the behavior of bulky, well-organized institutions. Institutional inertia, path dependence, and other status quo tendencies make it virtually impossible to shift institutional positions in the short run. This is especially true when such institutions truly believe in the merit of their stance, as has been argued is the case with the Pakistani military. Another paradox is also all too apparent: the military's guardian mindset has undermined political processes and, in turn, maturity among the ranks of the civilian political elite; yet, it is only these civilians who can push back on the status quo thinking. Moreover, as mentioned, the legitimacy of pursuing the India factor goes well beyond the military and even resonates among influential sections of the political enclave.

Also to be noted, while this chapter has not dealt with Indian posturing, there is a fairly credible case to be made that Indian behavior and military posturing over the years do not allow one to be completely dismissive of the Pakistani military's concerns. India's less-than-flexible attitude on the key issues reinforces the primacy of the India factor; it makes it even tougher to imagine normative arguments creating a buy in with the Pakistani Establishment.

The second path—making it impossible for Pakistan to maintain the status quo in terms of the India factor—has an obvious route: taking away Pakistan's capability to do so, perhaps by forcing it into submission.

Historically, such situations have most often come about following major debacles. For instance, loss of a major war or a break up of Pakistan could cause this. For obvious reasons, one need not delve into this option any further; no Pakistani decision-maker would ever wish for such an outcome.

The only realistic scenario that carries positive undertones, then, is a gradual improvement in the Pakistan-India relationship whereby both sides can be convinced of the merit in mutual gains. In other words, the importance of the India factor would reduce with a decline, forced by circumstances as it must be, in the intense competition between the two sides. Indeed, it is hard to imagine any scenario in which Pakistan is able to stabilize and progress swiftly or where India can truly acquire a global power status without having normalized bilateral ties. While even this will not be an easy transformation due to the multitude of institutional anomalies discussed here for Pakistan and an equally complex set of issues on the Indian side, it is, respectively, more likely and more desirable than the first two scenarios.

Ironically, India's swift rise over the past decade or so combined with Pakistan's worsening problems seems to have opened up a window of opportunity for rapprochement. While India finds no reasons to soften its stance on issues such as Kashmir and remains uninterested in making unilateral concessions to its neighbor, it is increasingly wary of a further weakened and possibly radicalized Pakistan on its border. For Pakistan, active competition with India is all but impossible given its internal weaknesses, and while it has not given up on seeking a revision to the status quo on outstanding disputes, it is being compelled to focus energies inward. Moreover, with the advent of nuclear weapons, there is much greater interest from within and from external parties to see the two sides normalize and lower the risks of a nuclear exchange.

Indeed, these and other compulsions have been playing out positively over the past few years. Notwithstanding the persistent mistrust, recurring crises, and ongoing foreign and domestic policy disagreements, these two rivals have made serious efforts to move beyond their longstanding impasse. They initiated a dialogue process in 2004 that was fairly successful in terms of implementing a number of important confidence-building measures, especially when it came to Kashmir. At one point, they were even fairly close to agreeing on a formula to resolve the dispute over Kashmir.[26] There has also been more appetite to talk about regional ventures, for instance, in the energy sector, and about liberalizing bilateral trade ties.[27] In Pakistan, the Establishment's support for these positive overtures is especially encouraging. Moreover, in a trend that bodes well for the future, the Establishment itself is under tremendous pressure (for reasons unrelated to its stance vis-à-vis India) as its de facto veto power over foreign policy decisions has begun to wane and multiple new poles of power are beginning to challenge its supremacy internally. While this argument cannot be carried too far given the weaknesses within civilian ranks discussed earlier, there is certainly movement on the issue of how easily the Establishment can exercise its veto.

It is too soon to tell whether these two rivals will manage a substantial breakthrough in the short to medium term. Will internal dynamics in Pakistan force the military to relinquish some of its political space and allow civilian principals to chart a new foreign policy on India? Equally important, will India see Pakistan's weakness as an opportunity to kick it hard when it's down, or will it show greater maturity and choose to reciprocate Pakistani concessions? As the two sides have reengaged in a holistic dialogue, reviving ties stalled after the 2008 Mumbai attacks, it seems that the decision-making enclaves on both sides do see the necessity of moving forward positively. This is welcome as the Pakistani state's ability to reduce the primacy of the India factor hinges on greater progress and eventual normalization of relations.

Notes

1. For some of the most prominent explanations on Pakistan's civil-military imbalance, see Jalal (1990), Jalal (1995), Siddiqa-Agha (2007), Haqqani (2005), Alavi (1973), and Chadda (2000).

2. In 1949, India devalued its currency—a steep devaluation by one-third of its original value. Pakistan refused to follow suit. This move sparked a crisis, and economic relations between the two countries deteriorated. Pakistan canceled a shipment of over 500,000 bales of raw jute, while India canceled its supply of coal to Pakistan. India subsequently ordered a trade blockade against its neighbor. For a more detailed commentary on trade relations in 1949, see Burki (2011, 71–73).

3. The term *Establishment* is used fairly loosely in the Pakistani context. As described here, it goes beyond the military and includes parts of the civilian decision-making apparatus, especially parts of the bureaucracy tasked to run foreign policy, as well as segments of the political elite. The broader definition is to recognize the fact that support for Pakistan's stance on the India factor is considerably broader and deeper in official circles than is often believed to be the case.

4. For more on the makeup of the institutions inherited from British India in 1947, see Lieven (2011, 60–63, 177–84).

5. Colin Gray defines *strategic culture* as the "social constructed and transmitted assumptions, habits of mind, traditions, and preferred methods of operation—that is, behavior—that are more or less specific to a geographically based security community" (Gray 1999, 28).

6. Several scholars have attempted to explain Pakistan's failure to consolidate democracy and have ended up focusing on various aspects of the military's behavior as a key determining factor. Some of the relevant works include Alavi (1973), Jalal (1990; 1995), Chadda (2000), Wilkinson (2000), Haqqani (2005), and Staniland (2008).

7. Pakistani military rulers have inevitably opted for local governance models that seek to sideline political parties and provinces and give greater weight to individual candidates. General Ayub Khan instituted the Basic Democracies Ordinance (1959) and the Municipal Administration Ordinance (1960). General Zia ul Haq introduced local government ordinances between 1979 and 1980, and then insisted on party-less elections. General Pervez Musharraf's decentralization program, the Local Government Ordinance, was perhaps the most comprehensive of the three but ultimately suffered from the same shortcomings. For more on local government structures in Pakistan, see Cheema et al. (2006).

8. General Asad Durrani, former director general of the ISI, disclosed in a formal affidavit that ISI's political cell had provided monetary support to the IJI for the 1990 election campaign. In an interview with the author, Durrani explained that the rationale for the military's support was to ensure that Pakistan did not emerge as a one-party state that allowed any one political actor to dictate terms without check. Several scholars also cite evidence that the ISI worked to assemble and fund the IJI by putting together a coalition of Islamist and pro-military to serve the interests of the military in making sure that Benazir Bhutto's PPP did not sweep the polls in the elections of 1988 (see Nasr 1992; Haqqani 2005; Abbas 2004; Lieven 2011).

9. Perhaps the best recent explanation of patronage-based networking as defining of Pakistani politics is provided in Lieven (2011, 204–33).

10. As calculated from Table 1–5 of Government of Pakistan (2011).

11. Data extracted from World Bank (2011).

12. See "Real Figure of Defense Budget," *The News*, June 12, 2010.

13. For detailed figures of U.S. assistance to Pakistan from 1948 to 2000, see Kronstadt and Epstein (2011), Fig. A–1.

14. For a detailed account of Pakistan's role in developments in Afghanistan during the 1990s, see Rashid (2010).

15. Pakistan has received US$33.6 billion in economic aid and US$8.93 billion in military assistance from the United States over the past fifty years, according to USAID data. For exact figures, see USAID's U.S. Overseas Loans and Grants (Greenbook) information for 2006, available on several websites. On average, the amount of aid given during each year of military rule has exceeded that disbursed to civilian governments in Pakistan. For a more detailed explanation of this trend, see Murad Ali (2009).

16. The Kargil conflict was a result of Pakistani infiltration across the line of control in Kashmir. Pakistan's outreach to China to enlist its support for its position was uncharacteristically unsuccessful, as China merely encouraged a swift scale back of tensions and nudged Pakistan to pull back. For one view on China's motives in pursuing neutrality, see Singh (1999, 1083–94).

17. Saudi Arabia, Malaysia, Iran, and Egypt have supported India joining the OIC as an observer. Pakistan has blocked any such move on grounds of Kashmir and, more specifically, criteria that it advocates that a member country should not be involved in any dispute with another member. For more details, see Ahmed and Bhatnagar (2010).

18. The notion of linkages between trade and conflict suggest that the more trade and regional interdependence among countries, the less likely they are to enter into a scenario of conflict. "Increased trade flows are likely to engender technical efficiency, improve resource allocation and allow countries to create niches by specializing in different products within a given industry" (Kahn, Shaheen, and Yusuf 2009, 85). The caveat here is that a certain degree of institutional and political stability is necessary to foster economic liberalization measures, an environment that South Asia has been unsuccessful in developing (Kahn, Shaheen, and Yusuf 2009).

19. While Pakistan's recent promise to grant India MFN status and a consequent move toward creating a "negative list" are positives, to date, Islamabad has maintained a "positive list," which has very few items with import potential from India listed among the approximately nineteen hundred items on it. For more information on how this policy impedes regional trade, see Taneja (2007a; 2007b, 9).

20. Baroncelli uses the gravity model to estimate potential for trade flows between India and Pakistan. She bases her model on this question: what would the trade between India and Pakistan have been if they were not involved in a military confrontation? For a detailed review of her methodology, see Baroncelli (2007).

21. Initially, the Federation of Indian Chambers of Commerce and Industry (FICCI) had proposed this grouping as a viable sub-regional bloc, with visions of Calcutta being the hub of the suggested rim. Pakistan's exclusion from BIMSTEC was justified on the basis of it not geographically falling within the Bay of Bengal rim (see "Ficci Moots New Trade Bloc—Bay of Bengal Rim," *The Financial Express*, November 9, 2002).

22. ECO, initially established in 1985, is an extension of its forerunner, the Regional Cooperation for Development, which was established in 1977 with the signing of the Treaty of Izmir by Pakistan, Iran, and Turkey. For more information on ECO's mission and history, see the ecosecretariat.org website.

23. For a discussion of the role of the Pakistani state's relationship to irregular warfare in the context of its strategic interests—and the internal implications of these choices—see Hussain (2007, 13–29).

24. A number of religious clerics launched a call for jihad in Pushtun-dominated areas of Pakistan's northwest and organized groups of young men to fight American troops. Perhaps the most high profile of these recruiters was the now infamous Sufi Muhammad, leader of the Tehreek-i-Nifaz-i-Shariat-i-Muhammadi, who took ten thousand volunteers across the border before subsequently abandoning them and returning to Pakistan (see Imtiaz Ali 2009).

25. "Casualty Scorecard," released by the Embassy of Pakistan, Washington DC, February 2011.

26. For a detailed rundown on the progress on Kashmir, see Steve Coll, "The Back Channel: India and Pakistan's Secret Kashmir Talks," *The New Yorker* 85/3 (2009).

27. Some of these measures include Pakistan agreeing to grant India MFN status and coming up with a negative list of tradable items. Talks are also being held between the oil ministers of both countries on a pipeline agreement that would import gas from Turkmenistan (See "Pakistan, India Report Progress on Key Pipeline," *Dawn*, January 25, 2012).

Reference List

Abbas, Hassan. *Pakistan's Drift into Extremism: Allah, the Army, and America's War on Terror.* New York: M. E. Sharpe, 2004.

Ahmed, Zahid Shahab, and Stuti Bhatnagar. "Gulf States and the Conflict Between India and Pakistan." *Journal of Asia and Pacific Studies* 1/2 (2010): 259–92.

Alavi, Hamzah. "The State in Post-Colonial Societies: Pakistan and Bangladesh." In *Imperialism and Revolution in South Asia*, edited by Kathleen Gough and Hari P. Sharma. New York: Monthly Review Press, 1973.

Ali, Imtiaz. "Militant or Peace Broker? A Profile of the Swat Valley's Maulana Sufi Muhammad," *Jamestown Foundation Terrorism Monitor* 7/7 (2009).

Ali, Murad. "U.S. Aid to Pakistan to Democracy." *Policy Perspectives* 6/2 (July–December 2009): 247–58.

Baroncelli, Eugenia. "The 'Peace Dividend,' SAFTA, and Pakistan-India Trade." In *The Challenges and Potential of Pakistan-India Trade*, edited by Zareen F. Naqvi and Philip Schuler. Washington DC: World Bank, 2007.

Behera, Navnita. "SAARC and Beyond: Civil Society and Regional Integration in South Asia." Paper no. 19. South Asia Center for Policy Studies (SACEPS). (2009).

Burki, Shahid-Javed. *South Asia in the New World Order: The Role of Regional Cooperation*. Oxon: Routledge, 2011.

Chadda, Maya. *Building Democracy and South Asia*. Boulder, CO: Lynne Rienner Publishers, 2000.

Chari, P. R., and Ayesha Siddiqa-Agha. "Defence Expenditure in South Asia: India and Pakistan." *RCSS Policy Studies* 12 (2000).

Cheema, Ali, et al. "Local Government Reforms in Pakistan: Context, Content and Causes." In *Decentralization and Local Governance in Developing Countries: A Comparative Perspective*, edited by Pranab K. Bardhan and Dilip Mookherjee. Cambridge: MIT Press, 2006.

Easterly, William. "The Political Economy of Growth Without Development: A Case Study of Pakistan." *Development Research Group at the World Bank* (Washington DC: World Bank, 2001).

Ganguly, Sumit, and Nicholas Howenstein. "India-Pakistan Rivalry in Afghanistan." *Journal of International Affairs* 63/1 (Fall-Winter 2009): 127–40.

Garver, John W. *Protracted Contest: Sino-Indian Rivalry in the Twentieth Century*. Seattle: University of Washington Press, 2001.

Government of Pakistan. "Chapter 5: Fiscal Development." In *Economic Survey of Pakistan 2006–2007*. Islamabad: Economic Adviser's Wing (EAW), 2007.

———. *Pakistan Economic Survey 2009–2010*. Islamabad: Economic Adviser's Wing (EAW), 2010.

———. *Economic Survey of Pakistan 2010–2011*. Islamabad: Economic Adviser's Wing (EAW), 2011.

Gray, Colin. *Modern Strategy*. Oxford: Oxford University Press, 1999.

Gul, Nazia, and Hafiz M. Yasin. "The Trade Potential of Pakistan: An Application of the Gravity Model." *The Lahore Journal of Economics* 16/1 (Summer 2011): 23–62.

Haqqani, Hussein. *Pakistan: Between Mosque and Military*. Washington DC: Carnegie, 2005.

Hasan, Parvez. *Pakistan's Economy at the Crosroads: Past Policies and Present Imperatives*. Oxford: Oxford Univeristy Press, 1998.

Huntington, Samuel. *Political Order in Changing Societies*. New Haven, CT: Yale University Press, 1968.

Hussain, Zahid. *Frontline Pakistan: The Struggle With Militant Islam*. New York: Columbia University Press, 2007.

IMF (International Monetary Fund). *Country Report 10/158*. Washington DC: IMF, 2010.

———. *Direction of Trade Statistics Yearbook 2011*. Washington DC: IMF, 2011.

Jalal, Ayesha. *The State of Martial Rule: The Origins of Pakistan's Political Economy of Defense*. Cambridge: Cambridge University Press, 1990.

———. *Democracy and Authoritarianism in South Asia: A Comparative and Historical Perspective*. Cambridge: Cambridge University Press, 1995.

Khan, Shaheen Rafi, Faisal Haq Shaheen, and Moeed Yusuf. "Managing Conflict Through Trade: The Case of Pakistan and India." In *Regional Integration and Conflict Resolution*, edited by Shaheen Rafi Khan, 130–64. New York: Routledge, 2009.

Kronstadt, Alan K., and Susan B. Epstein. "Pakistan: U.S. Foreign Assistance." In *CRS Report for Congress* (July 2011).

Lieven, Anatol. *Pakistan: A Hard Country*. New York: Public Affairs Press, 2011.

Naqvi, Zareen F., and Philip Schuler, eds. *The Challenges and Potential of Pakistan-India Trade*. Washington: World Bank, 2007.

Nasr, Vali. "Democracy and the Crisis of Governability in Pakistan." *Asian Survey* 32/6 (June 1992): 521–37.

Nawaz, Shuja. "The Economic Impact of Defense Expenditures." *Finance and Development* 20/1 (1983): 34–35.

PIPS (Pakistan Institute for Peace Studies). *Pakistan Security Report 2010*. Islamabad: PIPS, 2011.

Rashid, Ahmed. *Taliban: Militant Islam, Oil, and Fundamentalism in Central Asia*. New Haven, CT: Yale University Press, 2010.

Siddiqa-Agha, Ayesha. *Military Inc: Inside Pakistan's Military Economy*. London: Pluto Press, 2007.

Singh, Swaran. "The Kargil Conflict: Why and How of Neutrality." *Strategic Analysis* 23/7 (1999): 1083–94.

Staniland, Paul. "The Poisoned Chalice: Explaining Cycles of Regime Change in Pakistan." Paper presented at the annual meeting of the American Political Science Association, Boston, August 28, 2008.

Taneja, Nisha. "India-Pakistan Trade: The View from the Indian Side." In *The Challenges and Potential of Pakistan-India Trade*, edited by Zareen F. Naqvi and Philip Schuler, 69–86. Washington DC: World Bank, 2007a.

———. "India-Pakistan Trade Possibilities and Non-Tariff Barriers." ICRIER Working Paper No. 200 (2007b).

Yusuf, Moeed. "Using Trade as a Driver of Peace: Prospects in the Indo-Pak Context." *Criterion* 2/3 (2007).

UNDP (United Nations Development Programme). *Human Development Report 2011*. New York: UNDP, 2011.

USAID (United States Agency for International Development). *Facilitating Freer Trade Under SAFTA: Issues in Pakistan, India, and Afghanistan*. Washington DC: USAID, 2006.

Waltz, Kenneth. *Man, the State, and War: A Theoretical Analysis*. New York: Columbia University Press, 1959.

Wilkinson, Steven. "Democratic Consolidation and Failure: Lessons from Bangladesh and Pakistan." *Democratization* 7/3 (Autumn 2000): 203–26.

World Bank. *World Development Indicators 2011*. Washington DC: World Bank, 2011.

Editors and Contributors

Editors

Anita M. Weiss received her doctorate in sociology from the University of California– Berkeley and is now professor and head of the Department of International Studies at the University of Oregon. She has published extensively on social development, gender issues, and political Islam in Pakistan. Her books include *Power and Civil Society in Pakistan* (co-editor with Zulfiqar Gilani, Oxford University Press, 2001) and *Walls Within Walls: Life Histories of Working Women in the Old City of Lahore* (Westview Press, 1992, republished by Oxford University Press, 2002 with a new preface). Recent publications include "Crisis and Reconciliation in Swat Through the Eyes of Women" (in *Beyond Swat: History, Society, and Economy Along the Afghanistan-Pakistan Frontier,* ed. Magnus Marsden and Ben Hopkins [Hurst and Co., Columbia University Press, 2012]) and "Moving Forward With the Legal Empowerment of Women in Pakistan" (U.S. Institute for Peace Special Report 305, May 2012). Her current research project is analyzing how distinct constituencies in Pakistan are grappling with articulating their views on Islam, modernity, and women's rights, as well as exploring a range of social, political, and economic challenges confronting Swat. Professor Weiss is a member of the editorial boards of *Citizenship Studies* and *Globalizations*, is on the editorial advisory board of Kumarian Press, is a member of the Research Advisory Board of the Pakistan National Commission on the Status of Women, and is the vice president of the American Institute of Pakistan Studies (AIPS).

Saba Gul Khattak holds a Ph.D. in political science and is currently a member of the Planning Commission. She previously served as the executive director of the Sustainable Development Policy Institute (SDPI), Islamabad. She teaches occasionally as visiting faculty at Quaid I Azam University. Her research is guided by feminist and political economy approaches to understanding the intersections of development, security, gender, and governance. Her publications include "Women in Local Government: The Pakistan Experience," in *IDS Bulletin* (2010); "Women's Concerns in International Relations: The Crossroads of Politics and Peace in South Asia," in *Pakistan Journal of International Affairs* (2008); and "Living on the Edges: Afghan Women and Refugee Camp Management in Pakistan," in *Signs, Journal of Women in Culture and Society* (2007). Her current focus is on social protection concerns and women's land rights. She actively contributes to dialogues on these themes at different forums in Pakistan and internationally. She serves on a number of national and international committees and boards in a voluntary capacity.

Contributors

Aitzaz Ahsan studied law at Cambridge University, U.K., and was called to the bar at Grays' Inn. He is a barrister-at-law at Aitzaz Ahsan and Associates Law Firm, Lahore, and a senior advocate at the Supreme Court of Pakistan. He is also a writer, human rights activist, politician, former federal minister for Law and Justice, Interior, Narcotics Control, and Education. Elected to the Senate of Pakistan in 1994, he eventually succeeded to the positions of leader of the House and leader of the Opposition between the years 1996 and 1999. He is a past president of the Supreme Court Bar Association. He was integrally involved in the Pakistan Lawyers' Movement, 2007–10.

He is an actively engaged human rights activist and a founding vice president of the Human Rights Commission of Pakistan. He has been incarcerated under arbitrary detention laws many times by military and authoritarian regimes. During one such prolonged detention, he wrote *The Indus Saga and the Making of Pakistan* (Oxford University Press, 1996). He is co-author (with Meghnad Desai) of *Divided by Democracy* (Roli Books, 2006). He also wrote the poem "Kal Aaj Aur Kal," which became the theme song of the Lawyers' Movement. He has contributed articles to local and international newspapers.

Aasim Sajjad Akhtar earned his Ph.D. in political sociology at the School of Oriental and African Studies (SOAS), University of London. He is now assistant professor of political economy at the National Institute of Pakistan Studies, Quaid-e-Azam University, Islamabad. He previously taught at the School of Humanities and Social Sciences at Lahore University of Management Sceinces (LUMS). He co-authored (with Foqia Sadiq and Shahrukh Rafi Khan) *Initiating Devolution for Service Delivery in Pakistan: Ignoring the Power Structure* (Oxford University Press, 2007) and has written numerous articles for journals and newspapers. Dr. Akhtar is actively involved with trade and student unions, farmers groups, urban squatters, and progressive political organizations.

Nazish Brohi is currently an independent researcher and development consultant with twelve years of experience in the nonprofit sector in Pakistan. Her research interests are gender and violence, agency, citizenship, conflict, and political Islam. She has authored *The MMA Offensive: Three Years in Power, 2003–2005* (ActionAid International, 2006) and has published in various journals. As a consultant, she has worked with the Government of Pakistan, NGOs, international development agencies, and the United Nations. In the past she has established a crisis center for women survivors of violence, headed the women's rights program at ActionAid International, developed research programs at the Sustainable Development Policy Institute, and taught at the postgraduate level at the Gender Studies Department at Quaid-e-Azam University. She writes sociopolitical analysis for national newspapers and is also an activist with women's movements in Pakistan.

Shahrukh Rafi Khan is currently a Copeland Fellow at Amherst College. He has formerly served as executive director of the Sustainable Development Policy Institute, Islamabad, and taught at the University of Utah, Vassar College, and Mount Holyoke College. He has published extensively in refereed journals and authored eleven books (three co-authored), and edited four (three co-edited). His recent authored and co-authored books include *Basic Education in Rural Pakistan: A Comparative Institutional Analysis of Government, Private, and NGO Schools* (Oxford, 2005), *Harnessing and Guiding Social Capital for Rural Development* (Palgrave/Macmillan, 2007), *Initiating Devolution for Service Delivery in Pakistan: Forgetting the Power Structure* (Oxford, 2007), and *Export Success and Industrial Linkages: The Case of Garment Production in South Asia* (Palgrave/ Macmillan, 2009). His recent edited and co-edited books include *International Trade and the Environment: Difficult Policy Choices at the Interface* (Zed Books, 2002) and *Market as Means or Master: Towards New Developmentalism* (Routledge, 2010). He has twice won the Akhtar Hameed Khan book prize and engaged in academic consulting for several international organizations including the UNDP, UNESCO, UNEP, UNICEF, and the World Bank.

Muhammad Khalid Masud, former chairperson of the Council of Islamic Ideology, Pakistan (2004–10), and professor and academic director of the International Institute for the Study of Islam in the Modern World (ISIM), Leiden, the Netherlands (1999–2003), obtained his M.A. in1962 from Punjab University, an M.A. and Ph.D. in Islamic studies from McGill University in 1969 and 1973, respectively. He has published extensively on Islamic law and contemporary issues and trends in Muslim societies. His most recent publications include *Travelers in Faith: Studies on Tablighi Jama'at*, edited volume (Brill, 2000); *Dini akhlaqiyat ke Qur'ani mafahim*, translation of T. Izutsu's *Ethical Terms in the Qur'an* into Urdu (Lahore, 2005); *Dispensing Justice in Islam: Qadis and Their Judgements*, co-edited with David S. Powers and Ruud Peters (Brill, 2006); edited *Barr-i-Saghir men dini fikr ke rahnuma* [Renaissance of Muslim Thought in Eighteenth-Century India] (Islamabad, 2008); and *Islam and Modernity: An Introduction to Key Issues and Debates*, co-edited with Armando Salvatore and Martin van Bruinessen (Edinburgh University Press, 2009).

Peter C. Miller has been working in population and public health since 1970; his experience has included research, research management, program management, technical assistance, and capacity building. He has worked with a variety of international agencies and for twenty-four years has lived and worked in developing countries, including the Philippines, Egypt, Bangladesh, Pakistan, and Indonesia. He is now country director for the Population Council in Vietnam. Mr. Miller lived in Pakistan from 1995 to 2001, from 2003 to 2007, and from 2009 to 2011. During that time he worked closely with the Ministry of Population Welfare and the Ministry of Health, conducting research and providing technical assistance in population and reproductive health. He worked under a variety of different governments and administrations and was able to observe closely the political and technical debates taking place.

John Mock holds M.A. and Ph.D. degrees in South and Southeast Asian studies from the University of California–Berkeley and is a lecturer in Hindi and Urdu at the University of California, Santa Cruz. Dr. Mock has worked as a consultant on community-based conservation, tourism development and promotion, ecotourism, and wildlife conservation in Afghanistan and Pakistan for the Wildlife Conservation Society, Aga Khan Foundation (Afghanistan), Deutsche Gesellschaft für Technische Zusammenarbeit (GTZ), The International Union for Connservation of Nature, the World Wide Fund for Nature (WWF), and the Snow Leopard Conservancy. He is co-author of Lonely Planet's *Trekking in the Karakoram and Hindukush* and contributor to Lonely Planet's *Pakistan and the Karakoram Highway* and *Afghanistan* country guidebooks. His most recent research, as a Fulbright senior scholar in Pakistan and a Fulbright regional scholar in Tajikistan, is on the oral traditions of the Wakhi people of Pakistan and Afghanistan. He is an elected member of the executive council of the Association for Nepal and Himalayan Studies (ANHS).

Hasan Askari Rizvi, an independent political and defense analyst, is professor emeritus and former chairperson, Department of Political Science, University of the Punjab, Lahore. He received an M.A. and Ph.D. in political science and international relations from the University of Pennsylvania, and an M.Phil. in politics from the University of Leeds. He was the Allama Iqbal Professor at Heidelberg University, Germany, from 1988 to 1991; the Quaid-e-Azam Distinguished Professor of Pakistan Studies at Columbia University from 1996 to 1999; and Visiting Professor with the South Asia Program of the School of Advanced International Studies (SAIS), Johns Hopkins University, Washington DC, in 2007 and 2008. He is author of several books, chapters, and articles on the Pakistan army and its impact on Pakistani society, including *Military, State, and Society in Pakistan* (Palgrave Macmillan, 2000); *The Military and Politics in Pakistan 1947–1997* (Sang-e-Meel Publications, 2000); and "At the Brink?" in *The Future of Pakistan*, ed. Stephen P. Cohen et al., 182–98 (Brookings Institution Press, 2011).

Zeba Sathar received her master's and Ph.D. degrees in the United States and the United Kingdom. She has spent more than fifteen years at the Pakistan Institute of Development Economics, where she has held the position of chief of research in demography. She also has considerable international experience having worked with the World Bank, World Fertility Survey, London School of Hygiene and Tropical Medicine, and Population Council in New York and in Pakistan. She has published widely in books and peer-reviewed journals and has diverse academic interests in population ranging from the more pure demographic topics of fertility and mortality to issues of gender and their association with demographic processes. She has also worked extensively on education and poverty and their associations with demographic outcomes.

Dr. Sathar has advised and assisted the Government of Pakistan in formulating the 2002 Population Policy and is currently working on the 2010 Population Policy and preparation of the Tenth Five-Year People's Plan (2010–15) in conjunction with the Government of Pakistan Ministry of Population Welfare and the Planning Commission. She was instrumental in forming the Population Association of Pakistan and served as its president from 2002 to 2004. She is the first elected member from Pakistan on the governing council of the International Union for the Scientific Study of Population (IUSSP). She has worked with the Population Council since 1994 and is currently its country director in Pakistan. In recognition of her meritorious service to the development sector in Pakistan, Dr. Sathar was awarded the Tamgha-I-Imtiaz by the president of Pakistan on March 23, 2006.

Saeed Shafqat is the founding director of the Centre for Public Policy and Governance at Forman Christian (College) University, Lahore. He obtained his Ph.D. from the University of Pennsylvania, Philadelphia. Dr. Shafqat was executive director of the National Institute of Population Studies (NIPS), Islamabad, 2005–7. Prior to that, he was Quaid-e-Azam Distinguished Professor of Pakistan Studies, Columbia University (2001–5), and adjunct professor at Columbia (2005–10). His research on culture, politics, security, and various aspects of public policy, governance, and civil service reform on Pakistan have been published in journals of international repute. His books include *Political System of Pakistan and Public Policy: Essays in Interpretation* (Progressive Publishers, 1989); *Civil-Military Relations in Pakistan: From Zufikar Ali Bhutto to Benazir Bhutto* (Westview Press, 1997); *Contemporary Issues in Pakistan Studies* (Gautam Publishers, 2000, 3rd ed.); and *New Perspectives on Pakistan: Visions for the Future* (Oxford University Press, 2007). He is currently working on a monograph, *Assessing the Dynamics of Pakistan–U.S. Relations in the First Decade of the Twenty-First Century and Implications for the Future.*

Abid Qaiyum Suleri, executive director of the Sustainable Development Policy Institute (SDPI), Islamabad, since 2007, earned his Ph.D. in food security from the Natural Resources Institute, University of Greenwich, U.K. Prior to joining SDPI, he served as head of programs, OXFAM GB Pakistan Program. He is a member on the board of studies at the University of Agriculture, Faisalabad, and GC University Lahore. His current research interests include food security, rural livelihoods, regional integration, international trade, nontraditional security threats, and energy governance. He is a member on the board of directors of Pakistan State Oil (a state-owned oil-marketing company). He has served on the National Planning Commission's Task Forces on Climate Change and Social-Sector Development and heads the Regional Steering Committee of Imagine a New South Asia, a broad-based network of civil society organizations and individuals working for a New South Asia free from social injustice, conflict, poverty, hunger, diseases, and hegemonic regimes. He is the co-chair of Climate Action Network South Asia (CANSA) and also the vice chair of the executive board of South Asia Watch on Trade, Economics, and the Environment. He led the SDPI team that formulated the National Sustainable Development Strategy (NSDS) in collaboration with the Ministry of Environment and the UN Environmental Programme (UNEP). He is the lead author of *Food Insecurity in Pakistan 2009* (jointly produced by SDPI and the World Food Program) and *Social Dimensions of Globalization: The Case of Pakistan* (published by University of Zurich). He is a prolific writer who regularly contributes to various national and international publications on food security, climate change, regional economic integration, and nontraditional security threats. Dr. Suleri is a member of the Advisory Council formed by the Ministry of National Food Security and Research, part of the team formulating a national policy on food security for the Government of Pakistan. He is heading the SDPI-WFP team that is preparing the "State of Food Insecurity in Pakistan 2013 Report."

Ashley J. Tellis earned his Ph.D. in political science from the University of Chicago. He also holds an M.A. in political science from the University of Chicago and both B.A. and M.A. degrees in economics from the University of Bombay. He is currently senior associate at the Carnegie Endowment for International Peace, specializing in international security, defense, and Asian strategic issues. While on assignment to the U.S. Department of State as senior adviser to the undersecretary of state for political affairs, he was intimately involved in negotiating the civil nuclear agreement with India. Previously, he was commissioned into the U.S. Foreign Service and served as senior adviser to the ambassador at the U.S. Embassy in New Delhi. He also served on the National Security Council staff as special assistant to the president and senior director for strategic planning and Southwest Asia. Prior to his government service, he was senior policy analyst at the RAND Corporation and professor of Policy Analysis at the RAND Graduate School.

He is the author of *India's Emerging Nuclear Posture* (RAND, 2001) and co-author with Michael Swaine of *Interpreting China's Grand Strategy: Past, Present, and Future* (RAND, 2000). He is the research director of the Strategic Asia program at the National Bureau of Asian Research and co-editor of its seven most recent annual volumes, including *Strategic Asia 2010–11: Asia's Rising Power and America's Continued Purpose*. In addition to numerous Carnegie and RAND reports, his academic publications have appeared in many edited volumes and journals. Dr. Tellis is a member of several professional organizations related to defense and international studies, including the Council on Foreign Relations, the International Institute of Strategic Studies, the U.S. Naval Institute, and the Navy League of the United States.

Moeed Yusuf is the South Asia adviser at the U.S. Institute of Peace Center (USIP) in the Center for Conflict Analysis and Prevention and is responsible for managing the institute's Pakistan program. He is expanding USIP's work on Pakistan to cover aspects that remain critical for the United States and Pakistan to better understand each other's interests and priorities. His current research focuses on youth and democratic institutions in Pakistan and policy options to mitigate militancy in the country. He has worked extensively on issues relating to South Asian politics, Pakistan's foreign policy, the U.S.–Pakistan relationship, nuclear deterrence and non-proliferation, and human security and development in South

Asia. Before joining USIP, Yusuf was a fellow at the Frederick S. Pardee Center for the Study of the Longer-Range Future at Boston University and concurrently a research fellow at the Mossavar-Rahmani Center at Harvard's Kennedy School. He has also been affiliated with the Brookings Institution as a special guest. In 2007, he co-founded Strategic and Economic Policy Research, a private-sector consultancy firm in Pakistan. He has also consulted for a number of Pakistani and international organizations. From 2004 to 2007, he was a full-time consultant with the Sustainable Development Policy Institute (SDPI).

Mr. Yusuf taught in Boston University's Political Science and International Relations Departments as a senior teaching fellow in 2009. He had previously taught at the Defense and Strategic Studies Department at Quaid-e-Azam University. He has published widely in national and international journals, professional publications and magazines, and appears regularly as an expert on both U.S. and Pakistani media.

Afiya Shehrbano Zia is a feminist researcher and activist based in Karachi, Pakistan. She is author of *Sex Crime in the Islamic Context* (ASR, 1994), *Watching Them Watching Us: Representation of Women in Pakistani Print Media, Sept. 1994–Dec. 1995* (ASR, 2003), and has edited a series of books on women's issues. In recent years she has authored several essays carried in the *Feminist Review,* the *Journal of International Women's Studies, Economic and Political Weekly, Global Policy, OpenDemocracy*, and the University of Cambridge Occasional Paper Series. In 2008 she was a fellow at the Gender and Religions Department at the School of Oriental and African Studies (SOAS), University of London, U.K., where her research work was on challenges to secular feminism in Pakistan.

Index

women's rights and, 162–165,
173, 176–182
Federally Administered Tribal Areas
(FATA), 10, 62, 64, 257
Foreign Relations and Security Issues
Abbottabad raid (May 2011) and,
217, 229, 234
Afghanistan and, 236, 252–253,
255, 256, 257
China and, 241, 252
civil-military relations and, 18,
242–247, 249–251, 258–259
defense spending and, 247–251
Establishment and, 59, 242–243,
245, 246, 247, 251, 252, 255,
256, 258, 259, 260, 261
historical roots of security paradigm, 241–246, 251–253, 256,
258–261
India and, 233, 236, 239–245,
247–261
Inter-Services Intelligence (ISI)
and, 233, 256, 257
Islamic world and, 252–253
Islamic militancy and, 90–92,
233, 256–258
Kashmir and, 241, 242, 252, 254,
255, 256, 257, 260
military role and, 92–93, 230,
239–240, 242–251, 256–261
9/11 and, 256
nuclear weapons and, 49, 62, 242,
252
political realism and, 240
regional integration and, 58–59,
236, 253–256, 259
United States and, 251–252

guardian military, 239, 243–245,
250, 259
gross domestic product (GDP)
comparisons with other countries,
25–27, 33, 146–147, 240

historical trajectory, 25–26,
50–51
low to middle income countries
(LMIC), 27, 29
growth diagnostics
benefits and weaknesses of, 15,
24–25

Harvard Advisory Group, 5
history of Pakistan since Independence, 3–8, 242–243
Human Development Index
ranking, 12, 96, 131, 132, 162,
247
reflections of equity within development, 132, 162
social sector development and,
131–132

Islam and politics
democracy and, 89–90
development and, 188–189,
191–192, 201–204
foreign policy and, 252–253,
256–258
historical relationship, 88–90
relationship with the state, 89–90,
97, 199–204
social welfare and, 126–129

Kargil crisis, 7, 59, 252
Kashmir
geopolitics and, 91, 241, 242,
252, 254, 255, 256, 257, 260

Lawyer's Movement (2007–9),
15–16, 74, 79
See also Rule of Law Movement
(2007–9)

nationalism
identity construction and the
state, 88–90, 211–222
India and, 241, 242

Also available from Kumarian Press

Nation-Building Unraveled?
Aid, Peace and Justice in Afghanistan
Edited by Antonio Donini, Norah Niland, Karin Wermester

"Written with passion, with intellectual verve, and with stunning moral seriousness, the book is not only immensely important for its discussion of what actually happened in Afghanistan, and for its teasing out of the political and institutional implications of the Afghan experience for other 'humanitarian interventions' in the crisis zones, it is also a profound work about power in the twenty-first century."
—From the Foreword by David Reiff

Living Our Religions
Hindu and Muslim South Asian-American Women Narrate Their Experiences
Anjana Narayan, Bandana Purkayastha

"Lucid in its narration and heartfelt in scholars' careful etching of their religious, culturally specific and spiritual selves as a rightful, albeit negotiated part of their lives in the USA, this volume of essays demonstrates the richness of everyday life in contrast to theoretical attempts at capturing the ethos of religion. In the process, it takes on some formidable binaries including modernity/tradition, West/East and secular/religious."
—South Asian Diaspora

Achieving Education for All: Pakistan
Promising Practices in Universal Primary Education
Fareeha Zahar
Published by Commonwealth Secretariat

Despite the enormous challenge of attaining the Education for All and UN Millennium Development Goal of universal primary education by 2015, Pakistan has taken up the challenge. In this handbook for education policymakers and practitioners, Pakistani educator Fareeha Zahar has identified and compiled good and promising practices that are working towards the achievement of universal primary education in her country. Policymakers internationally will find that the approaches adopted in Pakistan have much to tell them about how to address similar problems in their own countries.

Visit Kumarian Press at **www.kpbooks.com** or call
toll-free 800.232.0223 for a complete catalog.

Kumarian Press, located in Sterling, Virginia, is a forward-looking, scholarly press that promotes active international engagement and an awareness of global connectedness.